D0788494

EUI — Series D — 1
Kobold, Interest Rate Futures Markets and Capital Market Theory

European University Institute
Institut Universitaire Européen
Europäisches Hochschulinstitut
Istituto Universitario Europeo

Series D

Economics/Economiques/Wirtschaft/Economia

1

Badia Fiesolana — Firenze

Interest Rate Futures Markets and Capital Market Theory

Theoretical Concepts and Empirical Evidence

by

Klaus Kobold

1986

Walter de Gruyter · Berlin · New York

Library of Congress Cataloging in Publication Data

Kobold, Klaus.
  Interest rate futures markets and capital market theory.

  (Series D -- Economics = Economique ; 1)
  1. Interest rate futures. 2. Capital market.
3. Hedging (Finance) 4. Portfolio management.
I. Title. II. Series: Series D -- Economics ; 1.

HG6024.5.K63   1986   332.8'2   86-9001
ISBN 0-89925-178-1

CIP-Kurztitelaufnahme der Deutschen Bibliothek

Kobold, Klaus:
Interest rate futures markets and capital
market theory : theoret. concepts and empir.
evidence / by Klaus Kobold. — Berlin ; New
York : de Gruyter, 1986.
  (European University Institute : Ser. D,
  Economics ; 1)
ISBN 3-11-010903-4

NE: Istituto Universitario Europeo <Fiesole>:
European University Institute / D

Dust Cover Design: Rudolf Hübler, Berlin.
Printing: Hildebrand, Berlin. — Binding: Verlagsbuchbinderei Dieter Mikolai, Berlin.
Printed in Germany

ACKNOWLEDGEMENTS

The research leading to this publication was carried out at the European University Institute (EUI), Florence and led to a doctoral dissertation defended in 1985. A grant from the German Academic Exchange Service (DAAD) made the research project possible.

A project like this could not have been completed without the infrastructural support of a research institute such as the European University Institute. Throughout I have benefited above all from the contacts and fruitful discussions with staff and fellow researchers in the Economics Department of the EUI and the University of Mannheim.

It is impossible to name all people who have helped. I am most indebted to Prof. Dr. Manfred E. Streit, University of Mannheim and former member of the Economics Department of the EUI, who drew my attention to the importance of interest rate futures markets and guided my research from the first day until my thesis was finished. His encouragement and advice was very helpful at all stages.

Finally I would like to thank the Publications Committee of the Institute for rendering possible this publication within the Institute's series.

Klaus Kobold, Bonn

TABLE OF CONTENTS

CHAPTER III: INTEREST RATE FUTURES MARKETS IN THE CONTEXT
OF THE CAPITAL ASSET PRICING MODEL

1. THEORETICAL BASIS

2. ANALYSIS OF INTEREST RATE FUTURES MARKETS IN THE
FRAMEWORK OF THE CAPITAL ASSET PRICING MODEL

FIGURES

ILLUSTRATIONS

TABLES

ABBREVIATIONS

CAPM   Capital Asset Pricing Model

CD   Certificate of Deposit

CDR   Collateralized Depositary Receipt

CFTC   Commodity Futures Trading Commission

CME   Chicago Mercantile Exchange

FHA   Federal Housing Administration

FRN   Floating Rate Notes

GNMA   Government National Mortage Association

IMM   International Monetary Exchange

LIFFE London International Financial Futures Exchange

VA   Veterans Administration

INTRODUCTION

GENERAL AREA OF INTEREST

> Like a trail through dense
> undergrowth, a market comes
> into being only through use,
> and is improved through
> increased use.
> GRAY, R.W. 1960, p. 296.

On October 20, 1975 the Chicago Board of Trade (CBT) introduced futures trading in a completely new instrument: a contract in GNMA (1) mortgage-backed securities. The launching of this contract marked the start of interest rate futures trading (2). Futures trading in commodities characterized by high price volatility, such as agricultural products or raw materials, has had a long history (3). A contract requesting delivery of an interest-bearing instrument initiated a new era in futures trading. The importance of this step is self-evident since the new contract is not based on a simple commodity, but rather on interest rates, the price of money.

In market economies, prices and interest rates have important steering functions. Since most economic activities are affected by the price of money, interest rates are one of the most important variables in market economies. Consumption, saving and real investment decisions as well as capital allocation are affected by interest rates (4). Thus more or less all economic agents and activities are influenced to a

1) Footnotes appear at the end of each chapter.

greater or less extent by the price of money. From this
follows that the launching of futures trading in
interest-bearing securities may not only have an impact on
the price of money but also on the whole economy.

In the United States interest rates were remarkably stable
until the end of the 1960s. At the beginning of the 1970s
rates became more and more volatile. While the prime rate
changed 8 times from 1960 to 1969 we may observe 130
alterations in the following ten years. In 1980 the prime
rate underwent 39 alterations, varying in a range from 11.00
to 21.50 percent (see Table 1). Such a volatility in rates
is without precedent since the last war (5). Rates for
government debt and long-term instruments also fluctuated
vehemently during this period (Figure 1).

Given their allocative functions for economic activities,
interest rates are an important instrument for planning.
Heavily fluctuating rates hinder rational economic planning.
Uncertainty is increased if one important variable on which
plans are based becomes highly unstable and unpredictable.
An investment project may yield a sufficient profit with an
interest rate of x % but may be disasterous with a higher
rate y.
In financial markets increasing interest rates cause falling
prices for fixed-income securities and thus severe losses for
investors. With highly volatile rates the risk and
uncertainty of lending and borrowing decisions increases

Table 1:   Interest Rate Volatility in the United States

	Prime Rate Changes (number)	Prime Rate Range (%)
1960	1	4.50 - 5.00
1965	1	4.50 - 5.00
1970	5	6.75 - 8.50
1974	23	8.75 - 12.00
1975	21	7.00 - 10.50
1976	8	6.25 - 7.25
1977	6	6.25 - 7.75
1978	15	7.75 - 11.75
1979	15	11.50 - 15.75
1980	39	11.00 - 21.50
1981	25	15.50 - 20.50
1982	12	11.50 - 17.00

Figures are taken from the FEDERAL RESERVE BULLETIN, Table 1.33, different issues.

Figure 1: Long-Term Interest Rates

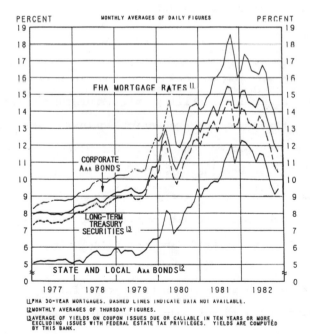

Figure from: Monetary Trends, Federal Reserve Bank of St. Louis, Dec. 21, 1982

significantly. The longer the investment period the greater the risk. As a reaction investors and financial intermediaries will request higher risk premiums and/or shorten their investment horizon, i.e. they will prefer to lend at shorter maturities. Consequently, reinvestment of matured funds will take place at shorter and shorter intervals, thus causing increasing instability. In addition, long-term capital formation will be undermined.

The reaction of banks to increasing interest rate volatility was the issuing of floating rate loans. In this way banks transferred the interest rate risk to their customers (6). The market share of flexible rate notes (FRN) at the US $ bond market increased from an average value of 1.9% in 1971-74 to about 37% in 1979 (7).

For planning and the rational conduct of business economic agents prefer price stability (8). Therefore, demand for an instrument that provides protection against risk caused by sudden and unexpected changes in the price of money emerged alongside the increasing volatility in interest rates (9). Among those who looked for protection against interest rate risk were investors, security dealers and customers of banks to whom the interest rate risk was transferred.

Therefore the emergence of interest rate futures markets can be regarded as a market reaction to highly volatile interest rates. These markets are a product of the inflationary

environment and an attempt to adjust to inflation and sudden
interest rate changes (10). They provide a useful instrument
for all those who handle money, either as investor,
intermediary or borrower, to deal with the uncertainty
stemming from interest rate changes.

The tremendous trading success of GNMA and of subsequent
interest rate contracts reflected the high demand - either
for hedging or speculative purposes - for these instruments.
These markets were termed as one of the most important
innovations in banking in the last decades (11) and the
fastest growing financial market in the world (12). The size
of traded GNMA contracts increased from 128,000 in 1976 to
953,161 (1978) to more than 2 million in 1980 (see Table 2).
The two contracts on government debt, the 90-day
Treasury-bill (T-bill) contract, introduced in January 1976,
and the T bond contract for long-term debt, launched in
August 1977, proved to be even more successful (Table 2). In
1979 about 2 million of each contract were traded. The
trading volume of T-bonds and T-bills in futures is three
times the size of the volume of the cash market (13).

The T-bond contract became the most actively traded futures
contract. In 1981 after 4 years of trading the contract
showed a higher trading volume than well-established
contracts such as the soybean, corn or gold contract. In
1982 about 17 million T-bond contracts were traded, which
represents a market share of more than 15% for all futures

6

Table 2: Volume of Interest Rate Futures Trading

Contract	GNMA (CBT)	Treasury Bill (IMM)	Treasury Bond (CBT)	Certificate of Deposit (IMM)	Euro $ Deposit (IMM)	Euro $ Deposit (LIFFE)
Contract Value	$ 100,000	$ 1 Mio	$ 100,000	$ 1 Mio	$ 1 Mio	$ 1 Mio
Start of Trading	Oct 75	Jan 76	Aug 77	July 81	Dec 81	Sept 82
1975	20,125					
1976	128,537	110,223				
1977	422,421	321,703	32,101			
1978	953,161	768,980	555,350			
1979	1,371,078	1,930,482	2,059,594			
1980	2,325,892	3,338,773	6,489,555			
1981	2,292,882	5,631,290	13,907,988	423,718	15,171	
1982	2,055,648	6,598,848	16,793,695	1,556,327	323,619	121,134
1983	1,692,017	3,789,864	19,550,535	1,079,580	891,066	160,766[1]

1) Jan - July

CBT: Chicago Board of Trade; IMM: International Monetary Market;
LIFFE: London International Financial Futures Exchange
Figures are taken from the Financial Times, Statistical Annuals of the CBT,
IMM Year Books (different years).

markets. The market share for all interest rate contracts amounted in 1982, eight years after the introduction of these new instruments, to more than 25%.

Besides the three contracts mentioned above a dozen contracts were introduced at futures exchanges in Chicago and New York. Of those instruments, the most important are: the 90-day Certificate of Deposit (CD) contract, introduced in July 1981, and the 3-month Eurodollar time deposit contract, introduced in December 1981 at the International Money Market (IMM) in Chicago. The maturity of securities traded ranges from 30 days (commercial papers) to up to 20 years (Treasury Bonds).

The idea of interest rate futures markets spread from the United States all over the world. At present, interest futures contracts are exchanged in Sydney (since 1979), Toronto and Montreal (1980), Winnipeg (1981) and London (Oct 1982) where 90-day domestic and Eurodollar time deposits, and a 20 year gilt contract are traded. In Singapore the introduction of a Eurodollar contract is planned. This would render possible futures trading in Eurodollar rates around the clock.

Participants in futures markets are often divided between
those who seek protection against unexpected price changes
(hedgers) and those who want to profit from absolute or
relative futures price changes. The latter group can be
divided into speculators and spreaders (14). Hedgers
contribute between 20 and 42.5% to the trading volume of
reporting traders (see Table 3).

Table 3: Commitments of Reporting Traders (%)

March 30, 1979

	Speculative	Spreading	Hedging
T-bond	11,0	55,1	33,9
GNMA	6,4	51,1	42,5
T-bill	29,9	50,2	19,9

Figures are taken from: Commodity Futures Trading Commission
(1981, part III, p. 19).

Table 4 where traders are split into occupational groups
provides more detailed information on the participants in
interest rate futures markets. Commercial traders provide up
to one third of market activities. Security dealers are
quite active in the T-bill and bond market, while mortgage
bankers and savings and loan associations are the most active
commercial users in the GNMA market (15).

The most active participants in the T-bill, T-bond and GNMA market were non-commercial traders such as the futures industry (floor traders, associated persons), commodity funds and individual traders. The last group includes all participants using the market for personal hedging or speculative transactions.

The above figures, which provide useful information on market participants stem from a market survey conducted in March 1979. Unfortunately, more recent data are not available. Nevertheless there are strong indications that commercial traders have become more active in recent years for several reasons (16). First, since interest rate futures markets were a completely new instrument, all participants had to learn how these markets work. Furthermore, for a long period no clear guidelines existed as to the extent to which commercial banks, savings and loan associations, pension funds and other commercial participants were allowed to trade in these markets. This uncertainty was resolved when regulatory agencies published trading rules (17).

Table 4: Commitments of Traders by Occupational Groups
March 30, 1979

	T-bonds	GNMA-CDR	T-bills
Commercial Traders	27.4	18.4	33.7
among			
Commercial Banks	3.3	1.1	3.0
Security Dealers	9.1	3.6	6.3
Saving and Loan Assn	0.9	4.3	0.4
Mortgage Banks	0.8	2.5	2.2
Other Financial Firms	2.8	2.4	11.2
Futures Industry	28.6	35.4	18.8
Commodity Pools & Funds	21.0	18.6	12.6
Individual Traders	23.0	27.6	34.9

Figures taken from: JAFFE, N.L.; HOBSON, R.B.
(1979, Tables II c and II d)

PURPOSE OF RESEARCH

The main purpose of the underlying research is to contribute to a better understanding of interest rate futures markets and their effects on individual economic agents, capital markets and the economy as a whole. To achieve this aim we shall investigate whether classical capital market theory such as the concept of portfolio theory (individual behaviour) and the capital asset pricing model (market level) can be applied to interest rate futures markets.

Above all the study is intended to shed more light on the following questions:
- the functioning of interest rate futures markets,
- the behaviour and transactions of economic agents in these markets,

  factors determining the results of transactions in interest rate futures markets.

Above we argued that these markets emerged in an environment of fluctuating interest rates to provide traders in financial markets with an instrument to deal with the risk stemming from unexpected price changes. It will be this hedging aspect of interest rate futures markets on which the following research is concentrated.

The main points to be investigated are:
- to what extent interest rate risk is reduced or even abolished,

- the effects of futures trading in interest-bearing securities on risk and return of single assets and portfolios,
- the consequences on the situation of participants in capital markets,
- optimal strategies to reduce the exposure to interest rate risk.

Given the answers to the above questions and points, which center on the effects of these markets for single economic agents, the remaining question to be dealt with concerns the effects of interest rate futures markets on capital markets and the economy.

OUTLINE

The <u>first chapter</u> will be an introduction to futures markets and futures trading in interest-bearing securities.

The term futures market will be defined and distinguished from its closest analogue, the forward market. A description of the market characteristics and the consequences of these characteristics will be presented. Next we shall analyse those transactions that can be carried out in futures markets, concentrating however on those aspects that are more particularly relevant for subsequent chapters of this publication. Different types of hedging and factors determining hedging outcomes will be discussed at some length. Other transactions, such as speculation, arbitrage and spreading will be surveyed and considered with reference to their contribution to the functioning of the market and the price formation process.

In the <u>second chapter</u> futures trading in interest bearing securities will be investigated in the context of portfolio theory.

First, the assumptions, decision criteria and main conclusions of portfolio theory will be summarized.

It will be shown that the analysis of futures trading using portfolio theory, covers two quite different concepts of hedging: that of the traditional theory of hedging, and Working's concept.
Next, we shall examine the behaviour of an economic agent who chooses his positions in futures markets based on portfolio theory decision criteria. Factors influencing traders' decisions and the importance of expectations will be elaborated.
The effects of futures trading according portfolio theory decision criteria on risk and return of assets and portfolios will then be evaluated theoretically and empirically.

Concluding this chapter, the results of the empirical investigation of hedging on risk and return, hedging effectiveness and optimal hedge ratios will be discussed. In addition, methods used to derive these results will be reviewed critically with respect to possible distortions brought about by this procedure of investigating the market.

The third chapter follows the question whether the capital asset pricing model (CAPM) can be applied to futures trading in interest rate bearing securities and whether it is possible to derive insights into the effects of these markets on risk and return of assets and portfolios, and on traders and capital markets.

In the first section, we present the market model, the extension of portfolio theory to riskless lending and borrowing, and the capital asset pricing model. Special attention will be drawn to the capital asset pricing model, which is an extension of portfolio theory to the macro level. A critical analysis of the assumptions underlying the model and methods applied for testing the CAPM will conclude the presentation of these theories.

The next section will examine whether the above-developped measures of security risk can be applied to spot, futures and hedged positions of interest-bearing securities and whether indications of the effects of futures trading on capital markets can be derived by using these measures.
Finally, values for systematic risk of interest-bearing securities will be calculated. Estimation procedures are outlined and the results discussed.

In the <u>last chapter</u> the main results of the publication will be summarized. Furthermore, based on these results, the effects of futures trading in interest-bearing securities on single economic agents and capital markets will be briefly investigated. Above all the effects on the informational situation in capital markets; on the volatility and the level of interest rates; and on the efficiency of capital markets will be discussed.

Footnotes to Introduction

1) GNMA stands for Government National Mortgage Association.

2) Interest rate futures belong to the group of financial futures which can be devided into currency, interest rate, and stock index futures. This thesis is limited to interest rate futures markets. Also options on interest rate futures are not considered. For a detailed analysis of these other financial futures markets see DUSHEK, C.J.; HARDING, C.J. (1979); KAUFMAN, P.J. (1984); FABOZZI, F.J.; KIPNIS, G. (1984).

3) See e.g. HIERONYMUS, T.A. (1977, pp. 71 ff.); TEWELES,R.J.; HARLOW,C.V.; STONE,H.L.(1977, pp. 5 ff).

4) See e.g. BRANSON, W.H. (1972, pp. 55 ff.); CLAASSEN, E.-M. (1980, pp. 28 ff).

5) HESTER, D.D. (1981, p. 171).

6) DEW, K.; MARTELL, T.F. (1981, pp. 27 f.).

7) OECD (ed.) (1979, p. 100).

8) WARDREP, B.N.; BUCK, J.F. (1982, p. 243).We shall mention an exception of the rule: for speculation - a rational business - price instability is a prerequisite.

9) BURNS, J.M. (1979, p. 24 or 1983 p. 53); Harding, J. (1979, pp. 12 f.).

10) CAGAN, P. (1981, p. 31).

11) New York Times, Dec. 28, 1978, p. D4.

12) HALL, W. (1981, p. VIII).

13) HOPKINSON, M. (1981, p. 1).

14) A detailed treatment of these different groups follows in the next chapter.

15) For an interpretation of these figures compare: JAFFE, N.L.; HOBSON, R.B. (1979, pp. 7 ff.).

16) See e.g. KOCH, D.L. e.a. (1982, pp. 4 ff.); VEIT, E.T. ; REIFF, W.W. (1983, pp. 283 ff.); DRABENSTOTT, M.; McDONLEY A. (1982, pp. 19 ff.); CBT, Monthly Bulletin (June 83, p. 1).

17) COMPTROLLER OF THE CURRENCY (1983); LOWER,R.C.(1982).

CHAPTER I :   THE INTEREST RATE FUTURES MARKET

1. DESCRIPTION OF FUTURES MARKETS

An analysis of interest rate futures markets as well as an investigation of their effects necessitates some basic understanding of these markets.   Therefore interest rate futures markets, their characteristics, and the transactions that can be carried out in these markets, will be discussed in this chapter. The characteristics outlined below refer to futures markets in Chicago. However, those of other places, e.g. London, do not differ significantly.

1.1. Characteristics of Futures Contracts and Markets

In futures markets standardized contracts on the future delivery of a commodity are traded at a highly organized and regulated exchange (1).   The   commodities   exchanged   at interest   rate   futures   markets   are   interest-bearing securities. The standardization of contracts refers to the type of interest-bearing security, its quantity and terms of delivery (place, time, payment). This standardization is an important prerequisite for trading contracts at an exchange. Prices of contracts are established by "open outcry" and thus are the only variable of a futures contract.

Futures contracts and the characteristics of futures trading will be thoroughly analyzed by contrasting the latter with its closest substitute forward markets (see also Table 1-1) (2).

In a classical forward market two contracting parties agree at any place on making or taking delivery of the relevant interest-bearing security at a specific date or period in the future. The terms of a forward contract, i.e. the quality and quantity of the securities, delivery date, delivery and payment procedure, are fixed by bilateral negotiations between buyer and seller. Thus contract terms are tailor-made to the individual needs of the two parties to the contract. Forward markets can, but need not be, organized. The interbank market for currencies exhibits some degree of standardization thus signifying an advancement of forward markets in the direction of futures markets (3).

In contrast to forward markets trading in futures markets takes place at an organized exchange. The contracts are standardized with respect to the quality and quantity of the interest-bearing security to be delivered and the terms of delivery. The date of contract settlement is standardized to the extent that only four delivery dates are traded within the year. For example: the T-bond contract exchanged at the CBT is based on an 8% issue with 20 years to maturity and has a face value of $ 100,000. Delivery dates are the 3rd Thursday of March, June, September and December (4).

Table 1-1 : Distinction between Forward and Futures Markets

	Forward	Futures
Date of contract's performance	in the future	in the future
Terms of contract	tailor-made to individual needs	highly standardized, homogeneous
Object of the contract	commodity	standardized contract on the delivery of a commodity
Place of trading	anywhere	premises of an exchange
Organization	in general unorganized	highly organized
Fixing of prices	negotiations	trading by open outcry
Price fluctuations	no daily limit	daily limit
Accessibility	limited to very large customers with high financial standing	open to nearly everybody via members of the exchange
Relation between buyer and seller	personal	clearing house is interposed between the two parties
Security deposit	normally no deposit	initial margin
Who takes risk of default	the two parties	clearing house
Performance of the contract	by delivery	delivery possible, but most transactions are offset before delivery
Information on trading	normally no published prices	public market, daily price quotations
Regulation	no regulation	government and self regulation

The number of contracts one buys or sells is not standardized, although there are reporting limits for individual traders established by the Commodity Futures Trading Commission (CFTC), the regulatory agency.

Prices are established by open outcry at the exchange. They are limited to the extent that minimum price fluctuations and a maximum deviation above or below the previous day's settlement price are set.

Access to futures markets is also standardized. Only members of the exchange are allowed to trade at the trading floor. To become a floor broker or trader a license of the CFTC is necessary the provision of which requires a high financial, moral and commercial standing (5). Individuals have access to the exchange through futures commission merchants and their floor brokers. Thus more or less everybody who is accepted by a broker can trade in futures market. In forward markets only persons or enterprises who have a sufficient reputation and credit standing can engage in trading.

In forward markets contracts are bilaterally exchanged between buyer and seller. In futures markets the clearing house is interposed between the contracting parties, after the trade has been established. The bilateral relation between buyer and seller is replaced by the buyer's and seller's commitment to the clearing house. In this way the clearing house becomes the opposite party to each participant and guarantees the fulfillment of the contract (6).

In contrast to forward markets, a security deposit must be paid to the clearing house with any position taken. This "initial margin" has to be deposited by the seller and the buyer of a contract as a guarantee of good faith (7). The initial margin amounts to up to 3% of the contract value, e.g. $ 1,250 for T-bond contracts (8). If prices moved against a participant and thus the margin is reduced by more than 25% the clearing house calls for an additional margin (margin call). When a contract is offset or delivery takes place, the clearing house settles the contract and refunds the remaining or increased margin (9). Other costs in establishing a futures position are brokerage fees which are negotiable and vary between $ 70 and 100 (10).

In forward markets, contracts are usually performed by delivery in the way specified in the agreement. After the contract is signed a contractor must renegotiate if he wants to perform in a way different from that specified.
Delivery in futures markets is exceptional. The subject matters of futures contracts are not the securities themselves but contracts for the future delivery of a security. Thus a commitment to take (make) delivery of a special type of security stemming from the purchase (sale) of a contract can be offset by an opposite transaction on the exchange. E.g. the buyer of one March T-bond contract can offset his commitment to take delivery of T-bonds with $ 100,000 face value at the 3rd Thursday in March by selling one March contract on the exchange.

In interest rate futures markets only about 2% of all contracts are settled by delivery (11). Nevertheless it is this provision of settling a contract via cash delivery that links prices in futures markets to those in cash markets (12).

The fact that only small numbers of contracts are fulfilled by delivery proves that the main reason for participating in futures markets is not making or taking delivery but serving other purposes such as to shift or take price risks.

Futures markets are public markets. The clearing house records all transactions and after a trading day publishes official prices (the highest, the lowest, opening and settlement price), the number of contracts traded, and the positions taken. In this way the public is kept informed about the market and prices quoted for future interest rates.

Futures markets are regulated markets. The Commodity Futures Trading Commission (CFTC) supervises and monitors the exchanges, approves contracts, sets margins and daily price movements. Futures commission merchants and floor traders have to be registered with the CFTC. The clearing houses are obliged by law to regulate themselves and their members (floor traders) (13).

To sum up, a futures market in contrast to a forward market is a highly organized and regulated market in which standardized contracts for the future delivery of interest-bearing securities are traded. The main reason for participation is not making or taking delivery but to get protection against unexpected price changes, or to profit from such changes. Hence delivery of securities is exceptional. Most positions are offset before a contract matures.

1.2. Consequences of these Characteristics

The characteristics of futures markets as discussed above lead to some important consequences for the functioning of these markets (14).

The interposition of the clearing house between the two contracting parties shifts the dealer's risk of counterpart default to the clearing house. In forward markets a trader has to make inquiries about the counterpart's standing and credit-worthiness. By this he tries to reduce the risk of the contracting partner running into financial difficulties in the interim and failing to fulfill the commitment agreed upon on the delivery day. These inquiries consume time and money. The risk of default of the contracting partner is one reason why there exist so few forward markets in the economy (15).

In contrast to forward markets, in futures markets the clearing house guarantees that contracts will be fulfilled.

Hence the risk of trader default is absent in futures markets. The soundness of both the clearing house and the clearing member is of paramount importance. As discussed above, both are subject to supervision by the CFTC and a self-regulatory body reducing substantially the risk of their default (16). The clearing house protects itself and market participants against default by claiming initial margins. Furthermore at the end of each trading day all outstanding contracts are settled (daily settlement), i.e. daily profits and losses are calculated and traders who have been affected negatively by price movements are called on to give additional margins to compensate for losses realized (17). By this system of daily settlement an accummulation of losses and consequent defaults is prevented. If the additional margin requirement is not met before the exchange opens on the following day the trader's position is offset by the clearing house. On the other hand, profits can be withdrawn at the end of a trading day.

The limitation of daily price movements (excluding the last weeks before a contract matures) is another safeguard. If the daily limit is reached trading is suspended (18). In this way the market is protected from extreme price movements and ensuing losses caused by (over-)reactions to some news item. While trading is suspended participants can reconsider their engagements and losers regroup their forces.

The organization of futures trading reduces risk of default to a minimum. Thus traders need not to be worried about the risk of default but can fully concentrate on trading price risks on the futures market.

The separation of the relation between buyer and seller of a contract through the interposition of the clearing house allows traders to offset positions at any time before the maturity of a contract. Thus a position can be closed out without difficulty if the aim of a transaction in futures markets has been achieved. The clearing house guarantees the fulfillment of the commitment to the contracting partner.

The standardization of contracts renders possible trading at an exchange because futures contracts are homogeneous products. The homogeneity of contracts concentrates a widespread demand and supply for different securities, different delivery dates, and different places, on some specified securities, delivery dates and exchanges. This concentration increases the number of contracts traded and thus provides liquidity for the market. A high trading volume ensures that large positions can be established or existing commitments offset without difficulty (uncertainty of whether an offsetting is possible at all or may affect the price adversely). Furthermore a large number of contracts traded reduces transaction costs, a fact attracting participants.

High liquidity in combination with a clearing house guaranteeing the fulfillment of a contract also attracts traders not showing a commercial interest in the securities traded but seeking opportunities to invest money for speculative purposes. Since the demand by hedgers for short positions usually is not met by hedgers' supply of long positions, speculators perform a very important function in futures markets by taking over this net long position (19). Additional participants provide additional liquidity for the market and reduce transaction costs. Consequently, further participants are attracted.

These factors - standardization of contracts and trading procedure, almost no default risk, and the possibility of offsetting commitments - are crucial for the working of futures markets since they attract participants to these markets. A large participation creates a liquid market which is an essential condition if markets are to be successful.

1.3. Contracts Traded

As discussed in the introduction about a dozen different interest rate futures contracts with maturity varying from 30 days to 20 years are traded in the United States. The following brief introduction to futures contracts and the related cash markets is limited to T-bonds and GNMAs since these two markets will be analyzed empirically.

T-bonds are long-term debt obligations issued by the Treasury for the US government (20). Maturity ranges from 10 up to 25

years. Recently most issues are callable in the last 5 years
before maturity. Since these securities are backed by the US
government they are regarded as default-risk free. T-bonds
are coupon securities with fixed rates of interest. Interest
is paid semi-annually. Prices are quoted as percentages of
their par value plus 32nds of a point. A price quotation of
96 8/32 means 96,25% of par value or a price of $ 962,50 if
we assume $ 1000 par value.

The Treasury issues T-bonds in quarterly auctions in
denominations from $ 1000 up to 1 million. The market for
long-term government debt is very liquid. At December 1982
T-bonds of a value of $ 104.6 billions were outstanding (21).
Single issues are of large amounts. The securities are
homogeneous, a fact encouraging the holding of T-bonds and
contributing to the very active sencondary market which is
made by government security dealers.

The T-bond futures contract as traded at the CBT is based on
an 8% coupon bond with 20 years to maturity (see also Table
1-2) (22). The contract has a face value of $ 100,000.
Prices are quoted similarly to the cash market as percentages
of par plus 32nds. A future price quotation of 102-04
indicates a contract price of $ 102,125 reflecting a yield of
7.81% (23). Minimum price fluctuations are 1/32 nds of a
point equal to $ 31.25 per contract ($100,00 contract value x
0.01 x 1/32). Daily price movements are limited to 64/32 or
$ 2000 above or below the settlement price of the provious

Table 1-2: Specification of Treasury Bond and GNMA Contracts

	Treasury Bond	GNMA
Basic trading unit	T-bonds with $ 100,000 face value, 8% coupon rate, 20 years to maturity	GNMA certificates, $ 100,000 principal, 8% coupon rate
Deliverable grade	T-bonds with at least 15 years to first call or maturity. Based on 8% standard	Modified pass-through GNMA certificate, with coupons of an equivalent principle balance based on an 8% coupon. 30 year certificate prepaid in the 12th year.
Price quotation	percentage of par value plus 1/32 of a point e.g. 102-04 = 102 4/32 = $ 102.125	percentage of par value plus 32nds
Minimum price fluctuation	1/32 of a point = $ 31.25	1/32 of a point
Daily price limit	2 points (64/32) = 2,000 $	2 points (64/32) = 2,000 $
	above or below the previous day's settlement price	
Delivery months	March, June, September, December	
Delivery Method	Federal Reserve book entry wire transfer system	GNMA Collateralized Depository Receipt
Number of consecutive delivery months traded	11	11

Source: CBT (ed.) (1982a, pp. 22 and 30).

day. Delivery dates are the 3rd Thursday of March, June
September and December. Eleven consecutive contract delivery
dates are traded at the exchange thus offering the
opportunity to trade up to 2 3/4 years in the future. If one
delivery month matures, trading in a new contract starts,
e.g. the September 84 contract will be replaced by the June
87 contract.

At maturity of a contract outstanding T-bonds with at least
15 years to maturity or first call date are accepted as
deliverable grade. Delivery takes place by Federal Reserve
book entry. Bonds with coupon rates different from 8% and
time to maturity different from 20 years have values
different from that quoted for the contract. Therefore
prices of bonds deviating from the contract standard must be
adjusted by a conversion factor. These factors are published
by the exchange. For bonds with coupons greater than 8%
conversion factors are above one, for those less than 8%
below one. Hence the invoice amount to be paid against
delivery will be at a premium or discount to the contract
value multiplied by the settlement price (24).

A Government National Mortgage Association pass through
certificate - in the following referred to as GNMA
certificate - is a fixed-income security (25). A GNMA
certificate is originated when a mortgage banker, thrift
institution, or savings and loan association, authorized by
the Federal Housing Association (FHA) or the Veterans

Administration (VA) pools together at least $ 1 million of single-family mortgages of the same coupon rate and maturity. This pool must be approved by the GNMA. Once a pool has been approved it is backed by the "full-faith and credit" of the US government (26). The securities (GNMA certificates) issued by the mortgage banker against this pool are guaranteed by the US government. Thus monthly interest payments and principal are insured. Default risk is supposed to be non-existant. This government guarantee explains the large amount of more than $ 100 billions of GNMA certificates outstanding by June 1981 (27). There is an active secondary dealer market.

Maturity of GNMA certificates is 30 years. But average maturity is about 12 years due to prepayments of principal. Yield calculations are based on the assumption that pre-payment occurs in the twelfth year. Price quotations are similar to the T-bond market: percentages of par value plus 32nds.

The GNMA CDR futures contract traded at the CBT stipulates the delivery of 8% GNMA certificates with a face value of $ 100,000 and 30 years of maturity prepaid in the 12th years (see also Table 1-2) (28). Certificates with a coupon rate different from 8% are deliverable, provided that prices are adjusted equivalently. Price quotations, minimum price fluctuation and the daily limit are similar to the T-bond contract. Delivery dates up to 2 3/4 years in the future can be traded since 11 consecutive contracts are offered at the exchange. A seller makes delivery by presenting a Collateralized Depositary Receipt (CDR), stating that the trader has deposited $ 100,000 of 8% GNMAs or an equivalent principal balance at an authorized bank.

2. TRANSACTIONS ON INTEREST RATE FUTURES MARKETS

There are four basic transactions that can be carried out in interest rate futures markets: hedging, speculation, arbitrage and spreading. Hedging and arbitrage always involve transactions in two markets, in cash (29) and futures; whereas speculation and spreading is restricted to one, the futures market. We shall treat hedging transactions very extensively since the analysis of futures trading in the following chapters is concentrated on this type of transaction.

2.1. Hedging

2.1.1. Definitions

Hedging can be defined as buying or selling a position in futures markets to counterbalance an existing or anticipated position in the spot market (30). Hedging always involves two markets, the market for actuals in which the hedger has a commercial or business interest and the futures market.

The position in futures is taken as a temporary substitute for an intended later transaction in the market for actuals (31). The substitution is temporary since the futures position will be offset when the planned purchase or sale in the cash market, which caused the engagement in futures, is carried out.

In the literature on hedging there is no unanimous agreement on the motives that cause traders to engage in hedging (32). The two views are that hedging is carried out either to reduce or even to abolish risk (33) or to profit (34) (35).

Risk reduction will be achieved by a more or less parallel movement of cash and futures prices. If prices move completely in parallel risk is abolished. This is the optimal case for a hedger seeking risk reduction. A trader establishing a hedge for profit motives, on the other hand, engages in futures trading in expectation of a non-completely parallel price movement, since the profit arises from different movements of cash and futures prices.

2.1.2. Types of Hedging

Two types of hedging can be distinguished: a short and a long hedge. A short hedge means selling a position in the futures market to counterbalance an existing or anticipated position in the cash market. A long hedger buys a position in the futures market as an opposite transaction to either an existing commitment to deliver a security at a future date in the cash market or a planned cash purchase.

These two types of hedging will be illustrated by the following examples.

Short hedge

An investor holds T-bonds with a face value of $ 100,000 in his portfolio. He plans to sell this position in two months. In the interim the investor is exposed to the risk of an interest rate increase which would cause the prices of fixed-income securities to decline and thus a loss from this T-bond position. To get protection against the expected increase in rates the investor could sell the T-bonds immediately in the cash market and invest the funds for two months in time deposits, try to sell the T-bonds in the forward market or establish a futures position. Since transaction costs are very low and there is no default risk in futures markets, the investor sells an equivalent amount of T-bonds in the futures market, i.e. he sells one futures contract. Hence his long position in actuals is balanced by an opposite short position in futures (see also Illustration 1).

After two months the investor sells the T-bond in the cash market. Since rates increased as expected the investor realizes a loss from his spot transaction. At the same time he closes out his futures position, i.e. the investor will now buy a futures contract after he sold one contract at the beginning of the hedge. As a consequence of the interest rate increase the price of the futures contract declined as did the cash price. The investor will pay a lower price to buy the contract back than he got when he sold one T-bond contract. (See Illustration 1). Hence he closes out his

Illustration 1:   SHORT HEDGE

Cash Market	Futures Market	Basis (s-f)
March, 2o An investor owns $ 1oo,ooo 8 1/4 T-bonds 2ooo/o5 quoted at 95-16 to yield 8.72%	Sale of one June T-bond contract for 94-24	24/32
May, 2o 8 1/4 T-bonds of 2ooo/o5 sold at 92-o4 to yield 9.1o%	Purchase of one June T-bond contract for 91-12	24/32
Loss of 3 12/32 points or $ 3,375	Profit of 3-12/32 points or $ 3,375	No change in basis

Transaction costs are neglected.

futures position with a profit. Since cash and futures prices moved completely in parallel the loss in actuals was exactly offset by a profit in futures. The aim of his transaction, to be protected against changing interest rates, was achieved.

If interest rates - contrary to the trader's expectations - declined in the interim, he could have sold the cash bonds with a profit. But parallel to the cash price futures prices would also have increased. Buying back the contract at a higher price would have caused a loss which at least partially offset the profit in the cash market. In a situation like this the trader would have reached his aim of being protected from changing interest rates but without hedging he would have been better off.

Long Hedge

A pension fund manager who will dispose of $ 1 million in three months time intends to lock in the current yield of 10.40% on GNMA certificates since he expects interest rates to decline and thus earnings from his planned investment to be reduced.

Therefore he buys 10 GNMA contracts in the futures market, each of a face value of $ 100,000. He anticipates his cash investment by purchasing an equivalent position in futures (see also Illustration 2).

Three months later when the funds are available and invested

Illustration 2: LONG HEDGE

Cash Market	Futures Market	Basis (s-f)
a) Basis change to hedger's advantage		
May, 1		
Pension fund manager wants to lock in yield of 1o.4o% on $ 1 mio investment in 8% GNMA quoted at 82-o8	Buys 1o Sept. GNMA contracts for 81-24 contract value 817,5oo	16/32
Aug, 1		
Purchase of $ 1 mio 8% GNMAs at 86-24 to yield 9.75%	Sells 1o Sept. GNMA contracts for 86-16 contract value 865,ooo	8/32
Opportunity Loss of 4-16 points or $ 45,ooo	Profit of 4-24 or $ 47,5oo	narrowing in basis of 8/32 or $ 2,5oo

Overall Result: Profit of $ 2,5oo or o,25%

b) Basis change to hedger's disadvantage		
May, 1		
8% GNMAs quoted at 82-o8	Sept. GNMA contract quoted at 81-24 contract value 817,5oo	16/32
Aug, 1		
8% GNMAs quoted at 86-24	Sept. GNMA contract quoted at 86-o4 contract value 861,25o	2o/32
Opportunity loss of 4 -16 or $ 45,ooo	Profit of 4-12 or $ 43,75o	widening in the basis of 4/32 or $ 1,25o

Overall Result: Loss of $ 1,25o or o,125%

Transaction costs are neglected.

in GNMAs rates actually had declined. Consequently the price
had increased. In our example the opportunity loss is of $
45,000. Investing the funds in the cash market, the fund
manager will offset his futures market position, i.e. he
will sell the 10 futures contracts. Since cash rates
declined, futures prices increased parallel to cash prices.
Selling the futures contract, will lead to a profit which
might balance the opportunity loss in the cash market.
Illustration 2 shows two different results: both outcomes
can be regarded as very successful since the opportunity loss
of $ 45,000 caused from a change in interest rates was
significantly reduced by hedging. In the first situation the
loss was more than offset by the profit in futures markets,
in the other case the loss was clearly reduced. The
different results were brought about by different movements
of cash and futures prices. A classification of possible
outcomes of hedging will be presented in the next section.

The short and long hedge were established with the aim to
reduce interest rate risk. The way in which hedgers
establish futures positions to get protection against prices
changes can be distinguished on the basis of whether
expectations are formed or not.
One type of hedger, the routine hedger, hedges every
outstanding or planned position in the cash market
automatically. He does not and need not form respectively
make use of expectations on price movements and consequently
hedges all positions, even if a price movement may be to his

advantage. The rationale behind this behaviour is the aim of abolishing or reducing any kind of price risk by shifting it through the futures markets to others who are willing to bear it.

Selective or discretionary hedgers establish futures positions based on expectations of future price movements (36). A hedge will only then be established if the trader expects interest rates to change to his disadvantage.

2.1.3. Classification of Hedging Outcomes

The outcome of a hedge depends on the direction and the extent of parallelism in cash and futures price movements. The following scheme (Table 1-3) summarizes all possible hedging results for long and short hedges in six pairs of symmetrical situations for rising and declining cash prices (37). Costs of transaction are neglected.

A) Perfect hedge. The loss in one market is exactly offset by a profit in the other market (as we saw in Illustration 1). Cash and futures prices move in the same direction to the same extent, i.e. the loss (profit) in the spot market is completely equalized by the profit (loss) in the futures market.

B) Overcompensating hedge. The outcome of the cash market is turned into the opposite by the futures transaction, i.e. a

Table 1-3: CLASSIFICATION OF HEDGING SITUATIONS

Type of Hedge	Price Movements		Outcomes			
	s	f	Short Hedger ("long" in spot)		Long Hedger ("short" in spot)	
			Unhedged Position	Hedged Position	Unhedged Position	Hedged Position
Perfect Hedge 1A	↓	↓	Loss	Neither profit nor loss	Profit	Neither profit nor loss
Overcompensating Hedge 1B	↓	⬇	Loss	Profit	Profit	Loss
Undercompensating Hedge 1C	⬇	↓	Loss	Loss, but smaller than unhedged loss	Profit	Profit, but smaller than unhedged profit
Aggravating Hedge 1D	↓	↑	Loss	Loss, but greater than unhedged loss	Profit	Profit, but greater than unhedged profit
Neutral Hedge 1E	↓	•	Loss	Loss, equal to unhedged	Profit	Profit, equal to unhedged
Determinative Hedge 1F	•	↓	Neither profit nor loss	Profit	Neither profit nor loss	Loss

s : spot price   ↓ price decrease   continued on
f : futures price   ↑ price increase   next page
                        • constant price

Table 1-3 continued

Type of Hedge	Price Movements		Outcomes			
			Short Hedger ("long" in spot)		Long Hedger ("short" in spot)	
	s	f	Unhedged Position	Hedged Position	Unhedged Position	Hedged Position
Perfect Hedge 2A	↑	↑	Profit	Neither profit nor loss	Loss	Neither profit nor loss
Overcompensating Hedge 2B	↑	⬆	Profit	Loss	Loss	Profit
Undercompensating Hedge 2C	⬆	↑	Profit	Profit, but smaller than unhedged profit	Loss	Loss, but smaller than unhedged loss
Aggravating Hedge 2D	↑	↓	Profit	Profit, but greater than unhedged profit	Loss	Loss, but greater than unhedged loss
Neutral Hedge 2E	↑	•	Profit	Profit, equal to unhedged	Loss	Loss, equal to unhedged
Determinative Hedge 2F	•	↑	Neither profit nor loss	Loss	Neither profit nor loss	Profit

This table is based on: YAMEY, Basil S. (1951, p. 3o8)

loser (winner) in the cash market becomes an overall winner
(loser) due to hedging (Illustration 2a). Cash and futures
prices move in the some direction but the futures price
changes by a greater amount than the cash price. The outcome
of the cash transaction is not only equalized as in the case
of a perfect hedge, but overcompensated. The result is a net
profit or loss given by the amount by which the futures price
movement exceeds the cash price change.

C) An undercompensating hedge is caused by price movements in
the same direction but the future price changes less than the
cash price. The loser (winner) in cash remains a loser
(winner) but the loss is reduced (Illustration 2b). The
difference in price changes determines the amount of the loss
(profit).

D) Aggravating hedge. The hedge causes an additional loss or
profit since cash and futures prices move in the opposite
direction, e.g. rising cash prices and declining futures
prices lead to losses from both positions in a long hedge.
The hedger would have been better off if he had not engaged
in futures trading.

Two further hedging situations will be mentioned in which
either the spot or the futures price remains stable while the
other price moves.

E) In a <u>neutral hedge</u> the futures price remains constant. The direction of the cash price change determines the hedging outcome. The only contribution of hedging are cost of transaction.

F) <u>Determining hedge</u>. Given constant cash prices the result of the hedge depends on the direction in which the futures price moves e.g. a decreasing futures price would cause a profit (loss) for a short (long) hedger.

2.1.4. The Basis as Determining Factor for Hedging Results

2.1.4.1. Explanations

The illustration of short and long hedging and the classification scheme clearly demonstrated the importance of the relation of cash and futures price movements for the outcome of a hedge. As long as spot and futures prices move in the same direction to the same extent the loss in one market is exactly offset by a profit in the other market - as shown by the short hedge and expressed by situation 1A and 2A of Table 1-3 (cost of transaction are neglected).

The difference between spot (s) and futures prices (f) is called "the basis" (s-f). As long as these two prices move completely in parallel the basis does not change, i.e. for a hedge established at date 0 and offset at date 1, the closing basis $(s_1 - f_1)$ is equal to the opening basis $(s_o - f_o)$. A situation like this characterizes a perfect hedge.

But for some reasons which will be discussed later, cash and futures prices normally do not move exactly in parallel and hedges end up with an overall profit or loss, as demonstrated by the example of the long hedge (Illustration 2) and expressed by all situations in the classification scheme except 1A and 2A.

Different cash and future price movements cause the basis to change, i.e. the closing basis is different from the opening basis: $(s_1 - f_1) \neq (s_0 - f_0)$.

Any change - widening or narrowing - in the basis over the life of a hedge reflects the overall result - profit or loss - of that hedge. A widening (narrowing) means that the closing basis is greater (less) than the opening basis.

A trader who engages in futures trading to reduce price risk faces a new type of risk, the basis risk. The hedger substitutes the risk of an absolute cash price change by the risk of a relative movement between cash and futures prices. Provided that basis changes are smaller than absolute cash price changes, a situation that normally occurs (38), hedging leads to risk reduction.

For the risk reducing hedger basis changes are unfavourable since they prevent complete risk reduction. The other type of hedger who wants to profit from hedging engages in futures trading in expectation of a favourable basis change.

2.1.4.2. Factors Influencing the Basis

At the maturity of a contract the futures price is determined
by the cash price (39). Weeks and months before the contract
maturity futures prices - and therefore also the basis - are
mainly influenced by
- cost of carry and
- expectations on the future level of interest rates
  and future cost of carry.

The cost of carry of securities is determined by the
relationship of short-term to long-term rates, or more
generally, by the net interest differential between the
interest earned on the investment and the cost of financing
this investment.
If short-term rates are below long-term rates there is a
"positive carry", i.e. costs of financing an inventory of
securities are lower than interest earnings. Consequently,
futures contracts should be quoted at a discount. E.g.,
short-term rates are at 6% and so are cost of borrowing for
half a year while T-bonds yield 8%. This situation reflects
a "positive carry" of 2% with an incentive to borrow and
invest the funds in T-bonds. An alternative to this
procedure is to buy a T-bond contract for delivery in six
months. With a positive carry of 2% and cash T-bonds quoted
at 100.00 an investor will only be willing to pay a price for
the contract which is less than the cash price of 100. A
price of 99.00 for a contract maturing in 6 months would

exactly reflect the positive carry of 2% (cost of transaction neglected; see also Figure 1-1).

A situation in which futures prices are below cash prices and subsequent futures prices are quoted at a discount is called backwardation, formally

$$s_{0,0} > f_{1,0} > f_{2,0} > f_{3,0}$$

(the first subscript refers to the date of delivery, the second to the date of price quotation).

Conversely, if short-term rates are higher than long-term rates there is a "negative carry". Consequently, futures contracts should be quoted at a premium, e.g. with T-bonds yielding 8% and cost of borrowing 11% the "negative carry" is 3%. The price of a T-bond contract for delivery in six months reflecting this "negative carry" should theoretically be 1 1/2 points above the cash price (see also Figure 1-1).

A situation like this - futures prices are above cash prices (f > s) and contracts for deferred delivery are quoted at higher prices than for nearby delivery - is called contango.

$$s_{0,0} < f_{1,0} < f_{2,0} < f_{3,0}$$

Expectations on future cost of carry influence futures prices too. An expected change in the cost of carry will result in

Figure 1-1: Cost of Carry and Expectations on Interest Rates

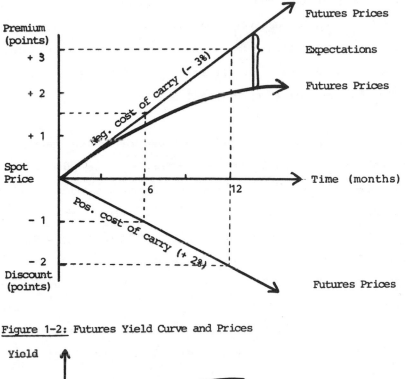

Figure 1-2: Futures Yield Curve and Prices

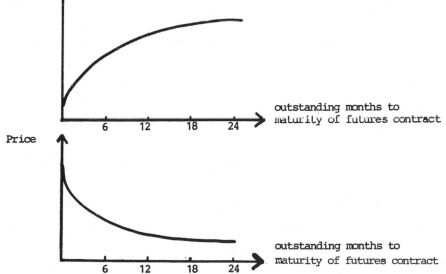

a greater or smaller discount/premium, to be reflected by a
steeper or flatter curved line in Figure 1-1. E.g. if
traders, given a negative carry, expect the difference
between short and long-term rates to diminish and thus cost
of carry to decrease, the futures price curve will become a
flatter curved line (Figure 1-1).

Besides cost of carry, the price of each successive quarterly
futures contract depends on expectations on the development
of interest rates in the future. If the market expects rates
to increase (decrease) over the outstanding months of a
contract this expectation is reflected in a discount
(premium). The futures prices for each successive delivery
month will be lower (higher) than the price of the preceding
contract (see also Figure 1-2). (A combination of negative
cost of carry of 3% and an expected decline in interest rates
might lead to a price curve as indicated in Figure 1-1).

Changes in the cost of carry or changing expectations on the
future level or structure of interest rates cause alterations
of futures prices and thus fluctuations in the basis.

2.1.4.3. Direction of Basis Changes and Hedging Outcomes

Whereas expectations on interest rates and cost of carry
determine the futures price and thus the basis in the months
and weeks before the maturity of a contract, at the maturity

date the futures price equals the spot price with the exception of cost of transaction and an amount reflecting the uncertainty on the grade of the securities to be delivered (e.g. coupon rate and maturity of the bonds). If contracts come closer to maturity the uncertainty on futures prices diminishes with more conclusive information on the cost of carry and the level of interest at the maturity date comming up. Price differences greater than cost of carry and transactions would initiate arbitrage transactions which keep cash and futures prices in line (40). Thus cash and futures prices start to converge in the final weeks of a contract.

Therefore any initial contango or backwardation will diminish during the final weeks, giving the basis a downward or upward tendency. The convergence of cash and futures prices in a backwardation favours a long hedge as the basis narrows in tho final weeks while a contango with a narrowing in the basis is to the advantage of a short hedger.

Thus basis changes and the direction of these changes should be taken into consideration when a hedge is initiated. Table 1-4 summarizes the possible outcomes of short and long hedges in different markets (contango or backwardation) and the situations known from Table 1-3 by which the widening or narrowing in the basis and thus losses or profits are brought about.

Table 1-4 explains e.g. to risk reducing hedgers to what extent they can expect price risk to be reduced in certain market situations. A short hedger facing a backwardation will be able to reduce price risk but will end up with an overall loss brought about by a narrowing in the basis. His optimal strategy may be not to use the nearby contract as hedging instrument but to use a more distant contract since this contract normally shows less convergence (41). The backwardation would be favourable for a risk reducing hedger if he establishes a long hedge since the basis is going to narrow. A narrowing can be brought about by the cash price declining as the futures price is rising (1D), the cash price rising less than the futures price (2B) or the futures price rising while the cash price remains constant (2F).

Furthermore Table 1-4 is a guide for trading the basis, i.e. for hedges that are established in expectation of a favourable basis change to profit. Assume a contango with futures prices above cash prices. A trader holding cash securities will sell a futures contract if he expects the basis to narrow, i.e. if he expects the futures price either to decline by an amount greater than the spot price (1B), or the futures price to decline while the cash price remains constant (1F) or increases (2D). Situations 2C and 2E show a profit too. But the profit stems from a favourable cash price movement and is reduced either by cost of transaction (2E) or a loss in futures (2C). Hence not to hedge would have been a better strategy. This type of hedging is also

referred to as carrying charge or arbitrage hedging. On the
other hand, given a backwardation, a profit orientated hedger
will sell his cash position and buy it immediately back in
the futures markets if he expects the basis to narrow and the
profit from this transaction to exceed cost of transaction
and the net interest differential.

Any type of profit orientated hedging requires the hedger to
form expectations on the relative movement of cash and
futures prices.

Table 1-4: Classification of Hedging Results Due to Type of Market and
Basis Change

	Change in Basis	Short Hedge	Long Hedge	Brought about by Situation	Unattractive Hedges[1]
CONTANGO	narrowing	Profit	Loss	1B 1F 2D	2C 2E
	widening	Loss	Profit	1D 2B 2F	1C 1E
BACK-WARDATION	narrowing	Loss	Profit	1D 2B 2F	1C 1E
	widening	Profit	Loss	1B 1F 2D	2C 2E

Costs of transaction are omitted.

1) These situations reflect a profit (loss) which occurs irrespectively of
   hedging. Hedging does not provide an opportunity for profit (loss) in
   these situations.

2.2. Speculation

Speculation means the sale (purchase) of a position and later re-purchase (re-sale) with the intention of profiting from an intervening price change (42). Whereas a hedge always involves two markets - cash and futures - a speculator establishes only one position in the futures market. Usually speculators are not involved in holding, trading or issuing the security they sell or purchase in futures. Speculators engage in futures trading on the expectation that they can predict prices better than the market does and thus profit from the expected price change. A speculator expecting long-term interest rates to increase and thus prices to decline will sell a T-bond contract, if the futures price does not yet reflect this expected price change. (This situation is similar to Illustration 1, however limited to only the right hand-side, which describes the futures market transactions).

Speculation does not depend on the existence of futures markets. However futures markets are extremely suitable for speculative engagements, since (43)

- funds invested and transaction cost (commissions and foregone interest on margins) are quite small whereas profit opportunities are enormous (in the example a profit of $ 3,375 is earned on a margin "investment" of 1,250 and commissions of $ 100),

- speculation is possible without being engaged in holding
  the security,
- positions can be immediately offset if personal
  expectations on price movements changed,
- long and short positions can be taken without
  difficulties.

Besides public speculators, a group of professional traders,
the locals, who are all members of the exchange act in the
market. The locals are distinguished by the period of their
speculative engagement (44). Scalpers trade on price ticks,
i.e. minimum price fluctuations of 1 or 2/32 which occur
with normal trading. Orders to buy or sell will bring the
price slightly away from its equilibrium level. Scalpers
step in immediately to profit from the price change, brought
about by the next order which will bring back the price to
its equilibrium level. Scalpers trade many times a day thus
providing liquidity to the futures market, lowering the
bid-ask spreads, and reducing transaction cost for hedging
(45). Day traders close out within the trading day.
Position traders speculate on more extended price movements,
taking positions for several days or weeks.

A vehement discussion has been and is still going on about
the effects of speculation on cash and futures prices.
Opponents to speculation argue that price movements are
exaggerated and thus speculative activities lead to
disruptive cash price movements whereas advocates of

speculation stress the contribution of speculation to more price stability (46). All this discussion can not neglect the fact that speculation is essential for futures markets since, as discussed above, the volume of short hedging is not met by the volume of long hedging. Speculators provide this net long position. The risk that hedgers want to shift is taken over by speculators in the hope of profit (47).

Speculators contribute to the markets liquidity which is of fundamental importance for effective hedging transactions. In addition speculators improve the informational efficiency of the markets by "contributing to the public the best judgment of minds that are generally alert, well-informed and capable" (48).

2.3. Arbitrage

Arbitrage means the simultaneous establishment of two opposite positions for the same security in two different markets (49). The motive is to earn a profit from the temporary price distortions between the two markets. The arbitrageur will purchase the security in the market with the low price and resell it immediately in the other market at a higher price. In contrast to speculation no expectations on the direction of price development are necessary. The transaction is of very low risk since the positions are established simultaneously at prices known in advance (50).

Arbitrage transactions between cash and futures markets are of great importance, since they keep prices in the two markets in line.

Given a contango, i.e. the futures price for T-bonds exceeds the cash bond price, the appropriate arbitrage strategy would be to buy T-bonds cash and resell the position simultaneously in the futures market. A transaction like this will pay for the arbitrageur if the difference between the futures and the cash price (f-s) exceeds the transaction cost and cost of carry. The cost of carry is the net interest differential between the interest earned on the investment and the cost of borrowing the funds to buy the T-bonds cash. The arbitrage transaction will be terminated when the price relationship has changed to the normal level or at the maturity of the futures contract.

Arbitrage differs from carrying charge or arbitrage hedging in that the cash position must first be established before it can be sold in futures.

Arbitrage increases the demand for cash T-bonds and thus causes cash prices to increase whereas the supply of futures contracts - either by arbitrage hedging or arbitrage - causes partial pressure on the futures price. Consequently, these transactions cause the contango to diminish and therefore keep cash and futures prices in line (51). Since arbitrage transactions are not limited by ownership or outstanding volume of cash securities the maximum value of a contango is given by the cost of carry and transaction. Any contango higher than this maximal value will be immediately used by arbitrageurs to profit.

A backwardation offers arbitrage opportunities if the difference between cash and futures prices (s-f) exceeds the net interest differential and cost of transaction. In contrast to a contango the amount of a backwardation is not automatically limited to a maximal value given by the interest differential and cost of transaction if cash holders are restricted to selling their cash positions, e.g. banks, and security dealers holding assets for business purposes (convenience yield), or investors who pledged their securities as collaterals (52).

The effectiveness of arbitrage between cash and futures markets is of fundamental importance for the success of hedging to reduce risk. Hedging is based on the assumption of an approximate parallel movement of cash and futures prices. If arbitrageurs did not keep cash and futures prices in line hedging would be similar to speculation.

Arbitrage transactions between different futures exchanges - e.g. the CD contracts traded at the CBT and the IMM or the Eurodollar contract of the IMM and the London International Futures Exchange (LIFFE) keep prices between different contracts in line.

2.4. Spreading

A spread is established by the simultaneous purchase and sale of related futures contracts (53). Spreading is a speculation on interest rate relationships. A spreader acts on the expectation that the price difference between the two contracts will change to his favour, e.g. the price of the contract bought will increase by more (fall by less) than the price of the contract sold.

The risk involved in spreading is less than in speculative but greater than in arbitrage transactions. Whereas the profit in arbitrage is more or less riskless and expectations on price movements need not to be formed, the profit of spreading depends on the spreader's abitility to anticipate relative price changes adequately. In contrast to speculation, the risk of spreading is quite small since no open positions are held and price movements of the two contracts are kept in line by carrying-charge hedging and arbitrage operations (54).

Three different types of spreads can be distinguished (55):

An interdelivery spread involves the purchase and sale of two different delivery months of the same contract, e.g. the sale of a T-bond contract in March and the purchase of a Sept. T-bond contract. In an intercommodity spread two different securities are sold and purchased for the same month, e.g. December T-bond and GNMA contracts. A spread based on the same security traded at different exchanges, e.g. the GNMA contracts traded at the CBT and the same contract traded in New York is called intermarket spread.

An interdelivery spread has to take the current and expected futures yield curve into account (56). Given a positive yield curve, the price of the nearby contract is at a premium over distant contracts. A spreader expecting interest rates to increase and thus also the premium of nearby over distant contracts to increase will sell the distant (e.g. Dec. 85). and buy the nearby (March 85) contract. The profit from the distant contract will overcompensate the loss from the nearby contract when both positions are offset after the expected movement in interest rates occured.

This and other spread transactions carried out to profit have an important effect on the price structure of interest rate futures contracts which is similar to the effects of arbitrage. While arbitrage keeps spot and futures prices in line, spreading keeps in alignment the prices for different futures maturities of the same security (interdelivery spread) or the price of different securities with the same maturity (intercommodity spread) or the prices of the same security traded at different exchanges (intermarket spread).

We have discussed different transactions that can be carried out in futures markets. Spreading, arbitrage and speculation are carried out by traders who need not necessarily have a commercial interest in the securities they sell or buy in futures or cash markets. They engage in these transactions for profit. Hedging can also be carried out for profit motives but also for risk reduction motives. Hedgers have a commerical relation to the securities they buy or sell in futures. The aim to reduce price risk stems from their commercial activities.

Footnotes to I.1. (Description of IRFM)

1) SANDOR, R.L.; SOSIN, H.B. (1983, p. 260); FITZGERALD, D.M. (1983, p. 1); MILLER, R. (1979, p. 4).

2) For a comparison of futures to forward markets see especially: STREIT, M.E. (1980, p. 534 ff.); GEMMILL, G.T. (1981, pp. 4 ff.); IMM (ed.) (1982, pp. 6 ff.).

3) In the interbank market quantities and delivery dates are standardized to some extent. These more standardized forward markets could not prevent the currency futures market from becoming a very sucessful market.

4) For detailed information on the T-bond contract see: CBT (ed.), (1982a, pp. 22 ff).

5) CME (ed.) (1978, pp. 7 f.).

6) See e.g. SANDER, G. (1981, pp. 13 f.); EDWARDS, F.R. (1983, p. 370 and 374).

7) POWERS, M.J.; Vogel, D.J.. (1981, p. 26).

8) CBT, monthly bulletin (Feb. 84, p. 4).

9) For a more detailed description of the margin system and its functions see the following section I.1.2.

10) WALT, H.R. (1981, p. 5).

11) HARDING, J. (1979, p. 4); CBT (ed.) (1982a, p. 4).

12) CBT (ed.) (1982b, p. 2); FITZGERALD, D.M. (1983, P. 11). See also section I.2.3..

13) For the regulatory aspect see e.g.: SCHWARZ, E.W. (1979, p. 4); ARNIM, von R. (1982, pp. 315 ff.); GEMMILL, G.T. (1983, pp. 298 f.).

14) Compare for this section: GOSS, B.A.; YAMEY, B.S. (1976, p. 9); STREIT, M.E. (1980, p. 537; 1981, pp. 186 ff.).

15) BERNHOLZ, P. (1979, p. 134).

16) The so called "Hunt-crises" in silver futures exhibited some weakness in regulation of futures markets. Nevertheless the crises proved the reliability and functioning of supervision in cases of emergencies. For detailed information see CFTC, (1981).

17) HIERONYMUS, T.A. (1977, p. 45); ARAK, M.; McCURDY, C.J., (1979/80, p. 35).

18) CME (ed.), (1978, p. 13); LOOSIGIAN, A.M. (1980, pp. 120 f.).

19) YAMEY, B.S. (1971, p. 414).

20) Information on the T-bond market is taken from: LOOSIGIAN, A.M. (1980, pp. 60 ff.); HARDING, J. (1979, p. 18);

21) FEDEREAL RESERVE BANK (ed.): Federal Reserve Bulletin, (April 1983, Table 1.41).

22) CBT (ed.) (1982a, pp. 22 ff.); KOLB, R.W.; CHIANG, R. (1981, p. 74).

23) 8% coupon rate, 20 years to maturity.

$$\text{Yield to Maturity} = \frac{\text{Coupon Rate} - (+) \dfrac{\text{Premium (Discount)}}{\text{Years to Maturity}}}{\text{Market Price} + \text{Par Value}) : 2}$$

$$7.81 = \frac{8.00 - \dfrac{2.125}{20}}{(1o2.125 + 1oo.oo) : 2}$$

24) A detailed description of adjusting bonds different from the contract standard can be found in SCHWARZ, E.W. (1979, pp. 96 ff.); CBT (ed.) (1982b, pp. 11 ff.).

25) See e.g. HOBSON, R. (1978, pp. 4 f.); ARDITTI, F.D. (1978, pp. 146 f.).

26) SANDOR, R.L.; SOSIN, H.B. (1983, p. 259).

27) CBT (ed.) (1982c, p. 4).

28) SCHWARZ, E.W. (1979, pp. 101 ff.); POWERS, M.J.; VOGEL, D.J. (1981, pp. 158 ff.).

Footnotes to I.2.   (Transactions carried out in IRFM)

29) The expressions cash and spot markets as well as markets in actuals are used as synonyms.

30) GOSS, B.A.; YAMEY, B.S.;   (1976, p.   17);   DAVIA, T.R.;   HARDING, C.J. (1979, p. 47). The CFTC definition of hedging is reprinted in POWERS, M.J.; VOGEL, D.J. (1981, pp. 172 f.).

31) WORKING, H. (1953b, p. 560; 1962, p. 442).

32) See e.g. POWERS, M.J.; VOGEL, D.J. (1981, pp.   173 ff.); YAMEY, B.S. (1983, pp. 28 ff.).

33) See e.g. HOFFMAN, G.W. (1932, p.   382); LOOSIGIAN, A.M. (1980, p. 316).

34) See e.g. WORKING, H. (1953a, p. 326); COOTNER, P.H. (1968, p. 117).

35) The different types of hedging will be analyzed explicitly in the following chapter.

36) WORKING, H. (1953a, p. 320).

37) This scheme of classification was first developped by YAMEY, B.S. (1951, pp. 307 ff.).

38) In the following sections we shall demonstrate that cash and futures prices are kept in line by arbitrage and spreading and thus basis changes on average are smaller than absolute cash price changes. Basis changes greater than cash price changes occur when cash price changes are extremely small or even zero, e.g. situation 1F and 2F of Table 1-3.   For a graphical display of basis and spot price changes see e.g.   CBT (1982b, p. 9).

39) For this section compare LOOSIGIAN, A.M. (1980, pp. 325 ff.);   DAVIA, T.R.; HARDING, C.J. (1979, p. 47); POWERS, M.J. VOGEL, D.J. (1981, pp. 184 ff).

40) For an explicit analysis of arbitrage transactions see section 2.3. of this chapter.

41) On the other hand, a contract with a maturity date different from the date of the cash transaction reflects prices quoted for this deferred date.   Thus hedging effectiveness may be reduced.   For optimal hedging strategies see e.g.   FITZGERALD, D.M. (1983, pp. 80 ff.).

42) KALDOR,N. (1939, p.1); HIRSHLEIFER,J. (1977, p.975).

43) Compare e.g. GOSS, B.A.; YAMEY, B.S. (1976, p.   29);
    ARAK, M.; McCURDY, C.J. (1979/80, p.   40).

44) HIERONYMUS, T.A. (1977, pp. 47 f.); FITZGERALD, D.M.
    (1983, pp. 133 f.).

45) SCHOLES, M.S. (1981, p.   267).

46) For this discussion see e.g. GOSS, B.A.; YAMEY, B.S.
    (1976, pp.   30 ff.); FROEWISS, K.C. (1978, pp. 22
    ff.). TREASURY/FED-Study on Futures Markets (1979, pp.
    6 ff.) and chapter IV.

47) This view led to Keynes' theory of normal
    backwardation, stating that hedgers have to pay a risk
    premium to speculators for taking over the risk they
    want to shift. KEYNES, J.M. (1930, p.   129). A
    critical evaluation of this theory can be found in
    TEWELES, R.J. et al. (1977, pp. 96 ff.); STREIT,
    M.E. (1980, pp. 542 f.).

48) MARSHALL, A. (1932, p.   262).

49) WATLING, T.F.; MORLEY, J. (1978, p.   133); POWERS,
    M.J.; VOGEL, D.J. (1981, p.   231).

50) Arbitrage transactions are often referred to as
    riskless. This is true to the extent that the
    difference between the two prices and hence the profit
    is known in advance. But this profit that will occur
    with certainty when the futures position is offset may
    be reduced by interest payments or foregone interest on
    additional margin payments to be provided in the
    interim.

51) Compare GOSS, B.J.; YAMEY, B.S. (1976, p.   13);
    STREIT, M.E. (1980, p.   544).

52) For this asymmetrie between the size of a contango and
    a backwardation see also: YAMEY, B.S. (1971, p.   421).

53) SCHWARZ, E.W. (1979, p.   135).

54) STREIT, M.E. (1980, p.   545).

55) LOOSIGIAN, A.M. (1980, p.   352); FITZGERALD, D.M.
    (1983, pp. 132).

56) See e.g. POWERS, M.J.; VOGEL, D.J. (1981, pp.   242
    ff.).

CHAPTER II :   INTEREST RATE FUTURES MARKETS IN   THE   CONTEXT
OF PORTFOLIO THEORY

1. CLASSICAL PORTFOLIO THEORY

1.1. Objectives and Assumptions

The theory of portfolio selection was developed by MARKOWITZ
and extended,   among   others,   by   TOBIN, SHARPE, LINTNER AND
MOSSIN (1).
Portfolio theory is a theory of investment behaviour   under
uncertainty (2).   It   deals   with   the decision problem of a
risk-averse investor who wants to increase his personal
wealth (3).   The investor is faced with different investment
opportunities, the possible outcomes of   which   he   does   not
know in advance with certainty. The uncertainty is given by
the fact that a trader, who is aware of the outcomes of
different actions (investments) given special states of the
world, does not know which state of the world will   occur   in
the next period (4). Hence the decision how much to invest
in which asset, and thus how to form an optimal portfolio is
a decision under uncertainty.

KNIGHT introduced a distinction between uncertainty and risk.
In the case of risk the probability of different possible

states of the world and thus also of the outcomes are known
to the agent, whereas the case of uncertainty is
characterized by the absense of probabilities (5).
Portfolio theory supposes that the category of risk is given
(6). If this condition is not met an analysis of investment
behaviour in probabilistic terms would not be possible (7).

Portfolio theory establishes two decision criteria for
evaluating the optimal composition of an individual
portfolio, i.e. the expected return of the investment and
the risk to which the investor is exposed of failure to
realize the expected return (8).

Portfolio theory is based on the following assumptions (9):

1. A one-period time horizon.
2. Investors maximize expected utility, E(U). They show
    diminishing marginal utility, i.e. they are risk-averse.
3. Investors evaluate investment outcomes by the rate of
    return on which they have probability distributions.
4. Risk is measured by the variability of the expected rate
    of return.
5. Investors base their decisions solely on the variables
    expected return, E(R), and risk, σ^2. Symbolically : U =
    $U(E(R),\sigma^2)$.
6. Furthermore, investors are assumed to behave rationally
    in the sense that they prefer, for a given level of risk,
    the portfolio with the highest expected return ($\partial U/\partial E(R)$

> 0) or, for a given expected return, the portfolio with lower risk is preferred to a portfolio with more risk $(\partial U/\partial \sigma^2 < 0)$.

The approach is restricted to the first two moments of the return distribution, mean and variance (return and risk). This procedure implies, given risk-averse traders, normally distributed returns if no restrictions are imposed on the utility function. If the utility function is quadratic all types of return distributions are allowed for (10).

An investor's procedure for deriving his optimal portfolio can be divided into three separate phases (11):

- Security analysis: Evaluation of future prospects of securities, i.e. their expected returns, their risks, and correlations between the returns of different securities.
- Portfolio analysis: On the basis of the predictions obtained in the first phase, expected returns and risks of combinations of securities (portfolios) can be derived. Out of the set of attainable portfolios the efficient portfolios are selected.
- Portfolio selection: Given his preferences the investor determines the optimal portfolio from the set of efficient portfolios.

Security analysis, the first step in portfolio selection, requires investors to form, at the beginning of the investment period, expectations on the future prospects of securities (12).

Since portfolio theory - unlike the capital asset pricing model (III.1.3.) - is not based on restrictive assumptions on traders' expectations we can speak of traders' subjective expectations. Even if a trader's expectations on the future prospects of securities are based solely on objective ex-post performance of these assets, we can still speak of subjective expectations since the trader subjectively believes that the ex-post performance will also occur in the future (13). He has an elasticity of expectations of 1.

Procedures for calculating expected rates of return have been developed in the literature but cannot be discussed here (14). All these procedures are in line with MARKOWITZ's recommendation to "combine statistical techniques and the judgment of practical men" (15).

1.2. Decision Criteria

To measure the outcome of an investment the rate of return is used not the absolute dollar return. The rate of return, R, is computed by formula (II.1), where s_0 and s_1 refer to the price of the security at the start respectively the end of

$$(II.1) \quad R = \frac{(s_1 - s_0) + d}{s_0}$$

the investment period and d stands for any dividends or interest payments received in the interim. Calculating returns according to (II.1) with ex-post data, leads to historical rates of return. At the beginning of an investment period the price of the security at the end of the period, $s_{1'}$, and sometimes also the income from the investment, d, are not known in advance, i.e. rates of return are uncertain. They can be interpreted as random variables. Investors derive expected rates of return by attributing a subjective probability, p_{i1}, to each possible outcome of an investment, R_{i1} (16). Given this probability distribution over all outcomes considered as possible, the expected value or mean of the random variable expected return, $E(R_i)$, can be written as:

$$(\text{II.2}) \quad E(R_i) = \sum_{n=1}^{n} p_{i1} \cdot R_{i1} \qquad (\text{with } \sum_{n=1}^{n} p_{i1} = 1)$$

$$0 \leq p_{i1} \leq 1$$

In a world of certainty the rate of return would be the best criterion for an investment decision. In a world of uncertainty the risk that the expected return may not be realized has to be taken into account by the investor (17). This risk of variability of return (18) around the expected value is usually measured by the variance

$$(\text{II.3}) \quad \text{Var}(R_i) = \sigma_i^2 = \sum_{i=1}^{n} p_{i1} \left[R_{i1} - E(R_i) \right]^2$$

or the standard deviation, $\sigma_i = \sqrt{\sigma_i^2}$. The greater the variance, the wider the range within which the actual return for a given probability level may fall and the greater the risk associated with this security.

Rates of return and risks of portfolios consisting of a combination of different securities are calculated in much the same way as for single assets. Portfolio theory assumes assets to be perfectly divisible (19). The proportion which a security i has in a portfolio is given by x_i, proportions for all the securities adding up to 1.

The expected return of a portfolio P, $E(R_P)$, consisting of n assets can be calculated from:

$$(II.4) \qquad E(R_p) = \sum_{i=1}^{n} x_i \cdot E(R_i) \qquad \text{(with } \sum_{i=1}^{n} x_i = 1 \\ x_i > 0 \text{)}$$

i.e. the expected portfolio return is a linear combination of the expected return of single assets weighted by their relative weights in the portfolio. Thus the portfolio return will always fall within the range given by the returns of the securities with the lowest and the highest return. The portfolio has the highest rate of return if it consists only out of the latter security. Such a portfolio is optimal if the rate of return were the only criterion for investment decisions. But as the return of the portfolio can vary considerably compared with the expected value, the variance of the portfolio has to be calculated:

$$(II.5) \quad Var(R_p) = \sigma_p^2 = \sum_{i=1}^{n} x_i^2 \sigma_i^2 + \sum_{\substack{i=1 \\ i \neq j}}^{n} \sum_{j=1}^{n} x_i x_j \, cov(R_i, R_j)$$

An important aspect of portfolio theory is diversification of risk, i.e. the combination of those securites in a portfolio that do not show perfect positive correlation of return (20). Writing for

$$(II.6) \quad cov(R_i, R_j) = \sigma_{ij} = \sigma_i \sigma_j \rho_{i,j}$$

we see that, for given standard deviations, the value of the covariance depends on $\rho_{i,j}$, the coefficient of correlation between two assets. This coefficient, which takes values between +1 and -1, indicates whether and to what extent the returns of two securities move in the same ($\rho > 0$), or opposite ($\rho < 0$) directions, or whether they vary independently of each other ($\rho = 0$).

In a portfolio consisting of two securities with perfect positive correlation ($\rho_{i,j}$ = 1) the covariance takes the greatest positive value and the portfolio risk, like the return, is a linear combination of single-security risks (see II.5). With less than perfect positive correlation

($\rho_{i,j}$ <1), the covariance is reduced and diversification of portfolios pays by a portfolio risk, smaller than the weighted sum of the single-security variances. Perfect negative correlation between two asset returns ($\rho_{i,j}$ = -1) leads to a negative covariance term and maximal possible reduction of portfolio risk.

After evaluation of expected return and risk we can turn to the following steps of portfolio analysis. The selection of an investor's optimal portfolio out of the set of attainable portfolios.

1.3. Efficient Portfolios

All portfolios constructed as a combination of securities are characterized by their expected rate of return and variance. They form the attainable set of portfolios (21). This set can be represented in a diagram where the expected rate of return is plotted on the vertical axis and the variance on the horizontal (See Figure 2-1).

From this set of attainable portfolios investors select efficient portfolios. According to the E-Var-rule (22), which is assumed to apply to all investors, efficient portfolios are those:

1. with minimum variance for given rate of expected
    return

2. with maximum expected rate of return for given
    variance

3. for which other portfolios with lower variance and
    higher expected return do not exist.

Efficient portfolios which dominate all other portfolios are
placed along a line at the left border of the attainable set.
This line is termed the efficient frontier (AB) (Figure 2-1).
All other combinations of securities below the efficient
frontier· are inefficient.

Figure 2-1: Efficient Frontier of Attainable Portfolios

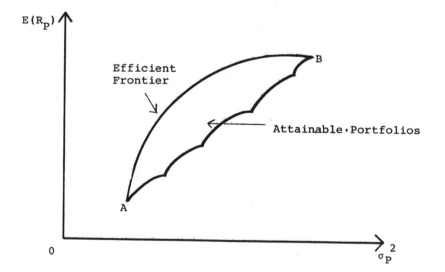

1.4. The Optimal Portfolio

From the portfolios on the efficient frontier an investor
will choose his optimal portfolio, i.e. that which maximizes
his individual utility. Even if investors have the same
expectations, and therefore the same efficient frontier, they
may choose different optimal portfolios, because they may
have different attitudes towards risk, i.e. different
preferences. As mentioned before (23) investors are
risk-averse. They prefer a larger expected return and
dislike risk. Preferences of risk-averse investors can be
represented by a set of convex indifference curves in the
mean-variance space (Figure 2-2). Utility increases with the
curves moving to the upper left. There are points of higher
return and less risk.

Figure 2-2: Determination of an Investor's Optimal Portfolio

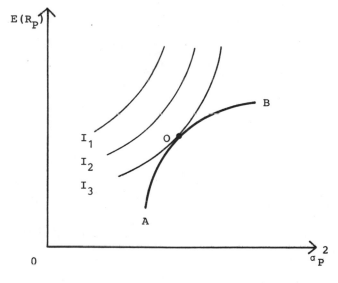

An investor's optimal portfolio and with this the optimal combination of risky securities is determined by the point where one of his indifference curves touches the efficient frontier (point 0 in Figure 2-2).

We have now outlined the procedure and tools with which an investor determines that combination of securities and their quantities maximizing his individual expected utility.

2. THE APPLICATION OF PORTFOLIO THEORY TO FUTURES TRADING

In this section we shall investigate in what way and to what extent portfolio theory as described in chapter II.1. can be applied to futures trading in interest-bearing securities. Portfolio theory allows investors to rank different investment opportunities and provides guidelines as to the optimal proportions for the different securities in a portfolio. In this study we analyse a portfolio consisting of a spot and an appropriate futures position and investigate the question whether the optimal proportions of these assets can be determined by the application of portfolio theory. This analysis will be carried out for hedging but if there are parallels with other transactions these will be taken into consideration.

2.1. The Portfolio Theory of Hedging

2.1.1. The Traditional Theory of Hedging

Holders of spot positions are exposed to the risk of unexpected price changes. Traditional hedging theory regards risk reduction as the motive for establishing a futures market position (24). In classical hedging theory the amount of the futures market position, x_F, hedgers take is equal to the amount with the spot position, x_S, but with opposite sign, i.e. $-x_F = x_S$ (25).

An application of the portfolio approach to the traditional theory of hedging, in anticipation of subsequent sections leads to the following formulae for the expected \$-return (loss or gain) of an unhedged spot position E(S)

$$(II.7) \quad E(S) = x_S E(s_1 - s_o)$$

and a spot position hedged in futures E(H)

$$(II.8) \quad E(H) = x_S E(s_1 - s_o) - x_F E(f_1 - f_o)$$

where s_o and f_o denote spot and futures prices at time 0; s_1 and f_1 at time 1 (26).

Traditional theory of hedging suggests that cash and futures prices move in the same direction. Whereas the naive view of hedging held at the beginning of this century assumed cash and futures prices to move completely in parallel (27), a price movement in the same direction but not exactly in parallel is a more realistic assumption (28). Hence with a price movement in the same direction, E(H) is smaller than E(S) and, consequently, Var(H) smaller than Var(S). Total risk avoidance occurs if cash and futures prices move completely in parallel. Then E(H) and Var(H) are zero and the hedge works out to a perfect hedge.

A perfect hedge can be formulated in basis terms. It occurs if the basis, defined as the difference between spot and futures prices, does not change between the beginning and the end of the hedge (29), i.e.

$$(s_1 - f_1) - (s_0 - f_0) = 0$$

In the classical approach of hedging risk reduction can be described by analyzing the variances of spot, Var(S), and hedged positions, Var(H), within the framework of portfolio theory (30).

According to equations (II.3) and (II.5) of classical portfolio theory and bearing in mind that the futures position enters with the sign opposite of the cash position we can write for the variances (31):

(II.9) $Var(S) = x_S^2 \sigma_S^2$

(II.10) $Var(H) = x_S^2 \sigma_S^2 + x_F^2 \sigma_F^2 - 2x_S x_F cov(S,F)$

Equation (II.10) is relevant for a hedger concerned with risk reduction. If cov(S,F) the indicator for the correlation between spot and futures price changes is positive, the third term of (II.10) turns out to be negative. Hence the variance of the hedged position would be smaller than the variance of the unhedged spot position: $\text{Var}(S) > \text{Var}(H)$.

We can show that the covariance turns out to be positive by writing the covariance as (32) (33):

$$\text{cov}(S,F) = E\left\{\left[(s_1 - s_o) - E(S)\right]\left[(f_1 - f_o) - E(F)\right]\right\}$$

$$= \sum_{t=1}^{n} P_t \left\{\left[(s_{1t} - s_{ot}) - E(S)\right]\left[(f_{1t} - f_{ot}) - E(F)\right]\right\}$$

With cash and futures prices moving more or less in parallel as assumed by classical hedging theory, the differences between the deviations of cash and futures prices from their expected values are either positive or negative and hence the covariance turns out to be positive.

Total risk avoidance caused by a complete parallel movement of cash and futures prices can be shown by writing $\sigma_S \sigma_F \rho_{S,F}$ for cov(S,F), with $\rho_{S,F}$ as the correlation coefficient between spot and futures price changes. We can write for (II.10)

$$(II.10a) \qquad \text{Var}(H) = x_S^2 \sigma_S^2 + x_F^2 \sigma_F^2 - 2x_S x_F \sigma_S \sigma_F \rho_{S,F}$$

With cash and futures prices moving in parallel to the same extent

$$\sigma_S^2 = \sigma_F^2 \;,\; \sigma_S = \sigma_F \;,\; \rho_{S,F} = 1$$

Further conventional hedging theory assumes that $|x_S|$ = $|x_F|$. Hence (II.10a) can be written as:

$$\text{(II.10b)} \qquad \text{Var(H)} = x_S^2 \sigma_S^2 + x_S^2 \sigma_S^2 - 2x_S x_S \sigma_S \sigma_S \cdot 1$$

With Var(H) = 0, the overall risk of a hedged cash market position is zero.

2.1.2. Working's Theory

WORKING contradicted the traditional theory that hedging is carried out solely for the purpose of risk reduction. In his concept, hedging decisions are based on the variable expected return. He stated that "hedging is not necessarily done for the sake of reducing risk" but "usually in the expectation of a favourable change in the relation between spot and futures prices" (34). Hence the motive for hedging is to profit from a basis change, i.e.

$$(s_1 - f_1) - (s_0 - f_0) \neq 0$$

Hedgers expect the basis to change to their advantage, so that

$$E(H) = x_S E(s_1 - s_0) - x_F E(f_1 - f_0) > 0$$

The other type of hedging WORKING analysed, discretionary or selective hedging, also incorporated a return component. A hedge is established if traders expect spot prices to change to their disadvantage (35). If traders expect a favourable change in spot prices they leave their positions unhedged to profit from this favourable price change whilst running the risk of losing from unexpected price movements.

2.1.3. The Synthesis of Portfolio Theory

Whilst in traditional hedging theory the hedger's decision is based solely on the variable risk and in WORKING's theory on the variable expected return, these two divergent theories of hedging can be integrated into one concept by the application of portfolio theory (36).

It has been shown above that one main aspect of portfolio theory is the combination of those securities that show less than perfect positive correlation of returns to reduce risk. This is precisely the motive for hedging in the traditional view, i.e. the combination of cash and futures positions for the sake of risk reduction or risk avoidance. The other decision variable of portfolio theory, expected return, leads hedgers to carry out transactions according to WORKING's theory of hedging. Hence the analysis of hedging in the concept of portfolio theory is not a completely new view of hedging but an integration of two hedging theories into an existing theory of investment behaviour under uncertainty.

The first studies that analysed the hedging process within the concept of portfolio theory were those of TELSER, JOHNSON and STEIN (37). It was JOHNSON who stated, based on empirical evidence, that the traditional concept and that of WORKING do "not account adequately for certain market phenomena" (38), and especially not for the fact "that an individual may held a mix of hedged and speculative positions in response to his expectations concerning absolute price changes" (emphasis in original) (39). Applying portfolio theory, it was possible to explain why hedgers held hedged and unhedged positions at the same time.

According to portfolio theory, hedgers in futures markets maximize their expected utility, E(U). Expected utility is a function of two variables, the expected income (which is for hedgers the expected return from a hedged position, E(H),) and the risk of not achieving this expected return, Var(H). Formally, we can write

$$E(U) = U(E(H), \sigma_H^2)$$

This approach to hedging, on which many formal analyses of futures trading are based (40), will be investigated in the following sections.

2.2. The Individual Agent's Optimal Position in Futures Markets

Traders in markets for financial securities which can also be exchanged on futures markets have to face two alternatives, i.e. holding the assets unhedged in the cash market and being exposed to the risk of price changes or hedging their cash holdings - either completely or partially - and bearing the risk of basis changes.

In the previous section it has been shown that hedgers were assumed to be either totally hedged (traditonal theory of hedging) or to leave cash positions completely unhedged (selective hedging, WORKING). In the following analysis, based on the decision criteria of expected return and risk, we shall explain the often observed phenomenon that agents hold both, hedged and unhedged positions. The extent to which traders hedge their cash market holdings will be determined and factors and expectations which may explain their behaviour will be derived. The analysis will be carried out graphically by applying JOHNSON's and STEIN's models developed for futures markets in commodities, and formally in the context of portfolio theory.

2.2.1. Point of Departure

The analysis is based on the following assumptions which deviate to some extent from the classical portfolio approach:

- There is only one investment opportunity in the cash market, a fixed-income security, e.g. T-bonds, T-bills or GMNAs. This is the only source of investors' income.
- All assumptions made by portfolio theory on investors' behaviour are valid (41).
- Agents' cash market holdings are viewed as fixed, i.e. the amount of the cash position is given and can be standardized at $x_S = 1$. Hence the agent is long in cash (42). In contrast to a farmer who sells a part of his crop futures although not knowing the size of the crop occuring in some months (43), a short hedger in financial assets knows the amount of securities he owns. A long hedger who wants to lock in a special interest rate also knows the sum he will receive and invest in some months time.
- Cash market holdings can be hedged in the futures market by a position of amount x_F; where $x_F < 0$ indicates a short position and $x_F > 0$, a long position. Futures contracts are divisible, i.e. any quantity can be bought or sold.

The agent has to choose the amount of the futures market position as a hedge for his outstanding cash holdings x_S, i.e. he has to determine his optimal x_F which might be

either a long or short position of an amount less than
(underhedging), greater than (overhedging), or equal to
(traditional theory of hedging), the cash position.
Furthermore he may decide to carry the cash position
unhedged, i.e. the amount of his futures holdings is zero.
Selecting his optimal futures position x_F, the hedger
proceeds as portfolio theory assumes agents to behave, i.e.
he maximizes his expected utility which is a function of
expected return and risk.

The return on the agent's cash position of amount x_S can be
split into two components: an assured interest income per
period, r, due to a fixed coupon rate and an additional
return, either positive or negative, of amount $(s_1 - s_0)$,
resulting from a spot price change between time 0 and 1 (44).
With the prevailing price in 1 unknown at time 0 the return
of this position is a random variable that can be
characterized by

$$(\text{II}.11) \quad E(S) = x_S \, E(s_1 - s_0) + x_S \, r$$
$$= x_S \, E(\Delta s) + x_S \, r$$

The variance of the cash position is

$$(\text{II}.12) \quad \text{Var}(S) = x_S^2 \sigma_S^2$$

Hedging the cash position via a trade in futures markets, the expected return of the hedged position is equal to (II.11) plus the expected price change of the futures position in this period, $E(f_1 - f_0)$, weighted by the amount invested in futures (45)

$$(II.13) \quad E(H) = x_S \, E(s_1 - s_0) + x_S \, r + x_F \, E(f_1 - f_0)$$

$$= x_S \, E(\Delta s) + x_S \, r + x_F \, E(\Delta f)$$

The risk is given by the variance (46)

$$(II.14) \quad Var(H) = \sigma_H^2 = x_S^2 \, \sigma_S^2 + x_F^2 \, \sigma_F^2 + 2x_S x_F \, cov(S,F)$$

Equations (II.13) and (II.14) define the two decision variables for the utility-maximizing trader: $E(U) = U(E(H), \sigma_H^2)$. To allow a decision it is assumed that the hedger's probability distribution over all possible spot and futures prices to prevail at time 1 is known. Therefore variances and covariances are given, with variances assumed to be greater than zero and less than infinity.

One deviation from classical portfolio theory needs special consideration, i.e. the amount of cash holdings x_S is assumed to be fixed and equal to one, whereas x_F is determined by the hedger and might be equal to x_S, or greater or less than x_S. This procedure is in contrast to classical portfolio theory where the proportions invested in the assets, x_i, sum up to one and hence the return of two assets can be expressed as a linear combination of the two asset returns. With $x_S = 1$ given, and x_F determined by the agent, the sum of x_S and x_F might exceed or be smaller than one. Hence it is possible that the expected return of the hedged position, as a combination of cash and futures holdings, exceeds the return of the cash position.

This deviation from classical portfolio theory is based on the assumption that cash and futures positions are not viewed as perfect substitutes (47). Whereas in portfolio theory one dollar can be invested in asset A, or B, or in a combination of both, in the following analysis the dollar can be fully invested in spot holdings, and futures positions can be established in addition. Hence investment of all funds in the cash asset and additional holding of futures positions does not violate the budget constraint.
This is due to the fact that establishing a futures position does not involve a financial investment. Pure transaction costs (brokerage fees) for futures positions are neglected as they are for cash positions. Other costs involved in futures trading are margin requirements. In practice margins can be provided by collaterals: traders deposit a proportion of their cash holdings as collateral to satisfy margin requirements (48). Hence establishing a futures position does not necessarily involve costs beyond those of

transaction (which, as usual, are neglected) and the budget constraint holds.

As a consequence, assuming a correlation between cash and futures returns of 1, expected return and risk of hedged positions cannot be expressed as a linear combination of expected returns and risks of spot and futures positions.

2.2.2. Graphical Analysis

STEIN and JOHNSON analyse in their models traders' transactions in commodity markets. Since fixed-income securities can be regarded as a special type of commodity these models are applicable to interest rate futures markets.

2.2.2.1. Stein's Theory of Holding Stocks

STEIN developed a simple geometric technique to determine a trader's optimal combination of hedged and unhedged stocks (49). The risk-averse trader maximizes expected utility, with expected return and risk as arguments of the utility function.

Unhedged stocks in actuals yield $E(S) = E(s_1 - s_o) - m$, with m for marginal net carrying costs, and bear risk of $Var(S) = Var(s_1)$ The return of a hedged stock position is $E(H) = E(s_1 - s_o) - E(f_1 - f_o) - m$, with a risk equal to $Var(H) = Var(s_1) + Var(f_1) - 2cov(s_1, f_1)$. .

To determine the optimal proportion of the cash position to be hedged, STEIN drew an opportunity locus HS for expected return and risk for various combinations of hedged and unhedged positions in an expected return-variance diagram (Figure 2-3). Assuming that unhedged stocks have a higher expected return and higher variance than hedged stocks the opportunity locus is positively sloped (50). At point H all stocks are hedged, yielding an expected return of E(H) with a risk of Var(H) while at point S all cash units are unhedged yielding E(S) with a risk of Var(S). The two points H and S in Figure 2-3 are based on given expectations for prices and risk.

Given a set of convex indifference curves, the optimal ratio of hedged to unhedged cash units is determined by the tangential point of an indifference curve with the opportunity locus HS. This is point P in Figure 2-3, indicating OA as the proportion of stocks in cash hold unhedged and 100 - OA as the proportion hedged in futures.

Figure 2-3: Proportion of Individuals' Cash Position to Be Hedged.

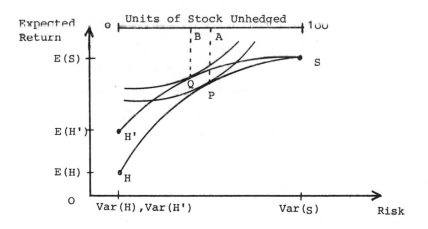

In a next step STEIN assumes a ceteris paribus futures price
increase. This price change leads to a higher expected
return for holding hedged positions given by H'. A new
opportunity locus H'S can be drawn which is touched by an
indifference curve of higher utility at point Q. Therefore,
in expectation of an increased return from hedged positions,
the ratio of unhedged to hedged units changes. The number of
hedged positions held increases by amount AB to a total of
100 - OB.

Stein not only showed that a hedger may hold parts of his
cash position unhedged, i.e. he is speculating to the extent
that he holds unhedged positions, but he also demonstrated
that the ratio of hedged to unhedged cash holdings is
modified with changing expectations on the return from
futures positions (51). He demonstrated that a hedger might
hold hedged and unhedged positions at the same time but he
could neither explain with his model why hedgers might be
overhedged nor the fact that hedgers might establish long
positions in futures in addition to unhedged stockholdings
(52). These shortcomings are overcome by the following
model.

2.2.2.2. Johnson's Model of Hedging and Speculation

JOHNSON presented a model with hedging and speculative
elements to explain various observable market phenomena by
traders' expectations of changes in the absolute level of
cash and futures prices (53). The trader is assumed to
establish positions in spot and futures in such a way that he
achieves his aim of an optimal combination of risk and return
subject to a risk minimization constraint in actuals (54).
Like STEIN the model specifies the proportion of hedged to
unhedged positions but determines beyond that the amount of
actual and futures holdings.

The following assumptions are made:
  - the risk-averse trader ranks all possible combinations
    of E(H) and Var(H) on a set of convex indifference
    curves in the expected return variance diagram.
  - the trader can engage in the following activities:
    • either he takes a long position in actuals at time 0
      which is sold at time 1;
    • or he goes long in cash and short in futures at time
      0 and offsets both positions which are assumed to be
      completely divisible at time 1.

As outlined above the amount of the spot position x_S is
assumed as given in this study. JOHNSON's model will be used
to illustrate the determination of the optimal futures
position for given x_S.

Market positions chosen by the trader at time 0 are shown in the coordinate system in Figure 2-4. Spot units purchased, x_S, are plotted on the horizontal axis. Since x_S is fixed the trader's cash position is indicated by point S on the horizontal axis. Every combination of this position with a futures position must lie on the vertical line AB through S. Futures units sold ($x_F < 0$) are plotted on the negative vertical axis, futures units bought ($x_F > 0$) on the positive vertical axis.

Expected return and risk (measured by the variance) of the trader's transactions can be expressed by equations (II.13) and (II.14). From (II.14) iso-variance of return ellipses with centre (0,0) can be drawn (55). Every point on such an ellipse represents a combination of spot, x_S, and futures, x_F, positions with a constant risk value.

On the basis of (II.13) $E(H) = x_S E(\Delta s) + x_S r + x_F E(\Delta f)$ iso-expected return lines of slope

$$ - \frac{E(\Delta s) + r}{E(\Delta f)} $$

can be drawn that describe combinations of x_S and x_F for which the expected return remains constant (56). The slope of iso-expected return lines is determined by the hedger's expectations on futures and cash price developments. If the trader's expectations on prices change, his set of iso-expected return lines changes too.

JOHNSON analysed the following situations (57):

1. The trader expects no changes in cash or futures prices, i.e. $E(\Delta s) = E(\Delta f) = 0$. Under these circumstances iso-expected return lines are vertical, such as lines AB, CD or any parallel, (see Figure 2-4), reflecting the fact that cash holdings yield the pure interest income r. All tangential points of iso-expected return lines with iso-variance ellipses form the opportunity locus OZ indicating combinations of x_S and x_F with minimum risk for given expected return.

Since in this analysis the amount of x_S is assumed as given, the intersection of a vertical line through S with the opportunity locus OZ determines the optimal futures position (58). At this point L the iso-expected return line is naturally tangent to an iso-expected variance ellipse.
The optimal futures position of amount $-x_{F_1}$ as a hedge against x_S has been determined for a situation in which the trader does not expect price changes. According to the trader's expectations on the variances and covariance, which are represented by the iso-variance ellipses, $-x_{F_1}$ need not necessarily be equal in amount to the spot holdings x_S.

2. Next JOHNSON analyses situations in which the trader expects a positive (negative) change in the cash market and constant futures prices, i.e. $E(\Delta s) > 0$ ($E(\Delta s) < 0$), $E(\Delta f) = 0$. Iso-expected return lines like AB or CD will remain vertical

Figure 2-4: Determination of a Hedger's Optimal Futures
Position with no Expected Futures Price Change

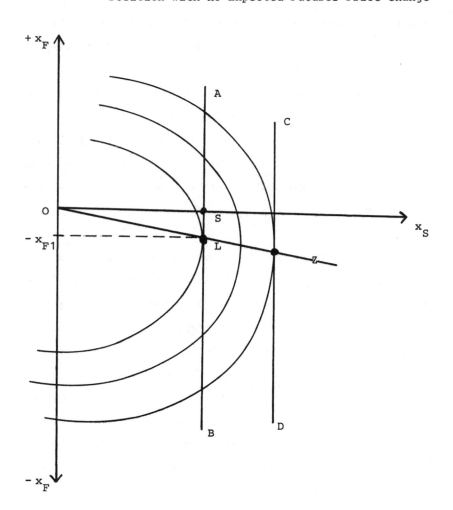

but will indicate higher (less) levels of expected return. Point L in Figure 2-4 will remain the tangential point to an iso-variance ellipse.

Hence neither the amount of the futures position $-x_{F_1}$ as a hedge against x_S will change, nor the risk of the overall position (59). In comparison to situation 1 (no expected price changes) point L will indicate values of higher (less) expected return at the same risk level.

3. If the trader expects constant cash prices and a price decline in futures, $E(\Delta s) = 0$, $E(\Delta f) < 0$, iso-expected return lines will be positively sloped like line EF and parallels in Figure 2-5. A new locus of tangential points OZ' of iso-expected return lines with iso-variance ellipses can be drawn. For given x_S the intersection of line AB with the opportunity locus at point M determines the optimal amount of the futures position $-x_{F_2}$ In response to an expected price decline in futures and, in consequence, an expected profit from the futures position, the trader extended his futures holdings from $-x_{F_1}$ to $-x_{F_2}$. The increase in the futures position is a speculative element (60).

4. The last situation to be analysed is an expected price increase in futures with constant cash prices, $E(\Delta s) = 0$, $E(\Delta f) > 0$. Iso-expected return lines will be negatively sloped like line GH in Figure 2-5. As in the analysis above the optimal amount of the futures position is given by the point where line AB (indicating the given spot position)

Figure 2-5: Determination of a Hedger's Optimal Futures
Position with Expected Futures Price Change

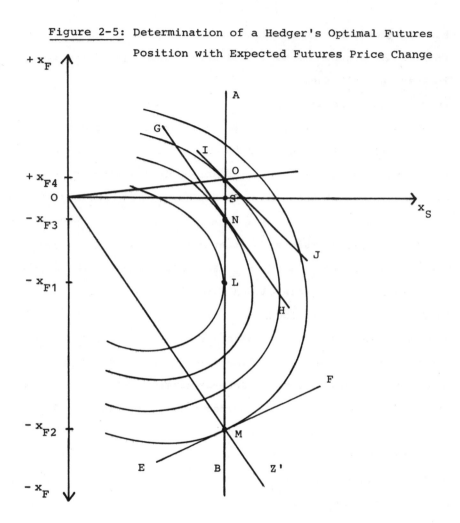

intersects the opportunity locus of tangential points between iso-expected return lines and iso-variance ellipses (point N with $-x_{F_3}$).

Since the slope of iso-expected return lines is determined by expected price changes, these lines will become flatter with increasing expected futures price changes (slope: $-E(\Delta s + r)/E(\Delta t)$, i.e. the larger the expected positive futures price change the more the agent will reduce the amount of short futures positions. In Figure 2-5 the agent will move upwards on line AB.

Two situations must be distinguished: Between points L and S the trader will take short positions in futures, e.g. of amount $-x_{F_3}$ as indicated by point N, although he expects futures prices to increase. He is willing to accept an expected loss from futures in order to reduce the overall price risk of the cash position S. In contrast to the situation with no expected price changes in cash and futures (point L in 2-5) the hedger holds a speculative element of $(x_{F_1} - x_{F_3})$.

In expectation of large positive futures price changes the trader will establish long positions in futures in addition to his long cash position. In Figure 2-5 these are points on line AB above point S, e.g. point 0 indicating a long position in futures of amount x_{F_4} (61). The trader has lifted his hedge completely. In fact he is speculating in both: actuals and futures.

Graphical analysis made it possible to derive the trader's futures position which maximizes, for given cash holdings, his expected utility as a function of expected return and risk. Furthermore it could be demonstrated that a hedger who has expectations on price movements takes hedged and unhedged (speculative) positions according to his expectations. By this procedure it was possible to overcome the traditional view that traders are either speculators or hedgers (62).

2.2.3. Formal Analysis

The determination of a trader's optimal futures market position as a hedge against his cash holdings will now be analysed formally. In this way factors determining the amount of futures positions can be analysed more precisely. Besides price expectations as an explanation of traders' transactions, variances and covariances between cash and futures prices, which were regarded as fixed in the previous graphical analysis, will also be taken into consideration.

The analysis uses a mean-variance representation of preferences (63). The situation is the same as described at the beginning of this section, i.e. a risk-averse trader with a given amount (x_S) of fixed-income securities wants to maximize his expected utility. The expected utility is given by a linear function of expected return and risk, where v is a positive parameter for the trader's risk aversion.

$$(II.15) \quad E(U) = E(H) - 0.5 \, v \, Var(H)$$

Expected return and risk are given by equations (II.13) and (II.14). Hence (II.15) can be written as

$$(II.15a) \quad E(U) = x_S \, E(\Delta s) + x_S \, r + x_F \, E(\Delta f)$$
$$- \, 0.5 \, v \, (x_S^2 \sigma_S^2 + x_F^2 \sigma_F^2 + 2 x_S x_F \, cov(S,F))$$

To determine the optimal position to be hedged (x_F^*) the utility function (II.15a) is maximized with respect to x_F (64).

$$(II.16) \quad \frac{\partial E(U)}{\partial x_F} = E(\Delta f) - \frac{1}{2} v \left[2x_F \sigma_F^2 + 2x_S \text{ cov}(S,F) \right]$$

Setting (II.16) equal to zero, the optimal amount to be hedged (x_F^*) can be written as

$$(II.17) \quad x_F^* = \frac{E(\Delta f)}{v \sigma_F^2} - \frac{\text{cov}(S,F)}{\sigma_F^2} x_S$$

This expression can be decomposed into two components (65), a speculative component given by the first expression in equation (II.17) and the pure hedge component (66). For a hedger both components are relevant in determining his optimal x_F^*. A speculator is only concerned with the first expression since he does not hold cash assets ($x_S = 0$) and hence the second component becomes zero.

2.2.3.1. Pure Hedge Component

The pure hedge component

$$(II.18) \quad x_{FP} = - \frac{\text{cov}(S,F)}{\sigma_F^2} x_S$$

determines a trader's futures market position who merely wants to reduce his overall price risk. This expression could also have been derived by minimizing the variance as given by (II.14) with respect to x_F (67). Rearranging (II.18) to

$$(II.19) \qquad - \frac{x_{FP}}{x_S} = \frac{\text{cov}(S,F)}{\sigma_F^2} = OHR$$

leads to the optimal hedge ratio (OHR) for a risk minimizing hedger.

For purposes of interpretation the cov (S,F) is decomposed and (II.18) can be written as

$$(II.20) \qquad x_{FP} = - \frac{\sigma_S}{\sigma_F} \rho_{S,F} x_S$$

This shows that the amount of the optimal futures position x_{FP} depends on the correlation coefficient between cash and futures price movements ($\rho_{S,F}$) and the relation between the two standard deviations (σ_S / σ_F).

A routine hedge would occur if the hedger expects $\sigma_S / \sigma_F \, \rho_{S,F}$ to be equal to one, i.e. equal standard deviations and total positive correlation of cash and futures prices. Cash and futures prices are expected to move always in the same direction to the same extent. Consequently $x_{FP} = -x_S$, the cash market position (long) is completely short hedged in futures. This situation is equivalent to traditional hedging theory (See II.2.1.1.).

If the hedger expects perfect positive correlation of cash and futures prices ($\rho_{S,F}$ = 1) but different standard deviations, i.e. a basis change, he will, according to the relation of σ_S/σ_F, take a short position in futures which may be smaller or greater than the cash position. If in this situation the correlation is less than 1 but greater than 0 the exact amount of the short futures position will be determined by (II.20).

With correlation coefficients equal to zero the futures position will be zero according to (II.20).

A negative correlation between cash and futures prices will always lead to a long position since

$$(\text{II.20a}) \quad x_{FP} = -\frac{\sigma_S}{\sigma_F}\left[-\rho_{S,F}\right]x_S$$

is positive. The amount of the long position the trader will take depends on his expectations of the relation between the standard deviations (σ_S/σ_F) and the correlation coefficient.

The pure hedge component describes the behaviour of a trader who intends to minimize risk. Based on his expectations on the correlation between cash and futures price movements and the relation between the standard deviation of cash and futures prices he determines the proportion of his optimal, i.e. risk minimizing, futures position. He might carry part of his cash position unhedged or take a futures position exceeding his cash holdings. Hence there is a speculative element in the pure hedge component of a risk minimizing hedger (68).

2.2.3.2. Speculative Component

Traders establish speculative positions to increase their expected return.

Expression (II.21) $\quad x_{FS} = \dfrac{E(\Delta f)}{v \, \sigma_F^2}$

shows that the speculative position a hedger takes depends on his expectations concerning the change in futures prices, $E(\Delta f) = E(f_1 - f_0)$, his risk aversion (v), and the variance of the futures price (σ_F^2) (69). The speculative position is independent of the trader's cash market holdings (x_S).
The amount held is inversely proportional to the hedger's parameter of risk aversion and the variance of futures prices. If the hedger is infinitely risk averse ($v \rightarrow \infty$) the speculative component will disappear. It will disappear too if he expects the futures price at time 1 to be equal to the price today, i.e. if he expects f_0 to be an unbiased predictor of f_1, or if he does not have any expectations on $E(\Delta f)$ at all.

If the trader expects futures prices to fall then $E(\Delta f)$ will be negative and so will be (II.21), $x_{FS} = -E(\Delta f)/v \, \sigma_F^2$. He will take a short speculative position. Thus the hedger is speculating on a futures price decline. The speculative component will be a long position if he expects a positive change in the futures price change, $E(\Delta f) > 0$.

Speculators in futures also establish positions according to the speculative component of (II.21). Wether it is a long or short position depends on the direction of the expected price change. The amount of the engagement depends on the expected futures price change and variance and speculators' risk aversion.

The hedger's <u>overall futures market position</u> consists of both, the pure hedge (x_{FP}) and the speculative (x_{FS}) component. All possible combinations of these two components, expectations on which these positions are established and overall futures market positions derived are shown in Table 2-1. Some situations will be treated in detail.

Let us assume a hedger who expects a positive correlation between cash and futures prices. Hence his pure hedge position will be a short position. If this trader expects a decline in futures prices, $E(\Delta f) < 0$, the speculative

Table 2-1 : Composition of the Overall Futures Market Position

Case	Pure Hedge Component		Speculative Component		Overall Futures Market Position
	position	given expectation	position	given expectation [1]	
I	short	$0 < \rho_{S,F} \le 1$	short	$E(\Delta f) < 0$	short
II			0	$E(\Delta f) = 0$	short
III			long	$E(\Delta f) > 0$	short or long
IV	0	$\rho_{S,F} = 0$	short	$E(\Delta f) < 0$	short
V			0	$E(\Delta f) = 0$	0
VI			long	$E(\Delta f) > 0$	long
VII	long	$-1 \le \rho_{S,F} < 0$	short	$E(\Delta f) < 0$	short or long
VIII			0	$E(\Delta f) = 0$	long
IX			long	$E(\Delta f) > 0$	long

1) We assume that $v \not\to \infty$ and $\sigma_F^2 \ne \infty$. Otherwise the speculative component would be zero.

component will also be a short position. The overall short position will be

$$x_F^* = x_{FP} + x_{FS} = - \frac{\sigma_S}{\sigma_F} \rho_{S,F} \; x_S + \left[\frac{- E(\Delta f)}{v \; \sigma_F^2} \right]$$

i.e. the amount of the overall position in futures will exceed the pure hedge component (x_{FP}) by the amount of the speculative component (case I of Table 2-1). This case can be compared to situation 3 described in the graphical analysis of the previous section where the short position was extended from point L of amount $-x_{F_1}$ to point M $(-x_{F_2})$ in expectation of a negative futures price change (70). There the increase of the short position from $-x_{F_1}$ to $- x_{F_2}$ was described as a speculative element.

If the same trader (short pure hedge component) expects futures prices to increase, $E(\Delta f) > 0$, his speculative component will be a long position, reducing the amount of the pure hedge component (case III of Table 2-1). In this situation it depends on the amount of the speculative component whether the overall futures market position will remain a short position (as indicated by N in Figure 2-5) or change to a long position (indicated by point O) (71).

A hedger expecting a negative correlation between cash and futures prices will hold a long pure hedge component. With

an expected price decline in futures, this long pure hedge
component will be reduced by the speculative short component
(case VII in Table 2-1). Depending on the amount of the two
positions, the overall hedge position may be either long or
short.

2.2.4. Conclusions

In the previous section the amount of the futures position a
trader takes to hedge his cash holdings that were assumed as
given and fixed were derived and expectations governing his
transactions outlined. It was possible to show by applying
the decision criteria of portfolio theory, i.e. expected
return and risk, that a utility maximizing agent need not
necessarily be completely hedged or unhedged, as is assumed
in classical theory of hedging or WORKING's concept. The
futures position may be smaller than or greater than cash
holdings. A futures position equal in amount to the cash
position can occur but need not necessarily result.

A hedger establishes a futures position that consists of two
elements: a speculative and a hedge element.
The speculative component which is independent of his cash
holdings is zero if the hedger

    - is infinitely risk averse ($v \rightarrow \infty$),
    - has no expectations concerning futures prices,

- expects no change in futures prices, i.e. f_o is an unbiased predictor of f_1,
- considers the variance of the futures price to be infinitely high ($\sigma_F^2 \to \infty$).

Otherwise the speculative component will be a long or short position, determined by the trader's expectations on the direction and amount of change in futures prices, his risk aversion, and the variance of futures prices.

The <u>pure hedge component</u>

- will be zero if there is no correlation between spot and futures prices ($\rho_{S,F} = 0$),
- will be equal in amount to the spot position and of opposite (same) sign if the trader expects total positive (negative) correlation between spot and futures price changes, i.e. $\rho_{S,F} = +1$, ($\rho_{S,F} = -1$), and equal variances, i.e. $\sigma_S = \sigma_F$,
- may be greater or smaller than the spot position depending on $\sigma_S/\sigma_F \, \rho_{S,F}$. Whether it will be a long or short position depends on the sign of $\rho_{S,F}$.

Hence even the pure hedge component of a risk minimizing hedger may deviate in amount from his spot holdings, and thus may contain a speculative element due to the hedger's expectations on the covariance term.

The pure hedge and the speculative component together determine the trader's <u>overall position</u> in futures. For the risk-minimizing hedger the speculative component will be zero, hence he will take positions in futures according to the pure hedge component.

3. THEORETICAL EVALUATION OF THE EFFECTS OF HEDGING ON AN INDIVIDUAL TRADER

In the previous section we determined the amount of the futures position an agent takes according to his expectations. On the basis of these results we shall investigate whether and in what way a trader's single position or portfolio is affected if he acts according to the rules developed above within the framework of portfolio theory (72). That means, expected return, risk and location in the mean-variance space of hedged positions or portfolios will be compared to unhedged cash holdings.

3.1. Hedging a Single Asset

As in the previous analysis, we assume a hedger holding a given amount (x_S = 1) of fixed-income securities, e.g. T-bonds. To simplify, we neglect any type of transaction cost as well as pure interest income, x_S r. Given the trader's expectations on cash prices for the next period, s_1, his probability distribution over the expected cash return $E(S)$ is known (See Figure 2-6). Hence expected return, $E(S)$, and variance, $Var(S)$, can be calculated via equations (II.12) respectively (II.11), where we abstract from pure interest income, and delineated in the mean-variance diagram of Figure 2-7. Three situations are shown: an expected positive cash

Figure 2-6: Probability Distribution of Return for Hedged
and Unhedged Positions

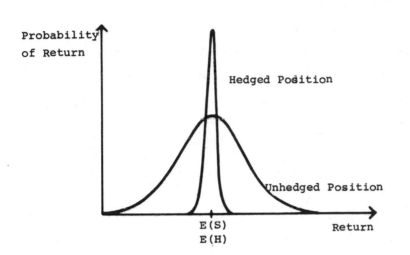

Figure 2-7: Spot and Hedged Positions of Risk-Minimizing
Hedgers in the Mean-Variance Space

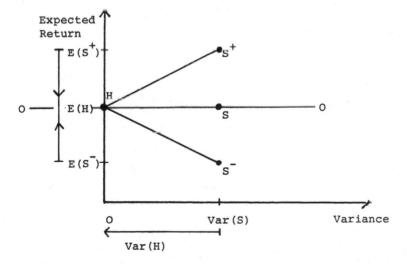

price change, $E(S) > 0$, represented by point S+, an expected negative cash price change, (S-), and expected constant prices leading to point S. The variance is assumed to be equal in all three cases.

The following analysis first investigates a hedger basing his decisions on the pure hedge component, before turning to the speculative and overall hedge (pure and speculative) positions.

3.1.1. Pure Hedge Component

A hedger acting according to the pure hedge component only seeks to minimize risk. Given his expectations, he will determine the futures market position as indicated by (II.18), the pure hedge component, x_{FP}. Substituting x_{FP} into equation (II.14), the variance of the hedged position, leads to (73)

$$(II.22) \quad Var(H) = x_S^2 \sigma_S^2 - x_S^2 \frac{cov(S,F)^2}{\sigma_F^2}$$

Decomposing the covariance term and rearranging, it follows that

$$(II.22a) \quad Var(H) = x_S^2 \left[\sigma_S^2 - \frac{\sigma_S^2 \sigma_F^2 \rho_{S,F}^2}{\sigma_F^2} \right] = x_S^2 \sigma_S^2 \left[1 - \rho_{S,F}^2 \right]$$

The expression $x_S^2 \sigma_S^2$ is the variance of the spot position. Thus the degree of risk reduction that can be achieved by holding the pure hedge component x_{FP} depends on the squared correlation coefficient between cash and futures prices which is the coefficient of determination, $\rho_{S,F}^2$. The greater $\rho_{S,F}$ the greater the risk reduction that can be achieved.

If $\rho_{S,F}$ is equal to ± 1, total risk reduction will occur, i.e. Var(H) will be zero (compare Table 2-2). No correlation between cash and futures prices, $\rho_{S,F} = 0$, leads to Var(H) $= x_S^2 \sigma_S^2$, i.e. the variance of an unhedged spot position. With $\rho_{S,F}$ between 0 and 1 the risk of a hedged position will be within the interval determined by the two extremes, i.e. $0 < \text{Var(H)} < \text{Var(S)}$.

Hence a futures position taken according to the pure hedge component will never lead to an enlargement of risk. In the worst case, correlation between cash and futures prices will be zero and Var(H) equal to Var(S). In all other situations, risk will be reduced, if $0 < \rho_{S,F} < |1|$, or completely abolished, if $\rho_{S,F} = |1|$ (74).

The probability of return of a position hedged according to the pure hedge component can be delineated in Figure 2-6 which shows that the variability of possible outcomes around the expected value is reduced to a large extent by hedging. Figure 2-6 is another way of presenting the risk reduction effects of hedging on cash holdings.

Substituting the expression of the pure hedge component in (II.13), and abstracting from pure interest income (x_S r), leads to an <u>expected return</u> of

$$(II.23) \quad E(H) = x_S \; E(\Delta s) \; + \; - \; \frac{\sigma_S}{\sigma_F} \; \rho_{S,F} \; x_S \; E(\Delta f)$$

Equation (II.23) indicates the return of a hedged position as combination of the spot return, x_S $E(\Delta s)$, plus or minus the expected return from the futures position, $E(\Delta f)$, multiplied by the amount of positions taken, x_{FP}.

If a correlation of 1 between cash and futures prices is expected, the futures return will always be of opposite sign to the cash return (compare Table 2-2) (75). Since the amount of the futures position is taken according to differences in the standard deviations between cash and futures prices (σ_S/σ_F) (76), the expected return of a hedged position will always be zero, $E(H) = 0$. With $\rho_{S,F} = 0$, no futures position will be established (see II.20), and $E(H)$ will be equal to $E(S)$ (Compare Table 2-2). A correlation coefficient between 0 and ± 1 will always lead to cash and futures price changes of opposite sign. If the expected return of a spot position was different from zero, $E(S) \neq 0$, an expected loss or profit in cash holdings will be reduced by the expected return of the futures position. Thus $E(H)$ will be in an interval between zero and $E(S)$, i.e. $0 < E(H) < E(S)$, if $E(S)$ was positive and $E(S) < E(H) < 0$, if $E(S)$ was negative (compare Table 2-2).

Table 2-2 : Expected Return and Risk of a Position Hedged According to the Pure Hedge Component

$\rho_{S,F}$	$E(H) = II.23$	$Var(H) = II.22a$
$+1$	$x_S \cdot E(\Delta s) + (- \frac{\sigma_S}{\sigma_F} \cdot x_S)\, E(\Delta f) = 0$	0
$0 < \rho_{S,F} < 1$	$x_S\, E(\Delta s) + (- \frac{\sigma_S}{\sigma_F}\, \rho_{S,F}\, x_S)\, E(\Delta f) \begin{array}{l} < E(S),\ \text{if } E(S) > 0 \\ > E(S),\ \text{if } E(S) < 0 \end{array}$	$x_S^2\, \sigma_S^2 (1 - \rho_{S,F}^2) < Var(S)$
0	$x_S\, E(\Delta s) = E(S)$	$x_S^2\, \sigma_S^2 = Var(S)$
$-1 < \rho_{S,F} < 0$	$x_S\, E(\Delta s) + (- \frac{\sigma_S}{\sigma_F} - \rho_{S,F}\, x_S)\, E(\Delta f) \begin{array}{l} < E(S),\ \text{if } E(S) > 0 \\ > E(S),\ \text{if } E(S) < 0 \end{array}$	$x_S^2\, \sigma_S^2 (1 - (-\rho_{S,F}^2)) < Var(S)$
-1	$x_S\, E(\Delta s) + (\frac{\sigma_S}{\sigma_F}\, x_S)\, E(\Delta f) = 0$	0

Traders acting according to the pure hedge component can obtain the following results:

1. With perfect correlation between cash and futures prices (either positive or negative) expected return and variance will be zero, a situation indicated by point H in Figure 2-7.

2. With no correlation a futures position will not be established. Hence this is identical to an unhedged spot position as indicated by points S, S+, or S- in Figure 2-7.

3. Correlation coefficients between 0 and |1|, lead to reduced variances and smaller absolute returns for hedged positions in comparison to spot positions. Points between S+ (S-,S) and H in Figure 2-7 describe these outcomes.

Hence we can conclude that risk-minimizing hedgers ex-ante reach their aim of risk reduction as long as the correlation between cash and futures prices is different from zero. Depending on traders' previous expectations concerning E(S), this risk reduction effect may be accompanied by an increase or decrease in return. Consequently, we may observe situations in which traders reduce the risk of their position while the return increases at the same time. Such an increase in expected utility can be shown in the mean-variance diagram of Figure 2-7 by any point moving from S- in the direction of H.

3.1.2. Speculative Component

Traders maximizing expected return, establish positions in futures as described by the speculative position. Such positions will always lead to a positive expected return in combination with an increase in risk.

Risk can be calculated according to $Var(F) = x_{FS}^2 \sigma_F^2$

Substituting for x_{FS} from (II.21) $E(\Delta f)/v \, \sigma_F^2$ leads to

$$Var(F) = \frac{E(\Delta f)^2}{v^2 \sigma_F^2}$$

We see that the speculative component is a risky position as long as $E(\Delta f) \neq 0$. $E(\Delta f) = 0$ would not lead to speculative trading.

Expected return is $E(F) = x_{FS} E(\Delta f)$. Since we saw above (77) that the futures position, x_{FS}, taken will be a long position if futures prices are expected to increase, and a short position if the trader expects the opposite price movement, expected return will always be positive.

According to the speculative position, expected results of futures trading can be analyzed for speculators and those hedgers who trade in futures not only for the sake of risk reduction.

3.1.3. Overall Hedge

A hedge consisting of the pure hedge and the speculative component is called - following above terminology (78) - an overall hedge. Effects on risk and expected return can be derived by substituting (II.17) into (II.14) or into (II.13). The risk inherent in the hedged position is

$$(II.24) \qquad Var(H^*) = x_S^2 \, \sigma_S^2 \left[1 - \rho_{S,F}^2\right] + \frac{E(\Delta f)}{\sigma_F^2 v^2} + 2 \frac{E(\Delta f)}{\sigma_F \, v} x_S \sigma_S \, \rho_{S,F}$$

It is equal to the variance of a position hedged according to the pure hedge component (II.22a), the latter of which we know to be smaller than Var(S) provided that $\rho_{S,F} \neq 0$, plus additional risk brought about by futures holdings according to the speculative component. Hence Var(H*) may be smaller or greater than Var(S). The exact value cannot be determined without knowledge of the parameters. From the graphical analysis of Figure 2-5 we know that both effects may result.

The expected return of the overall hedge is

$$(II.25) \qquad E(H^*) = x_S E(\Delta s) + \frac{\sigma_S}{\sigma_F} \rho_{S,F} x_S \, E(\Delta f) + \frac{E(\Delta f)^2}{v \, \sigma_F^2}$$

It consists of the expected return of the pure hedge component (II.23), the absolute value of which is smaller than the absolute value of the spot return, plus the expected return due to speculative trading. $E(H^*)$ might be less than $E(S)$ or exceed $E(S)$. Again, no precise value can be derived without knowledge of the parameters.

A theoretical investigation of new feasibility areas for the overall hedge in the mean-variance space is very difficult since the parameters that determine $Var(H^*)$ and $E(H^*)$ are not known. As indicated above, $Var(H^*)$ and $E(H^*)$ may be greater or smaller than equivalent values of a spot position. Hence combinations of $E(H^*)$ and $Var(H^*)$ in the mean-variance space are obtainable which lead to points of greater return with less or greater risk, or to points with less return and less risk in comparison with unhedged positions.

Possible results are shown in Figure 2-8. The graphical analysis of the previous section in Figure 2-5 will be used to support these indications (79). Point S in Figure 2-8 represents the spot position with no expected spot price change. It corresponds to point S in Figure 2-5 abstracting the fact that pure interest income $(x_s \ r)$ is neglected for the movement. The arrows indicate directions of new feasible areas:

Combinations of less risk and less return in the third quadrant correspond to points such as N in Figure 2-5 where traders take short futures poitions to reduce price risk although they expect futures prices to increase.

120

Figure 2-8: Feasibility Area for Hedgers (Overall Hedge)

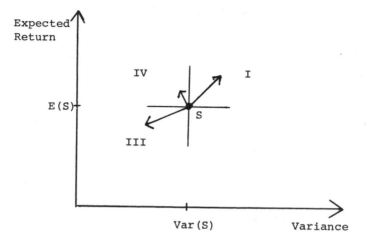

Points of greater return than S might be brought about by
additional short futures positions taken in expectation of a
futures price decline. These points might bear less risk
than S (fourth quadrant) or more risk (first quadrant). For
example point M from Figure 2-5 indicates a hedged position
with more return and more risk than a spot position.

The theoretical evaluation of the effects of taking overall
futures positions as a hedge against cash holdings led to the
conclusion that hedgers can improve their situation.
Compared to unhedged spot holdings new positions can be
reached that bear less risk with less or more return, or more
return combined with an increase in risk. Hence a trader

acting according to the rules developed by portfolio theory above can improve his situation, i.e. increase his utility, as shown in the mean-variance diagram of Figure 2-8. The point which he finally may choose depends on his preferences.

3.2. Hedging a Single Asset as Part of a Portfolio

In the previous section we analysed effects of hedging on
expected return and risk of single fixed-income securities.
The following investigation discusses consequences of hedging
on risk and expected return of portfolios.   The portfolio
consists of n-assets, stocks, or fixed-income securities and
an unhedged position, e.g. T-bonds.

The question is in which way expected return and risk of a
portfolio will   change if the fixed-income security i-s hedged
according to the pure hedge component (80).

3.2.1. Analysis of Expected Return

The expected return of a portfolio including an unhedged
fixed-income security (S), $E(R_{PS})$, can be calculated from
formula (II.4) leading to (81)

$$(II.26) \quad E(R_{PS}) = \sum_{i=1}^{n} x_i \, E(R_i) + x_S \, E(R_S)$$

$$\text{with } \sum_{i=1}^{n} x_i + x_S = 1, \quad x_i \geq 0, \quad x_S > 0$$

where x_S indicates the T-bond proportion in the portfolio.
If the T-bond is completely hedged its contribution to the
expected return changes to $x_H E(R_H)$, with x_H equal in amount
to x_S .   The previous analysis showed that the expected
return of a hedged position - whether or not we consider the

pure hedge or overall hedge component - may be equal to, greater, or less than the expected return of the unhedged position. This statement must be repeated for the hedged portfolio. A more precise result can only be derived if the parameters are known.

3.2.2. Analysis of Risk

3.2.2.1. With Respect to One Hedged Position

The risk of the portfolio consisting of n-assets and the fixed-income security, referred to as portfolio 1, can be described by equation (II.5) as:

$$(II.27) \quad \text{Var}(R_{PS}) = \sum_{i=1}^{n} x_i^2 \sigma_i^2 + \sum_{\substack{i=1 \\ i \neq j}}^{n} \sum_{j=1}^{n} x_i x_j \text{cov}(R_i, R_j) \quad (a)$$

$$+ \quad x_S^2 \sigma_S^2 \quad (b)$$

$$+ 2x_S \sum_{i=1}^{n} x_i \text{cov}(R_i, R_S) \quad (c)$$

Hedging the fixed-income security, the risk of this hedged portfolio, referred to as portfolio 2, is expressed by

$$(II.28) \quad \text{Var}(R_{PH}) = \sum_{i=1}^{n} x_i^2 \sigma_i^2 + \sum_{\substack{i=1 \\ i \neq j}}^{n} \sum_{j=1}^{n} x_i x_j \text{cov}(R_i, R_j) \quad (a)$$

$$+ \quad x_H^2 \sigma_H^2 \quad (b)$$

$$+ 2x_H \sum_{i=1}^{n} x_i \text{cov}(R_i, R_H) \quad (c)$$

A comparison of (II.27) with (II.28) to evaluate which of the two portfolios bears less risk, shows that the variances and covariances of the n-assets are not influenced at all by hedging the T-bond. Hence component (a) expresses equal risk for both portfolios.

Components (b) and (c) change if the T-bond is hedged. While in portfolio 1 the variance of the spot position $(x_S^2 \sigma_S^2)$ contributes as component (b) to the portfolio risk, in portfolio 2 it is the variance of the hedged position $(x_H^2 \sigma_H^2)$. From the previous analysis we know that the variance of an unhedged spot position, $\text{Var}(R_S)$, is greater than the variance of the hedged position, $\text{Var}(R_H)$, provided that the correlation between spot and futures prices is different from zero, $(\rho_{S,F} \neq 0)$. Assuming $\rho_{S,F} \neq 0$ (82), we can conclude that component (b) leads to a risk reduction of portfolio 2 in comparison to portfolio 1.

Component (c) expresses the sum of weighted covariances between the unhedged T-bond and all other securities in portfolio 1, $2x_S \sum_{i=1}^{n} x_i \text{cov}(R_i, R_S)$, or the sum of weighted covariances between the hedged T-bond and all other securities of portfolio 2, $2x_H \sum_{i=1}^{n} x_i \text{cov}(R_i, R_H)$. Since x_S is equal in amount to x_H and all x_i-s remain unchanged, the covariance terms of asset S or H with all n-assets determine values and signs of component (c). Decomposing the covariance terms, we have to compare

$$\sum_{i=1}^{n} x_i \sigma_i \sigma_S \rho_{i,S} \gtrless \sum_{i=1}^{n} x_i \sigma_i \sigma_H \rho_{i,H}$$

The σ_i-s do not change when the fixed-income security is hedged, hence they are equal on both sides. Assuming $\rho_{S,F}$ different from zero, we recognize that $\sigma_S > \sigma_H$. Hence we can so far conclude that component (c) bears less risk in the hedged portfolio than in portfolio 1. Values and signs of the sum of weighted correlation coefficients are unknown:

$$\sum_{i=1}^{n} x_i \rho_{i,S} \underset{<}{\overset{>}{=}} \sum_{i=1}^{n} x_i \rho_{i,H}$$

If $\sum_{i=1}^{n} x_i \rho_{i,S}$ is equal in amount or greater than $\sum_{i=1}^{n} x_i \rho_{i,H}$ then component (c) of portfolio 1 exceeds the same component of portfolio 2, and the unhedged portfolio 1 will bear more risk than the hedged portfolio 2.

With $\sum_{i=1}^{n} x_i \rho_{i,S}$ smaller than $\sum_{i=1}^{n} x_i \rho_{i,H}$ component (c) would make portfolio 2 more risky than 1, under the further assumption that the amount of risk increase of portfolio 2 according to component (c) is larger than the amount of risk reduction according to component (h).

For another situation a judgment is possible. If the hedge works out to a perfect hedge, the hedged position has a variance of zero, $\sigma_H^2 = 0$. Hence whilst $\sum_{i=1}^{n} x_i \rho_{i,S}$ is positive, component (c) of portfolio 2 will be less than the equivalent component of portfolio 1 and the hedged portfolio will bear less risk.

A definite answer to the question whether hedging one asset of a portfolio reduces overall portfolios risk cannot be derived as long as the sum of weighted correlation coefficients or covariance terms is unknown. We can state that these terms determine the overall risk of the two portfolios, and that a correlation between the n-assets and the spot position equal to or greater than the correlation between n-assets and the hedged position leads to risk reduction for the hedged portfolio:

$$\text{Var}(R_{PS}) > \text{Var}(R_{PH}) \quad \text{if} \quad \sum_{i=1}^{n} x_i \rho_{i,S} \geq \sum_{i=1}^{n} x_i \rho_{i,H}$$

3.2.2.2. With Respect to a Decomposed Hedged Position

The above analysis of the risk of a hedged and unhedged portfolio did only lead to a limited result. Therefore the hedged position in portfolio 2 will be decomposed, i.e. attention will be drawn to a hedged portfolio 3 consisting of n-assets, a spot T-bond and a futures T-bond position. The variance of this portfolio 3 is:

$$(II.29) \quad \text{Var}(R_{PH}^{=}) = \sum_{i=1}^{n} x_i^2 \sigma_i^2 + \sum_{\substack{i=1 \\ i=j}}^{n} \sum_{j=1}^{n} x_i x_j \text{cov}(R_i, R_j) \quad \text{(a)}$$

$$+ x_S^2 \sigma_S^2 + x_F^2 \sigma_F^2 + 2x_S x_F \text{cov}(R_S, R_F) \quad \text{(b)}$$

$$+ 2x_S \sum_{i=1}^{n} x_i \, \text{cov}(R_i, R_S) \quad \text{(c)}$$

$$+ 2x_F \sum_{i=1}^{n} x_i \text{cov}(R_i, R_F) \quad \text{(d)}$$

A comparison of (II.29) with the risk of the unhedged

portfolio 1 leads to the result that component (a) is again equal for both portfolios. The same is valid for component (c) since the weighted covariances between the spot T-bond and all other assets in the market, $x_S \sum_{i=1}^{n} x_i \, cov(R_i, R_S)$, do not change. To judge on component (b), the spot T-bond variance, $x_S^2 \sigma_S^2$, of portfolio 1 has to be compared with

$$x_S^2 \sigma_S^2 + x_F^2 \sigma_F^2 + 2x_S x_F \, cov(R_S, R_F).$$

Since this expression is the variance of a hedged position, $x_H^2 \sigma_H^2$, we come to the same result as above: component (b) is of smaller risk in portfolio 3 than in the spot portfolio 1 (under the assumption that $\rho_{S,F} \neq 0$).

To summarize the results reached sofar: components (a) and (c) are equal in amount, whilst component (b) is smaller for the hedged portfolio 3.

A component (d) contributes to the risk of the hedged portfolio 3 which does not exist for portfolio 1. Thus if this component is either negative, which would mean risk-decreasing, or positive but of smaller amount than the risk-decreasing effect of component (b), we may conclude that hedging a fixed-income security of a portfolio reduces the overall portfolio risk.

Therefore component (d), expressing the weighted covariances between all assets i and the futures position, $2x_F \sum_{i=1}^{n} x_i \, cov$ (R_i, R_F), has to be analysed. Decomposing the covariance term, we find:

$2x_F \sum_{i=1}^{n} x_i \sigma_i \sigma_F \, \rho_{i,F}$. Values for x_i, σ_i and σ_F are not negative. The signs of x_F and $\rho_{F,i}$ must be discussed.

From the previous analysis (83) we know that x_F has a negative sign which expresses a short position if the covariance between cash and futures returns is positive, $\rho_{S,F}$ > 0. In the following analysis we shall assume a positive correlation between cash and futures prices (84). Under this assumption the sign of component (d) depends on the sum of weighted correlation coefficients between the futures position and the n-asset in the portfolio, $\sum_{i=1}^{n} x_i \, \rho_{i,F}$. If this sum is positive, component (d) will be negative, due to $- x_F$, and the hedged portfolio 3 will bear less risk than portfolio 1.

If the sum of the correlation coefficients is negative component (d) will take a positive value; hence it will add to the risk of portfolio 3. As long as the n-covariances of component (d) are not trivial in magnitude relative to the variance of the hedged position (component (b)), overall risk of portfolio 3 is much more likely to be determined by the n-covariances (R_i, R_F) than by the risk of the hedged position (85). That means, that component (d) will probably be of higher amount than component (b) and determine the overall risk of portfolio 3. Hence, given a negative correlation between futures position and the n-assets, portfolio 3 will be more risky than portfolio 1.

The decomposition of the hedged position led also to a limited result, i.e. if we assume a positive correlation between cash and futures prices then hedging will lead to risk reduction if the sum of the weighted correlation coefficients between the n-assets of the portfolio and the futures position is positive, i.e.

$$\text{Var } (R_{PS}) > \text{Var}(R_{P\overline{H}}) \qquad \text{if } \sum_{i=1}^{n} x_i \rho_{i,F} > 0$$

$$\text{given } \rho_{S,F} > 0$$

An ultimate evaluation of the effects brought about by hedging one asset of a portfolio on risk and expected return of this portfolio is possible only if the values of all relevant parameters are known. As long as this is not the case, we can only define circumstances under which hedging has positive effects - defined in a risk-return framework - on portfolios. This question can only be finally clarified by an empirical investigation of interest rate futures markets.

3.3. Different Way of Analysing the Risk Contribution of a Single Asset to a Portfolio

The contribution of a single asset i to the risk of a portfolio consisting of n-assets is characterized by $x_i^2 \sigma_i^2 + 2x_i \sum_{j=1}^{n} x_j \, cov(R_i, R_j)$ where i referred to any asset in the portfolio, i.e. either a share or a spot, futures or hedged fixed-income security.

Rearranging equation (II.5) the overall risk of a portfolio can be expressed in terms of the standard deviation as

$$(II.30) \qquad \sigma_P = \left[\sum_{i=1}^{n} \sum_{j=1}^{n} x_i x_j \, cov(R_i, R_j) \right]^{1/2}$$

If the amount of asset i in the portfolio, x_i, varies, the overall risk of the portfolio will vary too. The marginal contribution of asset i to the portfolio risk is (86)

$$(II.31) \qquad \frac{\partial \sigma_P}{\partial x_i} = \frac{0.5 \left[2x_i \sigma_i^2 + 2 \sum_{j=1}^{n} x_j \, cov(R_i, R_j) \right]}{\left[\sum_{i=1}^{n} \sum_{j=1}^{n} x_i x_j \, cov(R_1, R_j) \right]^{1/2}}$$

We assume that the number of assets in the portfoliio is very large (87). Hence the contribution of the variance of asset i, $(x_i^2 \sigma_i^2)$ to the portfolio risk is negligibly small, whereas the n-1 covariances between asset i and the other securities in the portfolio will primarily determine the risk contribution of asset i (88).

Since the expression $\sum_{j=1}^{n} x_j \text{cov}(R_1, R_j)$ is the covariance of asset i with the n-1 securities in the portfolio we can write for this expression $\text{cov}(R_i, R_p)$. The denominator of equation (II.31) is the standard deviation of the portfolio. Therefore from (II.31) follows

$$(II.32) \qquad \frac{\partial \sigma_P}{\partial x_i} = \frac{\text{cov}(R_i, R_j)}{\sigma_P}$$

(II.32) expresses the risk contribution of an asset i to a portfolio as the covariance of this asset with all other assets of the portfolio standardized by the portfolio standard deviation.

Hence the risk contribution of a spot T-bond to a portfolio cannot only be described by $x_S^2 \sigma_S^2 + x_S \sum_{i=1}^{n} x_i \text{ cov }(R_S, R_i)$ but also by $\text{cov}(R_S, R_P)/\sigma_P$ · For futures and hedged positions similar expressions can be derived.

We shall show in the following chapter that this measure for the contribution of an asset to the risk of a portfolio can be calculated within the framework of the capital asset pricing model. In this way an answer to the question, that could not be found in the theoretical analysis of this section, whether hedging one asset of a portfolio affects the portfolio overall risk, can be derived.

4. TECHNICAL ASPECTS OF THE EMPIRICAL INVESTIGATION

Sections four and five will consist of an empirical investigation of interest rate futures markets. The theoretical framework developed up to this point will be applied to evaluate and complete the previous analysis of the effects of interest rate futures markets on risk and return of fixed-income securities. Above all, we shall investigate whether the effects of hedging on a single position can be confirmed, and whether a solution to the question of the consequences of hedging one asset of a portfolio on portfolio risk and return can be derived.
Technical aspects of this investigation will be outlined in the following section, whereas in section five results will be presented and discussed.

4.1. Markets and Periods Investigated

In the empirical analysis we shall compute rates of return and risk of spot and hedged positions and of portfolios containing such positions. These values will be analysed and the hedging effectiveness of interest rate futures markets derived.

The investigation concentrates on markets for T-bonds and GNMAs since these instruments are, apart from T-bills, the oldest and most actively traded securities in interest rate

futures markets. Furthermore the application of the capital
asset pricing model to futures trading in the next chapter
requires long-term securities.

Referring back to the theoretical investigation where agents
held a given amount of cash assets, we assume economic agents
to take a cash market position at the first day of the month
which is held till the end of that month. If this cash
holding is hedged, the futures market position is established
and closed out in parallel with cash market transactions.
Futures positions are closed out via an opposite transaction
at the exchange. Delivery of the cash position is not
investigated.

In the theoretical analysis we investigated traders acting
according to their subjective expectations. Since those
subjective expectations are unobservable traders are assumed
to establish futures positions according to the naive 1:1
hedging strategy, i.e. the amount of the futures position is
equal to the amount of the cash position but of opposite sign
(89). Thus speculative trading activities are not
investigated.

Futures trading in financial instruments started with the
GNMA CDR contract at the Chicago Board of Trade (CBT) on
October 20, 1975 (90). GNMA futures are investigated for the
period January 1977 to December 1982. This period excludes
the first 15 months when trading in this completely new

futures instrument was not very active. In January 1977 the number of open contracts had reached 6,680. This figure increased to 20,700 at the end of 1978 and to 115,000 at the end of 1980 (Compare also Table 2-14) (91).

Futures trading in T-bonds started at the CBT on the 22nd of August 1977. To exclude the first period when trading started and the market was quite thin the investigation starts in January 1978 when the market had gained some depth. In the first month of trading the number of open contracts was 1,090 which increased to 2,864 in December 1977. In March 1978 the volume was 6,091 and reached 41,246 open contracts in Dec 1978. At the end of 1981 this figure reached 222,000 contracts. The investigation ends in December 1982.

The period investigated shows a variability in interest rates that had not occured in the USA since World War Two. Interest rates (yields) for T-bonds increased from about 8 percent at the beginning of 1978 in a more or less stable trend, only interrupted in 1980, to a peak of about 15 percent in September 1981. Up to the end of 1981 interest rates fluctuated at this high level and then declined over 1982 to a value of about 10.5 % at the end of the year (92).

Interest rates for GNMAs were at 7.60 percent at the beginning of 1977. In the following period GNMAs showed a trend in interest rates parallel to the one of T-bonds with rates between 1/2 and 2 percent above bond rates. At the peak in September 1981 rates reached 17 % and then declined over 1982 to 12.60 % at December 1982 (93).

Hence the study analyses periods of increasing and decreasing trends in interest rates.

Data Sources: T-bond cash market data for single bond issues were taken from the Treasury Bulletin and the New York Times (Nov and Dec 1982) and the bond index quotations from the Federal Reserve Bulletin. Quotations for single bonds were prices for the last day of the month. T-bond price index quotations were average bid yields for the week including the last day of the month.

This point requires further explanation. 1. The use of ask prices for the purchase and bid prices for the sale of a cash position would better reflect the investment situation of the agent, but this procedure would introduce price changes of an asset during the holding period without any change in market rates. Thus the use of one price quotation only does reflect interest rate developments better. 2. Bid price quotations (like ask prices) are not automatically traded prices, and so a price quotation indicating an offer to sell but not a transaction may not adequately reflect actual market developments. The author is not aware of any statistic that distinguishes between these two categories of price quotations. Consequently the use of price quotations instead

of traded prices can be regarded as a second-best solution
dictated by the data available.

GNMA cash market data (bid prices) were taken from the
Statistical Annual of the CBT and the Wall Street Journal
(1982).

T-bond and GNMA futures market data for the last trading day
in the month were taken from the Statistical Annuals of the
CBT or the Wall Street Journal (1982).

The CBT Annuals do not publish a settlement price which is an
average of highest and lowest prices in the last 30 seconds
of trading and is used to settle all gains, losses and
deliveries (94). Instead two closing prices are published as
the highest and lowest price for the closing range. To
adjust these price quotations to the settlement price the
average of the two closing prices was taken.

4.2. Representative Indicator for the Cash Market

4.2.1. The Problem

To find a representative cash market price quotation
equivalent for T-bill futures quotations causes no
difficulties. Prices for T-bills as non-coupon instruments
are quoted as discount from their face value. Since T-bill
auctions take place weekly there will always be a cash
instrument with a maturity equal to the 13-week maturity of
the futures contract.

For GNMA contracts things are more complicated. In the cash
market prices are quoted for coupon rates ranging from 8 to
16 % whereas futures contracts assume an 8 % coupon. As far
as maturity is concerned, cash and futures price quotations
are based on the same maturity of 30 years. In practice GNMA
certificates have an average life of about 12 years because
of prepayments.

For T-bonds neither coupon rates nor maturity of cash and
futures instruments are identical. Futures price quotations
are based on a fictive bond with twenty years to maturity and
a coupon rate of 8 %. On the other hand cash bonds
deliverable against futures contracts on February 1, 1983
added up to 20 different issues with coupon rates between 7
5/8 and 15 3/4 % and outstanding maturity (or first call
date) between 15 1/2 and 24 1/2 years hence (95).

Hence any T-bond or T-bond portfolio chosen to reflect the cash market should (96):

- represent the cash market with respect to maturity and coupon rate and by this be a 'good trader', i.e. a bond that is traded daily so that its price changes do reflect day to day market changes,
- not reflect 'disturbances' or unsystematic influences affecting an individual issue, e.g. heavy trading on one day which brings prices out of line with the market,
- be in accordance with respect to maturity and coupon rate on which T-bond futures prices are quoted.

These points show that for an investigation period of 5 years, in which the maturity of every bond/portfolio chosen will decline, it will be quite difficult to find 'the representative' bond or portfolio which reflects the market. The selection of one bond or portfolio will always violate one or more of the criteria developed above.

4.2.2. Possible Solutions

Selecting a <u>single bond issue</u> will conflict with most of the requirements listed above. The bond must exist for the whole period hence neither coupon rate of a bond issued before 1978 nor a maturity that declines over the period investigated can reflect the market over the entire period. One single issue might contain 'disturbances' and with a coupon rate below market rates there are doubts whether one bond is a good trader. In addition price quotations for single bond issues over a five-years period will contain to some extent price changes reflecting the bond's decreasing time to maturity, and not changes in market rates. With respect to factors underlying futures price quotations one single cash bond may reflect the coupon of 8 % but cannot satisfy the 20-years-to-maturity condition.

On the other hand, the use of a single issue has an important advantage, in that, the analysis of the investment performance of a single bond is closest to the investor's situation assumed in the following investigation, i.e. holding a single cash asset for investment that can be hedged in the futures market.

Among the published bondindices on government securities (Moody's Governments, Salomon Brothers Governments) the index of the Federal Reserve Bank (97) comes closest to the requirements of this investigation. This index, in future referred to as Fedindex, "based on only recently issued, actively traded" (98) T-bonds, quotes yields adjusted to constant maturities of 20 years. Hence the index more or less excludes 'bad traders' and 'disturbances', represents the cash market, and fulfills the 20 years maturity requirement underlying futures bond quotations. Coupon rates different from 8 percent can be adjusted by use of a conversion factor.

Unfortunately the data of this index were not available on a daily basis. In the Fed bulletin only weekly average yields are published. Especially in times of extremely volatile price changes weekly average quotations do not adequately reflect prices of the last day of the month (99). Hence the use of this index which seems to fulfill most of the criteria developed above introduces a new type of disturbance.

To overcome the potential distortions caused by weekly average price quotations a new bondindex, also referred to as Ownindex, was constructed. Single bonds which reflect the market with respect to maturity and coupon rates, and which can therefore be regarded as 'good traders', were used to form the new portfolio. To exclude price distortions for the months when one bond was substituted by an up-to-date issue, the portfolio always included two bonds. This procedure also reduces disturbances which may be introduced by the use of a single bond.

This method of constructing the index circumvents the problem of weekly averages whilst most of the advantages of an index are maintained. With respect to the factors determining the futures price quotations coupon rates must be adjusted by inclusion of the conversion factor to a rate of 8%. Average maturity of such a portfolio is above 20 years. Since the yield curve for government securities turns out to be flat at the long end (maturities over 15 years) the effects of maturities different from 20 years can be expected to be very small (100).

The Ownindex can be critized for inconsistency in composition, a fact the author is fully aware of.

But we should remember the reasons why it is necessary to construct such an index. Single bond issues might contain disturbances, or may not be in accordance with coupon rates in the market. Fedindices are based on weekly average prices. These indices are inconsistent too since over the 5 years period new issues were added.

An opportunity to overcome this difficulty would be to construct a portfolio of two bond issues reflecting average coupon rates of the period under investigation. Since such a portfolio contains at least one bond that did not exist for the overall period, yield figures of a third low coupon bond must be converted into prices for this higher coupon bond for the period in which the high coupon bond did not yet exist. This procedure will lead to a consistent price series of the index and to coupon rates that reflect average market rates. But the average coupon rate chosen will never reflect - apart from a few months - actual market rates in the overall period. Since, as we shall see, bonds with coupon rates different from actual market rates are not good indicators for 'the market', the author has preferred the inconsistent index to a bond index that does not reflect market rates.

4.2.3. Indicators Selected

Because neither a single bond issue, nor the Fedindex or the
Ownindex can be regarded as an optimal indicator of 'the
T-bond market', the investigation makes use of all three
indicators.

Single Bond Issues: The fact that the bond required for the
investigation must have been issued before 1978 reduced the
selection to only 9 issues (Compare Table 2-3). Out of these
the 8 % issue was chosen because its coupon rate reflects
exactly the coupon on which futures price quotations are
based.   The first call date of this issue is 8/15/96.   Thus
for the last year of the investigation this bond, with 14
years to first call, is no longer a deliverable instrument.
Therefore the 8 1/4 % issue was analysed too. For the last
years of the investigation period high coupon bonds were also
examined.

Fedindex: Yield quotations as published by the Federal
Reserve Bulletin were transformed into prices assuming coupon
rates of 8, 10 and 12 percent. With a coupon rate of 8 % the
index perfectly reflects coupon rate and maturity of the
fictive bond on which futures prices are quoted.   Hence
comparability to the single bond issue is given.   The
selection of 10 and 12 % coupon rates does give a better
reflection of market developments in the 80s.

Table 2-3 : Deliverable Bond Issues Before 1978

Coupon Rate (%)	Issue Date	Maturity Date/ First Call
3	2/15/55	2/15/95
3 1/2	10/03/60	11/15/98
8 1/2	5/15/74	5/15/94-99
7 7/8	2/18/75	2/15/95
8 3/8	8/15/75	8/15/95
8	8/16/76	8/15/96-01
8 1/4	5/15/75	5/15/00-05
7 5/8	2/15/77	2/15/02-07
7 7/8	11/15/77	11/15/02-07

Source : Treasury Bulletin, Jan. 1978, p. 86.

Table 2-4 : Bonds Included in the Own Bondindex

Period	Bonds Included		Highest Lowest Yield in Period [1] (%)	
	Coupon Rate (%)	Maturity First Call	Highest	Lowest
1/78 - 1/79	8 8 1/4	8/15/96-01 5/15/00-05	7.99	8.99
2/79 - 11/79	8 1/4 9	2/15/94	8.82	10.44
12/79 - 2/80	9 10 3/8	11/15/04-09	10.24	12.59
3/80 - 12/80	10 3/8 11 3/4	2/15/05-10	10.15	12.43
1/81 - 5/81	11 3/4 12 3/4	11/15/05-10	12.48	13.75
6/81 - 7/82	12 3/4 13 7/8	5/15/06-11	13.22	15.55
8/82 -12/82	12 3/4 11 3/4		12.48	10.52

1) Yield figures are taken from the Treasury Bulletin
   (different issues). Index reflects T-bonds with a maturity
   adjusted to 20 years.

<u>Ownindex</u>: Two bond issues with coupon rates close to market rates formed the Ownnindex. Bond issues chosen are listed in Table 2-4.

An 8 percent coupon rate was chosen to represent the <u>GNMA</u> <u>market</u>. Hence maturities of cash and futures instruments are equal. Higher coupon rates were not available for the overall period. Since the investigation of the T-bond market will show (compare II.5.1.1. and III.2.2. of this study) that different coupon rates do not affect the results seriously, this procedure seems acceptable.

4.3. Calculating Return and Variance

4.3.1. Spot Positions

Calculating monthly rates of return for <u>single bond issues</u> has to reflect the fact that T-bond prices are always quoted without accrued interest (101) An investor buying a T-bond has to pay as invoice the dollar price quoted plus accrued interest (A).

The return for period t of one month, in percent per period, is calculated according to

$$(II.33) \quad R_{S,t} = \frac{(s_t + A_t) - (s_{t-1} + A_{t-1})}{s_{t-1} + A_{t-1}} \cdot 100$$

$$= \frac{(s_t + n \cdot c/m) - \left[s_{t-1} + (n-1)c/m\right]}{s_{t-1} + (n-1) \cdot c/m} \cdot 100$$

$$= \frac{(s_t - s_{t-1}) + c/m}{s_{t-1} + (n-1)c/m} \cdot 100$$

where s_t and s_{t-1} are the prices at the end of period t and t-1 respectively, c the periodic interest payment for 100\$ face value, m the number of months (holding periods) between two interest payments and n the number of holding periods accrued since the last interest payment (102).
The term c/m indicates the amount of interest accrued during one holding period. The periods are assumed to be equally

long (103). Interest payment received during the holding
period is assumed to be reinvested at the end of the month.
From transaction costs - brokerage fees, transfer taxes,
bid-ask spread (about 1/4%) - we abstract.

Hence the above formula expresses the percentage return of a
one month investment, where the investor paid the accrued
interest when the bonds was bought in t-1 and received
accrued interest when the bond was sold in t.

The rate of return of the Ownindex is the sum of weighted
returns of single bonds calculated according the formula
above.

Government bond index: The figures published in the Federal
Reserve Bulletin for the bond index are yield quotations. To
calculate monthly rates of return the yield figures must be
converted into prices (s). With an arbitrary assumption on
the coupon rate (C), given maturity (k) and yield (i), and
assuming the usual semi-annual interest payment the yield
figures were converted into prices according to the formula
(104):

$$(II.34) \quad S = \frac{C}{2} \left[\sum_{k=1}^{K} \frac{1}{(1 + \frac{i}{2})^{2k}} \right] + \frac{100}{(1 + \frac{i}{2})^{2k}}$$

On the basis of these prices monthly rates of return were
calculated from

$$(II.35) \quad R_{S,t} = \frac{s_t - s_{t-1} + c/m}{s_{t-1}} \cdot 100$$

In the denominator we do not take into account accrued interest since it is inadequate to fix arbitrarily two months when interest payments are received for an index of about 20 different bonds and thus about 20 different dates when interest is paid.

For GNMAs monthly rates of return are also calculated according to this formula because interest for GNMAs is passed through to the investor on a monthly basis (105).

Variances of monthly rates of return are calculated using the formula

$$(II.36) \quad Var(R_S) = \frac{1}{T-1} \sum_{t=1}^{T} (R_{S,t} - \bar{R}_S)^2$$

$$\bar{R}_S = \frac{1}{T} \sum_{t=1}^{T} R_{S,t}$$

4.3.2. Futures positions

Holding period returns - one month - of futures T-bond or GNMA positions are calculated on the assumption that the full contract value has been paid although in reality only a very small portion of this amount has to be deposited as margin. This assumption is justified by the fact that futures positions are not investigated as investment (speculative position) but as counterbalance to an existing cash position (hedging position).

Thus the holding period return is equal to the percentage price change of the futures contract (again neglecting transaction costs, about 70 - 100$ of commissions, plus foregone interest on the initial margin of $1.250 (106))

$$(\text{II.37}) \quad R_{F,t} = \frac{f_t - f_{t-1}}{f_{t-1}} \cdot 100$$

where f_t and f_{t-1} are futures price quotations for the same contract at the end of period t (t-1).

4.3.3. Hedged Positions

Calculation of monthly rates of return for hedged positions is based on the following assumptions:

- no transaction costs,
- the margin is paid by cash assets as collateral,
- cash and futures positions are established and closed out at the same day,
- a one month holding period,
- a hedge ratio of 1:1 (c.f. 4.3.3.1.),

- futures commitments are closed out by an offsetting
futures market transaction, not by cash delivery.

The holding period return for T-bonds, as percent per period,
is

$$(II.38) \quad R_{H,t} = \frac{(s_t - s_{t-1}) + c/m - (f_t - f_{t-1})}{s_{t-1} + (n-1)c/m} \cdot 100$$

The denominator is equal to that of the cash position return
formula (II.33), since to establish the futures position does
not involve expenses. The margin is provided by cash bonds
as collaterals and transaction costs are ignored.
For the own T-bond index the holding period return is the sum
of weighted hedged returns for single bonds as calculated
above To calculate returns for hedged GNMA and Fedindex
positions we abstract again from accrued interest ((n-1)*c/m)
in the denominator.

The variance is calculated from

$$(II.39) \quad Var(R_H) = \frac{1}{T-1} \sum_{t=1}^{T} (R_{H,t} - \bar{R}_H)^2$$

$$\bar{R}_H = \frac{1}{T} \sum_{t=1}^{T} R_{H,t}$$

4.3.3.1. Hedge Ratio

In this investigation an investor is analysed who has to decide on the hedging ratio at the beginning of the hedge period. In order to determine his ex-ante optimal hedge ratio, OHR = $-x_F/x_S$ he might use either

- subjective expectations,
- ex-post ratios or
- a naive 1:1 ratio.

Hedge ratios based on traders' subjective expectations cannot be applied since firstly subjective expectations of individual traders and therefore their subjective ex-ante hedge ratios are unobservable and secondly even if it were possible to derive such a measure for single traders, it would be impossible to aggregate this information into a "market expectation".

To use ex-post ratios, that were optimal for the past period, as optimal ex-ante ratios, would mean to assume that the price development of the preceding period will also occur in the future. This construct is often used in the analysis of financial markets but there are doubts whether it is an optimal procedure for this investigation. MANESS, (107) showed for the T-bill futures market that the use of the ex-post ratios in most cases led to worse results than the naive strategy of a 1:1 hedge ratio. MCENALLY and RICE (108)

found that this procedure outperformed the naive strategy in
only 50% of the cases.

For these reasons in the following analysis a 1:1 hedge ratio
is assumed.
Empirical results of investigations on optimal hedge ratios
support this procedure to a large extent. Studies of the
T-bill market arrived at optimal ex-post hedge ratios that
were different from one.   Ratios were in a range between
0.666 and 1.2, depending on time-periods investigated and the
duration of hedges, but less than half of these values were
significantly different from one.   (109).   EDERINGTON and
HEGDE computed optimal hedge ratios for the GNMA market of
between 0.845 - 1.010 (one week hedge), 0.840 - 1.070 (two
weeks) and of 0.980 for a four week hedge.   But all values
were not significantly different from one (110). HEGDE's
study is the only invostigation of the T-bond market.   He
analysed hedges with a duration of one or two weeks for a
period of 1 1/2 years. Hedge ratios derived were in the
range of 0.840 - 1.110 (one week duration) and 0.887 - 1.275
(two weeks). Only few values were significantly different
from one.

4.3.3.2. Nearby or Distant Contract

Among the 12 different contract delivery dates offered by the
T-bond futures market, one has to be chosen as hedging
instrument. Only contracts with a delivery date in the near
future show intensive trading, hence distant contracts are
not suitable as hedging instruments.

All studies of the T-bill futures market came to the
conclusion that the nearby contract, that is the contract
which matures within 0 and 3 months after the end of the
hedge, performed clearly better than the more distant
contracts (111).

EDERINGTON's results for the GNMA market are contradictory:
the two contracts following the nearby contract performed
slightly better, whereas the following contract led to less
hedging effectiveness (112). In HEGDE's analysis the nearby
contract outperformed the following contract (113).

In the following investigation not only nearby contracts (N)
are analysed but also the two following contracts (D,DD).
The results were in accordance with the studies mentioned
above. The nearby contract led to better hedging results
than the two following contracts (See the following section
II.5).

4.3.3.3. Period Between End of Hedge and Maturity of Futures Contract

With the investment period of one month given the interval between the end of the hedge and the maturity of the contract used as hedging instrument differs for single investment periods. Given the nearby contract, this period is either 2,6 or 10 weeks. We know that cash and futures prices converge when the contract comes closer to maturity. Hence hedges ending 6 or 10 weeks before the maturity of the futures contract might show worse results than those hedges maturing 2 weeks before contract maturity. This might influence the results of the study. On the other hand one should not forget that trading becomes quite thin two weeks before a contract matures.

PARKINSON (114) investigated this question when he analysed the hedging effectiveness of the T-bill market. His results showed a more or less stable hedging effectiveness for contracts maturing between 3 and 9 weeks after the end of the hedge. For an interval of 12 weeks the hedging effectiveness declined.

Hence we can conclude that different lengths of the periods between the end of the hedge and the contract maturity should not affect the results of this study seriously.

4.4. Measure for Hedging Effectiveness and Optimal Hedge
Ratio

In previous sections we developed tools for analysing hedging
effects by comparing absolute values for return and risk of
hedged and unhedged positions. In this part the indicator
hedging effectiveness is derived from the portfolio approach.
This measure will be used to investigate risk reduction
effects of T-bond and GNMA futures markets. Since this
indicator is a relative measure, direct comparisons between
different assets and periods can be carried out easily.
Furthermore, as a by-product, optimal ex-post hedge ratios
can be calculated.

Hedging effectiveness (HE) is measured by considering the
risk of a hedged position in relation to the risk of the same
position unhedged (115).

$$(\text{II}.40) \quad HE = \frac{Var(S) - Var(H)}{Var(S)} = 1 - \frac{Var(H)}{Var(S)}$$

This expression indicates the percentage risk reduction
brought about by hedging when the risk-minimizing hedge is
considered.
The value of Var(H), the risk of a position hedged according
to the pure hedge component, is known from section II.3.1.
as formula (II.22). Substituting the expression for Var(S)
and Var(H) into (II.40), leads to:

$$(II.41) \quad HE = 1 - \frac{x_S^2 \left[\sigma_S^2 - \frac{cov(S,F)^2}{\sigma_F^2} \right]}{x_S^2 \, \sigma_S^2}$$

$$= 1 - \left[1 - \frac{cov(S,F)^2}{\sigma_S^2 \, \sigma_F^2} \right] = \frac{\sigma_S^2 \, \sigma_F^2 \, \rho_{S,F}^2}{\sigma_S^2 \, \sigma_F^2} = \rho_{S,F}^2$$

Hence the measure of hedging effectiveness is the squared correlation coefficient between cash and futures price changes. This coefficient of determination is equivalent to the R-square value of an OLS regression of spot price changes on futures price changes:

$$\Delta S_t = \gamma_o + \gamma_1 \Delta f_t + \varepsilon_t$$

This regression leads to another useful value: γ_1, the slope coefficient of the regression line, is identical to the optimal hedge ratio (OHR) determined in the theoretical analysis (116):

$$(II.19) \quad OHR = \frac{cov(S,F)}{\sigma_F^2} = \gamma_1$$

Hence regressing spot price changes on futures price changes leads to values for the hedging effectiveness and the optimal hedge ratio.

All calculations and regressions in the following analysis were carried out using the SHAZAM programme (117).

5. RESULTS OF THE EMPIRICAL INVESTIGATION

5.1. Effects of Hedging on Risk and Return of Single Positions (118)

In the theoretical analysis the following results of hedging single assets according to the pure hedge component were derived (119), (120):

- the risk will be reduced if the correlation between the return of the cash asset and the return of the futures position is positive,
- the risk reduction is greater, the greater the value of the correlation coefficient,
- the risk is completely abolished with a correlation of one.

The previous investigation indicated for a correlation between cash and futures returns of (plus or minus) one an expected return for hedged positions equal to zero, or equal to the pure interest income if we do no longer abstract from this sort of income. For correlation coefficients between 0 and |1| expected return may be smaller or greater than the spot return. Hence no answer to the question where the hedged position is located in the mean-variance space compared to spot positions could be derived.

5.1.1. T-bond Market

5.1.1.1. Correlation between Cash and Futures Returns

Correlation coefficients for cash and futures positions are
in a range between 0.930 and 0.994 (See Table 2-5). Single
bonds like the 8%, 8 1/4%, and 11 3/4% issue indicate, with
coefficients between 0.980 and 0.994, more or less complete
risk reduction. Coefficients calculated for the Fedindices
are smaller (0.930 - 0.973) reflecting the fact that rates of
return of these indices are based on weekly average prices
instead of daily prices. This is reflected by coefficients
for the Ownindex of 0.991 - 0.993, values very close to
coefficients of single bonds.   Correlation coefficients
discussed so far are based on the nearby futures contract
(N). Computation of the 8% bond coefficients with distant
(D) or then following contracts (DD) display values slightly
smaller: N: 0.983, D: 0.980, DD: 0.975 (overall period).
These figures indicate declining hedging quality for more
distant contracts.
Coefficients for the 8 and 8 1/4% issue and Fedindices in the
subperiods 1978-6/80 and 7/80-1982 indicate a decreasing risk
reduction quality within the period under investigation, e.g.
the 8% bond coefficient decreases from 0.992 to 0.980, the
10% Fedindex from 0.973 to 0.930. The Ownindex on the other
hand indicates a constant risk reducing quality and the 11
3/4% bond coefficient for the second subperiod is very close
to the 8% bond coefficient for the first subperiod.

158

Table 2-5 :   Correlation Coefficients for Cash and Futures
              Returns (T bond and GNMA)

	1978-1982	1978-6/80	7/80-1982
8 % T-bond N	0.983	0.992	0.980
8 % T-bond D	0.980	0.990	0.976
8 % T-bond DD	0.975	0.985	0.971
$8\frac{1}{4}$% T-bond	0.986	0.994	0.984
$11\frac{3}{4}$% T-bond	---	---	0.991
8 % Fedindex	0.946	0.973	0.930
10 % Fedindex	0.947	0.973	0.930
12 % Fedindex	0.947	0.973	0.930
Ownindex	0.991	0.992	0.993
GNMA N	0.912	0.960	0.891
GNMA D	0.904	0.954	0.885
GNMA DD	0.896	0.937	0.881
	1977-1982	1977-1979	1980-1982
GNMA N	0.908	0.915	0.916

These values for correlation coefficients, in combination
with theoretical results derived above, allow the conclusion
that the T-bond futures market is very effective in reducing
risk caused by interest rate changes. Coefficients close to
one incicate nearly complete risk reduction.
This statement will be explicitly analysed in the following
section for single spot and hedged T-bond positions.

5.1.1.2. Variance of Spot and Hedged Positions

Figures of Table 2-6 strongly support the result derived
above of the enormous risk-reducing property of the T-bond
futures market. The 8% bond variance was reduced from 22.085
to 0.890 for the overall period. An even smaller risk was
computed for the Ownindex with a variance reduced from 17.561
to 0.389. The different Fedindices have a variance in the
range between 2.100 and 2.337. Values for the Fedindices
greater than those for single issues or the Ownindex were
indicated by smaller correlation coefficients.

The indication of decreasing risk reduction effectiveness of
the 8% and 8 1/4 % bond and Fedindices in the second
subperiod, given by correlation coefficients, is supported by
the variance values. But the figures also give a possible
explanation for this result: Risk in the T-bond market
increased significantly from the first to the second
subperiod, e.g. the 8% bond spot variance increased from

17.506 to 27.067, the 10% Fedindex from 17.893 to 23.823 and the Ownindex from 14.810 to 20.659. Hence higher variances of hedged positions in the second subperiod (8% bond 1.338 to 0.308, 10% Fedindex 3.213 to 0.992) reflect greater return variability in the cash market. Another explanation for reduced risk reduction quality might be the fact that the 8% bond and the Fedindices, which also contain low coupon bonds, are out of line with the interest rate level in the second subperiod.

The 11 3/4% bond variance of 0.385 for the second period is evidently smaller than the 8% bond variance for the same period and only slightly greater than the variance of this bond in the first period. The Ownindex displays in the second subperiod an even smaller variance than in the first subperiod (0.317 to 0.347). Analysis of variances for 1982 supports the indication of smaller risk reduction effects for the 8 and 8 1/4% issues and the Fedindices compared to high coupon bonds (11 3/4%, 12 3/4%, 13 7/8% issues) and the Ownindex in periods of high market rates. We observe variances between 0.215 and 0.318 for high coupon bonds and the Ownindex whereas the 8 and 8 1/4% bonds display variances of 0.638 and 0.491.

These relative high variance values for the 8 and 8 1/4 % bond issues in the second subperiod and in 1982 - either spot or hedged positions - reflect the fact that low coupon bonds

Table 2-6 : Variance of Spot and Hedged T-bond Positions

	1978–1982		1978-6/80		7/80–1982		1982	
	$Var(R_S)$	$Var(R_H)$	$Var(R_S)$	$Var(R_H)$	$Var(R_S)$	$Var(R_H)$	$Var(R_S)$	$Var(R_H)$
8% Bond N	22.085	0.890	17.506	0.308	27.067	1.338	16.545	0.630
8% Bond D		1.097		0.370		1.725		0.946
8% Bond DD		1.424		0.555		2.205		1.167
$8\frac{1}{4}$% Bond	21.268	0.684	17.487	0.249	25.414	0.953	15.091	0.491
$11\frac{3}{4}$% Bond	----	----	----	----	21.515	0.385	12.162	0.300
8% Fedindex	22.342	2.337	19.389	1.106	25.712	3.493	16.681	3.658
10% Fedindex	20.668	2.185	17.893	0.992	23.823	3.213	15.411	3.454
12% Fedindex	19.549	2.100	16.892	0.937	22.562	3.204	14.584	3.331
Own Index	17.561	0.389	14.810	0.347	20.659	0.317	11.696	0.252
GNMA	21.457	3.876	13.679	1.178	29.832	6.680	9.805	1.517
$12\frac{3}{4}$% Bond							11.097	0.318
$13\frac{7}{8}$% Bond							11.061	0.215

respond with a greater price volatility to a given yield change - other things being equal - than high coupon issues (121).

Whether the hedging quality of the bond market was affected by increasing interest rates and cash market variability will be analysed more completely in a separate section (II.5.3.).

Variances of hedged positions discussed so far are based on a hedge using the nearby (N) futures contract. If the distant (D) or next following (DD) contract had been used, results would not have been significantly different as demonstrated by the investigation of the 8% bond hedged with different contracts (See Table 2-6.).

Variance values of distant contracts - for the overall and the two subperiods - are slightly greater than those values for the nearby contract. The more distant contract displays the highest variance; a result indicated by smaller correlation coefficients for this contract. Nevertheless even this contract with the worst hedging results leads to variances of hedged positions that count for less than 10% of the unhedged position variance. The result of the nearby futures contract as the best hedging instrument, supports the procedure of concentrating the investigation on nearby futures contracts.

The analysis of risk reduction quality might also give some indications which of the different positions investigated might be the best indicator for the T-bond market. The comparison of single T-bond issues with different coupon rates clearly demonstrates that high coupon issues exhibit the smallest variance values (either hedged or spot). Hence a high coupon rate bond would be the better indicator since it automatically bears less interest rate risk than low coupon issues. But, for the overall period, only the 8% and 8 1/4% issue or bonds with even lower coupon rates existed. Compared to single issues the Fedindices display the same degree of risk for spot positions but higher risk for hedged positions caused by the fact that combining weekly average spot data with daily futures prices, reduces the hedging quality. The 12% Fedindex expresses the smallest variance of all three Fedindices due to the above mentioned fact that the greater the coupon rate the lower the price volatility.

The Ownindex, constructed to reduce the deficiencies of single bonds (disturbance) and Fedindices (weekly average price), presents values for risk of spot and hedged positions superior to single assets in the overall period and the more volatile second subperiod. For the first subperiod the values are slightly greater than those of the 8 and 8 1/4 bond. The Fedindex is outperformed in all periods.

Therefore we can conclude that the newly constructed bondindex seems to be a very good indicator for the T-bond cash market.

The empirical results clearly demonstrate the risk reduction effectiveness of the T-bond futures market with an underlying

naive hedging strategy no matter which issue or index is
taken as indicator for the bond market. This is strong
evidence that the T-bond futures market fulfills the task of
risk reduction excellently.

5.1.1.3. Return of Spot and Hedged Positions

The influence of hedging on return is presented in Table 2-7.
We observe for the overall and the two subperiods an increase
in return, i.e. all hedged positions - either single issues
or indices - exhibit greater rates of return than related
spot positions. Return values of hedged positions differ
only slightly.
Even if transaction cost, from which we abstract, were taken
into account the results would remain the same. Assuming 100
$ commissions for a 100,000 $ T-bond contract, monthly
returns of hedged positions would be reduced by 0.1 % which
is much less than the return increase for hedged positions.

The overall period can be divided into a period of increasing
interest rates till the end of 1981 and a period of
decreasing rates in 1982. Hence, till the end of 1981
average returns of spot positions reflect pure interest
return reduced by depreciation of the asset price, e.g.the 8%
bond cash price declined from 97.875 in Jan 1978 to 62.875 in
Dec 1981. The hedged position on the other hand was
protected against this price decline.

Table 2-7 : Return of Spot and Hedged T-bond Positions (in %)

	1978–1982		1978–6/80		7/80–1982		1982	
	R_S	R_H	R_S	R_H	R_S	R_H	R_S	R_H
8% Bond N	0.617	1.057	0.201	0.774	1.032	1.339	2.983	1.222
8% Bond D		1.075		0.817		1.333		1.362
8% Bond DD		1.051		0.795		1.308		1.466
$8\frac{1}{4}$% Bond	0.589	1.060	0.167	0.757	1.011	1.361	3.048	1.297
$11\frac{3}{4}$% Bond	---	---	---	---	0.966	1.272	2.905	1.145
8% Fedindex	0.592	1.048	0.178	0.773	1.006	1.322	3.411	1.570
10% Fedindex	0.628	1.084	0.227	0.823	1.029	1.345	3.343	1.531
12% Fedindex	0.654	1.110	0.262	0.858	1.046	1.362	3.298	1.506
Own Index	0.551	1.001	0.198	0.725	0.904	1.249	2.814	1.065
GNMA	0.631	1.050	0.368	0.934	0.893	1.167	3.016	1.748
$12\frac{3}{4}$% Bond							2.801	1.053
$13\frac{7}{8}$% Bond							2.784	1.033

The reverse situation for 1982 with decreasing interest rates is shown in Table 2-7: Spot positions earned additional profit from increasing cash prices. Therefore spot positions returns are greater than hedged positions returns.

Furthermore we observe rates of return for hedged positions above pure interest income, e.g. the 8% bond yields a monthly return of 0.667 $ due to interest rate payments, whilst return values computed for hedged positions are 1.057, 0.774 and 1.339% (122). Similar results can be derived for the other single issues or indices for all periods (123). In the year of decreasing interest rates most hedged positions - the 12 3/4 and 13 3/4 bonds excluded - showed rates of return exceeding pure interest income.

If the hedges had worked out to perfect hedges, returns of hedged positions would have been equal to pure interest income received. Rates observed are greater than pure interest return, indicating a basis change to the short hedger's advantage. Since we are analysing short hedges, a basis change to the hedger's advantage means - on average - a widening in the basis when cash prices exceed futures prices (backwardation) and a narrowing in the basis when cash prices fall below futures prices (contango) (124). During the period under investigation cash prices normally exceeded futures prices (125).

Table 2-8 presents average values of basis changes for selected assets. As indicated these values are positive.

Table 2-8 : Basis Changes ($)

	1978-1982	1978-6/80	7/80-1982	1982
8 % T-bond N	0.118	0.012	0.224	0.164
8 % T-bond D	0.130	0.047	0.215	0.260
8 % T-bond DD	0.109	0.025	0.193	0.336
$11\frac{3}{4}$% T-bond	---	---	0.221	0.074
$12\frac{3}{4}$% T-bond	---	---	---	-0.016
$13\frac{7}{8}$% T-bond	---	---	---	-0.043
GNMA N	0.109	0.129	0.089	0.508
GNMA D	0.140	0.163	0.118	0.622
GNMA DD	0.158	0.175	0.142	0.706

The 8% bond exhibits with 0.012$ in the first subperiod the
lowest basis change. Consequently, as Table 2-7 shows, the
bond earns in this subperiod the lowest return (0.774)
whereas the second subperiod with an average basis change of
0.224 leads to the greatest return of 1.339. For the 8% bond
hedged with the next following futures contracts (D,DD) we
also observe basis changes in the second subperiod clearly
greater than those in the first period. Hence with
increasing interest rate variability in the cash market the
basis and changes in the basis increased. For the 12 3/4%
bond we register negative basis changes for 1982 explaining a
return below pure interest income.

Analysis of returns for the 8% bond hedged with the distant
and next following contract led to results very similar to
those of the nearby contract. The distant contract led to a
greater the then following contract to a slightly smaller
return in the overall period. Again different changes in the
basis explain different return values (See Table 2-7 and
2-8).

5.1.1.4. Spot and Hedged Positions in the Mean-Variance
         Space

Comparisons of spot and hedged positions for all bond issues
and indices according the MARKOWITZ criterion (a portfolio
dominates others if it has 1. lower variance for given rate

of return, or 2. greater return for given variance or 3. higher return and lower variance than other portfolios) allows the conclusion that all hedged positions dominate the spot positions (Compare Table 2-6 and 2-7). Graphically hedged positions are located in the north-west region of the mean-variance diagram, indicating - independently of the risk-averse trader's utility function - an improvement of the hedger's situation: he earned higher return at a significantly lower level of risk (See also Figure 2-9).

This result of hedged positions being superior compared to spot positions was derived for the overall period and the two subperiods.

For 1982 with decreasing interest rates and, consequently, greater returns for spot than for hedged positions, an evaluation of the trader's situation is not possible as long as no utility function of an individual trader or 'the traders' is specified (See also Figure 2-10). The large reduction in risk is accompanied by a return reduction (Compare Table 2-6 and 2-7). It depends on the trader's attitude towards risk, whether the sacrifice of some return for a reduction in risk increases or decreases his utility.

Empirical results for T-bond markets demonstrate, as consequence of hedging, a clear improvement in the trader's situation in the mean-variance space for periods with increasing interest rates. Whereas for periods with decreasing rates no statement of a trader's situation can be made without knowing his utility function.

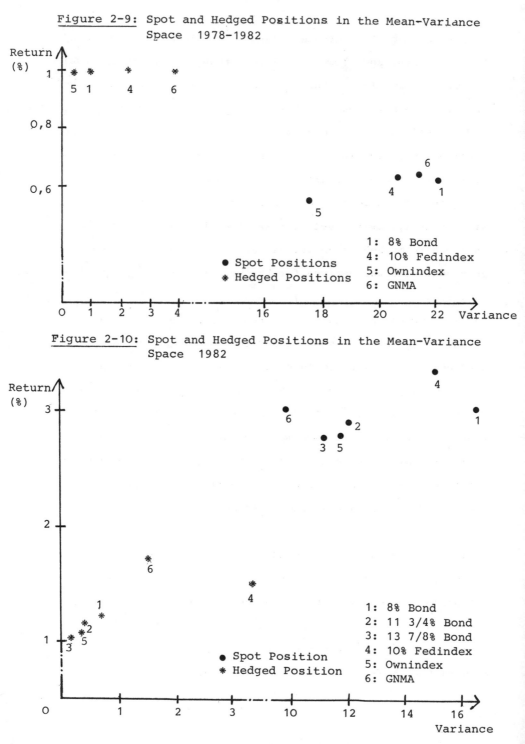

Figure 2-9: Spot and Hedged Positions in the Mean-Variance Space 1978-1982

Figure 2-10: Spot and Hedged Positions in the Mean-Variance Space 1982

5.1.2. GNMA Market

5.1.2.1. Correlation between Cash and Futures Returns

Correlation coefficients for spot and futures GNMA positions
range between 0.912 and 0.960 (period 1978-82) respectively
0.908 - 0.916 (1977-82,nearby contracts see Table 2-5).
These values are smaller than figures obtained for the T-bond
market, what suggests less parallelity in cash and futures
price movements and a lower risk reduction effectiveness for
the GNMA market. Nevertheless, with correlation coefficients
not too distant from one, the GNMA futures market can be
regarded as a very effective instrument to reduce risk.

Correlation coefficients for following contracts are slightly
smaller than values for the nearby contract (0.904 and 0.906
instead of 0.912 for the nearby contract (period 1978-82))
indicating slightly smaller correlation between cash and
futures returns. Hence we also expect somewhat lower hedging
effectiveness for these contracts.

5.1.2.2. Variance of Spot and Hedged Positions

Hedging a GNMA position by the naive 1:1 strategy reduced
risk significantly. Variance values for the overall period
(1977-82) declined from 18.004 to 3.339 (Compare Table 2-9).

Table 2-9 : Variance and Return of Spot and Hedged GNMA Positions

	Spot	Hedged	Spot	Hedged	Spot	Hedged	Spot	Hedged
	1978–1982		1978–6/80		7/80–1982		1982	
VARIANCE								
GNMA N	21.457	3.876	13.679	1.178	29.832	6.680	9.805	1.517
GNMA D		4.057		1.245		6.978		1.534
GNMA DD		4.433		1.642		7.338		1.368
RETURN								
GNMA N	0.631	1.050	0.368	0.934	0.893	1.167	3.016	1.748
GNMA D		1.089		0.966		1.212		1.917
GNMA DD		1.119		0.984		1.254		2.037
	1977–1982		1977–1979		1980–1982			
VARIANCE								
GNMA N	18.004	3.339	3.118	0.586	32.956	5.935		
GNMA D		3.497		0.712		6.108		
GNMA DD		3.824		0.810		6.604		
RETURN								
GNMA N	0.560	0.925	0.093	0.575	1.027	1.276		
GNMA D		0.961		0.596		1.326		
GNMA DD		0.986		0.577		1.394		

Variances of hedged positions account for less than 20% of spot position variances. This figure refers to the first subperiod (1977-79) with relatively low variability of spot returns as well as to the second subperiod (1980-82) that exhibits a spot return variablilitly ten times larger. Risk reduction quality for the year 1982 with interest rates decreasing does not differ from periods of increasing rates.

Table 2-9 also presents variance values for positions hedged with the next two following contracts. As indicated before, we observe variances slightly greater for the more distant contracts, i.e. an increase from 3.339 (N) over 3.497 (D) to 3.824 (DD). Only in 1982 does the nearby contract not lead to the best hedging result.

5.1.2.3. Return of Spot and Hedged Positions

Return values for GNMA spot and hedged positons show features similar to the T-bond market (Compare also Table 2-9):

- Higher returns for hedged positons in the overall period and the two subperiods (whether or not we look at the 77-82 or 78-82 periods).
- Lower returns for hedged positions in the year of decreasing interest rates 1982, than in the period of increasing rates.
- Returns for hedged positions exceed pure interest income

(0.667) in periods of decreasing as well as increasing interest rates (126).

- Rates of return above pure interest income are also caused by basis changes to the hedger's advantage which he could not necessarily expect (Compare Table 2-8).
- For positions hedged with distant contracts we observe slightly greater rates of return.

5.1.2.4. Spot and Hedged Positions in the Mean-Variance Space

According to the Markowitz criterion we can conclude for the overall period and the two subperiods (whether or not the 77-82 or 78-82 overallperiod is taken into consideration) that hedged positions display lower variances and higher returns. Hence a trader using GNMA futures would have improved his overall situation. This result also applies to positions hedged by using distant futures contracts (Compare Figures 2-9 and 2-10).
Similar to the T-bond market, no statement can be made for the year 1982 with less variability but smaller return for the hedged position compared to the spot position without knowledge of the trader's utility function.

5.1.3. Comparison of T-Bond and GNMA Futures Markets

Both markets prove to be very effective in reducing interest
rate risk. They exhibit broad parallelism in spot and hedged
position return variability.   Table 2-6 describes the GNMA
cash market as a market with less risk for the overall and
the first subperiod compared to the market for T-bonds,
(Comparison based on the 8% issues).   But hedged GNMA
positions bear a risk four times higher than related T-bond
positions, applying a linear risk evaluation. In the second
subperiod GNMA spot markets indicate slightly higher risk
than the T-bond market (29.832 to 27.067) whereas the risk of
hedged positions exceeds the T-bond risk clearly (6.680 to
1.338). This leads to the conclusion of a GNMA market being
very effective in risk reduction but being also clearly
inferior to the risk reduction effectiveness of the T-bond
market. Reasons for these differences will be discussed
under point II.5.3.

5.2. Effects of Hedging on Risk and Return of Portfolios

The theoretical analysis did not give an answer to the question whether hedging one asset of a portfolio reduces the overall risk of this portfolio. This was due to the fact that correlation coefficients of the hedgeable fixed-income security - either as spot, futures or hedged position - with the other assets of the portfolio were not known.

It was derived that hedging one asset of a portfolio leads to risk reduction

- if the sum of weighted correlation coefficients between the spot asset return and the other assets in the portfolio ($\sum_{i=1}^{n} x_i \, \rho_{i,S}$) is greater or equal to the sum of weighted correlation coefficients of the same asset hedged with the rest of the portfolio ($\sum_{i=1}^{n} x_i \, \rho_{i,H}$):

$$\text{Var}(R_{PS}) > \text{Var}(R_{PH}) \quad \text{if} \quad \sum_{i=1}^{n} x_i \rho_{i,S} > \sum_{i=1}^{n} x_i \rho_{i,H}$$

or

- if correlation coefficients of the futures position return with other portfolio assets sum up to a positive number (given a positive correlation between cash and futures prices) (127):

$$\text{Var}(R_{PS}) > \text{Var}(R_{P\bar{H}}) \quad \text{if} \quad \sum_{i=1}^{n} x_i \rho_{i,F} > 0$$

$$\text{given} \quad \rho_{S,F} > 0$$

The question whether and in which way portfolio return changes if one of the assets out of this portfolio is hedged, could not be solved in the theoretical investigation.

5.2.1. Correlation between   Spot,   Futures   and   Hedged
        Positions and Other Assets

Correlation coefficients for T-bond and GNMA positions (spot,
futures and hedged) with other bonds and stocks were
calculated (Compare Table 2-10).   Other bonds were
approximated to by the 10% Fedindex, and stocks by the
Standard & Poor's Composite Index (128).

T-bond and GNMA _futures_ positions show a positive correlation
with the stock market index in the range between 0.327 and
0.420, and 0.930 to 0.973 with the Fedindex. In combination
with a positive correlation of cash and futures prices, as
derived   above (Table 2-5), these values indicate risk
reduction for the overall portfolio including a hedged
position.

The analysis of _spot_ position correlation coefficients with
the stock market presents values in the range between 0.280
and 0.437. These values are clearly greater - regardless of
T-bond or GNMA position and period chosen - than coefficients
of _hedged_ positions with the stock market (-0.178 to 0.261).
These values and the results of the theoretical analysis
indicate less risk for a stock portfolio including a hedged
fixed-income security, compared to the same portfolio with
the fixed-income security unhedged.

Table 2-10 :   Correlation Coefficients for T-bond and GNMA Positions
               with Other Assets

SPOT POSITIONS	1978 - 1982	1978 - 6/80	7/80 - 1982
8 % T-bond - 10% Fedindex	0.956	0.988	0.934
8 % T-bond - Stock Market	0.377	0.315	0.418
$8\frac{1}{4}$% T-bond - Stock Market	0.380	0.311	0.437
$11\frac{3}{4}$% T-bond - Stock Market	---	---	0.406
10 % Fedindex - Stock Market	0.349	0.280	0.408
Own Index - Stock Market	0.377	0.343	0.407
GNMA - Stock Market	0.336	0.361	0.328
FUTURES POSITIONS			
8 % T-bond - 10% Fedindex	0.947	0.973	0.930
8 % T-bond - Stock Market	0.378	0.327	0.420
GNMA - Stock Market	0.366	0.352	0.379
HEDGED POSITIONS			
8 % - 10% Fedindex	0.459	0.481	0.468
8 % T-bond - Stock Market	0.157	0.014	0.203
$8\frac{1}{4}$% T-bond - Stock Market	0.172	0.042	0.261
$11\frac{3}{4}$% T-bond - Stock Market	---	---	0.097
10 % Fedindex - Stock Market	-0.074	-0.160	-0.070
Own Index - Stock Market	-0.048	0.065	-0.178
GNMA - Stock	0.117	0.179	0.112

The correlation between a spot bond and the Fedindex is close
to one, the adequate value for the bond hedged with the Index
clearly smaller (0.459 - 0.481).

Therefore estimates of correlation coefficients between
fixed-income securities and the bond or stock market lead to
the conclusion that hedging not only reduces the risk of
single assets but also the overall risk of portfolios
including a hedged asset.

The following empirical investigation of portfolios including
a hedged asset is limited to the T-bond position as the
hedged asset in the portfolio. Since GNMA positions exhibit
correlation values close to the bond market (compare Table
2-10), we expect similar results for both markets.

5.2.2. Variance of Portfolios Partially Hedged

Stock Portfolio

Variances of stock portfolios including a hedged T-bond
position were calculated with different bond proportions
increasing from 10 to 25 to 50 to 75 percent. The 8% bond
represented the hedged bond position. As a result we observe
for all periods an explicit reduction of risk for portfolios
including hedged bond position, $Var(R_{II})$, compared to the same
portfolio with the bond unhedged, $Var(R_S)$, (See Table and
Figure 2-11). Risk decreased as the bond proportion

increased. Whereas the pure stock portfolio had a variance of 21.297 this was reduced to 17.383 if the hedged bond accounted for 10% of the portfolio proportion. A hedged bond proportion of 25% reduced overall portfolio risk by half. For the subperiods and the year 1982 similar results can be observed. As with single positions, portfolios exhibit in the second subperiod greater risk for spot and hedged positions than in the first subperiod.

Inclusion of the 11 3/4% bond instead of the 8% issue for the second subperiod led to similar results with even lower risk values.

Bond Portfolio

Inclusion of different proportions of hedged T-bonds in a normal bond portfolio demonstrated a clear risk reduction effect for the overall portfolio over the entire period and in the two subperiods (Compare Table and Figure 2-12). Risk decreased as the hedged bond proportion increased.

5.2.3. Return of Portfolios Partially Hedged

Including hedged bonds, increased the return of stock port-folios in times of increasing interest rates (See Table 2-11). For 1982 we observe a return reduction for stock portfolios including hedged bonds. These two effects - similar to the situation observed above for single bonds - are strengthened as the proportion of hedged bonds increases.

Table 2-11 : Variance and Return of Stock Portfolios Including Hedged
and Unhedged T-bonds

Stock Bond Proportion (in %)		1978–1982		1978–6/80		7/80–1982		1982	
VARIANCE									
		$Var(R_S)$	$Var(R_H)$	$Var(R_S)$	$Var(R_H)$	$Var(R_S)$	$Var(R_H)$	$Var(R_S)$	$Var(R_H)$
100	0	21.297	21.297	20.607	20.607	22.718	22.718	30.431	30.431
90	10	18.942	17.383	17.943	16.701	20.580	18.654	27.342	24.949
75	25	16.422	12.291	14.927	11.624	18.444	13.360	23.417	17.769
50	50	14.928	5.888	12.517	5.246	17.745	6.678	18.765	8.583
25	75	16.816	2.088	13.377	1.474	20.619	2.670	16.474	2.872
00	100	22.085	0.890	17.506	0.308	27.067	1.338	16.545	0.638
RETURN									
		R_S	R_H	R_S	R_H	R_S	R_H	R_S	R_H
100	0	0.758	0.758	0.715	0.715	0.802	0.802	1.280	1.280
90	10	0.744	0.788	0.663	0.720	0.825	0.856	1.450	1.274
75	25	0.723	0.833	0.586	0.729	0.860	0.936	1.706	1.266
50	50	0.687	0.907	0.458	0.744	0.917	1.071	2.132	1.251
25	75	0.652	0.982	0.329	0.759	0.975	1.205	2.557	1.237
0	100	0.617	1.057	0.201	0.744	1.032	1.339	2.983	1.222

Table 2-12 : Variance and Return of Bond Portfolios Including Hedged and Unhedged Assets

Bond Portf. Proportion (in %)	Asset Hedged	1978–1982		1978–6/80		7/80–1982		1982	
VARIANCE		$Var(R_S)$	$Var(R_H)$	$Var(R_S)$	$Var(R_H)$	$Var(R_S)$	$Var(R_H)$	$Var(R_S)$	$Var(R_H)$
100	0	20.668	20.668	17.893	17.893	23.823	23.823	15.411	15.411
90	10	20.637	17.104	17.815	14.700	23.835	19.785	15.233	12.911
75	25	20.622	12.419	17.715	10.508	23.983	14.474	15.088	9.588
50	50	20.896	6.374	17.591	5.115	24.577	7.610	15.170	5.185
25	75	21.370	2.531	17.521	1.715	25.605	3.322	15.655	2.202
0	100	22.058	0.890	17.506	0.308	27.067	1.338	16.545	0.638
RETURN		R_S	R_H	R_S	R_H	R_S	R_H	R_S	R_H
100	0	0.628	0.628	0.227	0.227	1.029	1.029	3.343	3.343
90	10	0.627	0.671	0.224	0.282	1.029	1.060	3.307	3.131
75	25	0.625	0.735	0.220	0.364	1.030	1.106	3.253	2.813
50	50	0.622	0.842	0.214	0.500	1.031	1.184	3.163	2.283
25	75	0.619	0.949	0.207	0.637	1.031	1.261	3.073	1.752
0	100	0.617	1.057	0.201	0.774	1.032	1.339	2.983	1.222

183

Figure 2-11: Risk of Stock Portfolios Including Varying
           Proportions of Hedged T-bonds   1978-1982

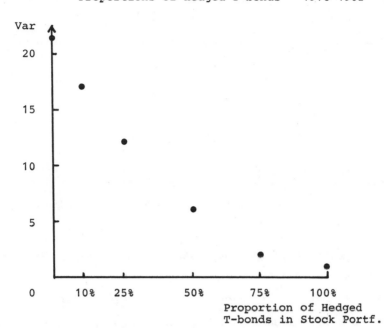

Proportion of Hedged
T-bonds in Stock Portf.

Figure 2-12: Risk of Bond Portfolios Including Varying
           Proportions of Hedged T-bonds   1978-1982

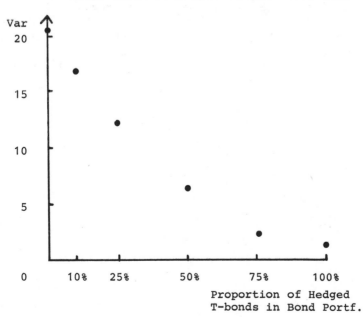

Proportion of Hedged
T-bonds in Bond Portf.

<u>Bond Portfolios</u>, including hedged bonds display an increase in return for the overall period and the subperiods, and a decrease in return during 1982 similar to the development observed for stock portfolios (compare Table 2-12).

5.2.4. Portfolios in the Mean-Variance Space

Hedging a bond position of a stock or bond portfolio, improved a trader's overall situation and hence enlarged his utility in the periods under investigation, i.e. risk of such portfolios was clearly reduced while the return increased simultaneously. This statement must be qualified for the period of decreasing interest rates in that the explicit risk reduction is accompanied by a return reduction. Hence a judgement based on the MARKOWITZ criterion of a change in a trader's situation in the mean-variance space is not possible without knowledge of the trader's utility function.

5.3. Analysis of Hedging Effectiveness

Table 2-13 presents empirical results concerning hedging effectiveness and optimal hedge ratios for the T-bond and GNMA market. The following statements can be derived:

1. The indicator of hedging effectiveness strongly supports the result derived in the previous section which judged the T-bond futures market to be a highly effective market for reducing risk caused by interest rate changes. For the overall period hedging with the nearby contract reduced 96.8% of the 8% bond and 97.6% of the 8 1/4% bond risk. The conclusion that the T-bond futures market led in periods of low interest rates and price variability to better hedging results for low coupon bonds than in periods of high rates and volatility, is supported by the greater hedging effectiveness for the first subperiod of 98.4% compared to 95.7% in the second subperiod for the 8% issue, and of 98.8% to 96.7% for the 8 1/4% issue. The use of the following contracts confirms this result.

The hedging effectiveness of 98.5% for the 11 3/4% bond issue in the second subperiod demonstrates that the hedging effectiveness did not decrease if bonds with coupon rates closer to market rates were investigated. This value is in the same range as those for the 8 and 8 1/4% bonds in the first subperiod (98.4 and 98.8%) and clearly better than hedging effectiveness values for those two low coupon bonds in the second subperiod (95.7 and 96.7%).

Table 2-13 : Hedging Effectiveness and Optimal Hedge Ratios

	1978–1982		1978–6/80		7/80–1982	
	HE	γ_1	HE	γ_1	HE	γ_1
8% T-bond N	0.968	1.051 [1] (0.025)	0.984	1.023 (0.025)	0.957	1.075 (0.043)
8% T-bond D	0.962	1.069 [1] (0.028)	0.980	1.022 (0.027)	0.949	1.115 [1] (0.049)
8% T-bond DD	0.951	1.100 [1] (0.033)	0.971	1.045 (0.034)	0.939	1.156 [1] (0.056)
$8\frac{1}{4}$% T-bond	0.976	1.074 [2] (0.022)	0.988	1.066 (0.022)	0.967	1.078 (0.038)
$11\frac{3}{4}$% T-bond					0.985	1.349 (0.032)
GNMA N	0.843	1.129 [1] (0.064)	0.905	1.055 (0.065)	0.808	1.201 (0.110)
GNMA D	0.827	1.088 (0.065)	0.894	0.993 (0.065)	0.794	1.190 (0.114)
GNMA DD	0.812	1.104 (0.069)	0.867	0.998 (0.073)	0.790	1.220 (0.119)

Values in paranthesis are standard errors. Numbers of observations: 60 overallperiod, 30 subperiod.

1) Significantly different from 1 (95% level of significance).
2) Significantly different from the 1:1 hedge ratio adjusted by the conversion factor.

Hence we can conclude that the hedging effectiveness of the T-bond futures market did not decrease as interest rates became more volatile. The market displays constant hedging effectiveness for bond issues close to market rates, but decreasing hedging effectiveness for low coupon issues in periods of high and extremly volatile interest rates. This result supports indications given by the correlation coefficients and variance values derived in previous computations (129).

2. The GNMA market proves to be not as efficient in risk reducing as the T-bond market. For the 1978 - 1982 period hedging effectiveness reached values between 80.8% and 90.5%, clearly below equivalent results for the T-bond market (nearby contract). This outcome was indicated by lower correlation between cash and futures returns for the GNMA market. It might be explained by lower daily trading volume compared to the T-bond futures market (Compare Table 2-15). The volume of sales in the T-bond market exeeded the GNMA market six times in 1981.

Another explanation for the lower hedging effectiveness might be that T-bonds are more homogeneous securities than GNMA certificates which are issued by different mortgage banks and might be prepaid after 12 years although maturity is of 30 years (130).

3. Values for hedging effectiveness in the GNMA market indicate an improvement in hedging quality. EDERINGTON derived for the period 1976/77 a hedging effectiveness of 78.5% for the nearby contract (131). Our study computed greater values for following periods: 77/79: 81.9%, 78 - 6/80: 90.5% and 7/80 - 82: 80.8%. In the first two years trading in GNMA futures, which was the first interest rate futures contract ever introduced, was quite low. At the end of 1976 monthly volume of sales reached 15,000 contracts, and 42,000 contracts at the end of 1977 (Compare Table 2-14). With an increase in trading the effectiveness seems to be improved (132).

4. Parallel to the T-bond market, the GNMA futures market shows higher hedging effectiveness for the 8% coupon issue in periods of lower interest rates and interest rate changes. In the first subperiod hedging effectiveness reached 90.5% whereas in the second subperiod only 80.8% of the interest rate risk was reduced. The reason for this reduction in hedging effectiveness seems to be the same as in the T-bond market: a 8% coupon rate of the asset investigated that is different from actual market rates in the second subperiod.

5. The analysis of <u>hedging effectiveness</u> of three <u>different futures contracts</u> clearly proves the superiority of the nearby contract to distant contracts. Hedging effectiveness unquestionably decreased for GNMAs or bonds in all periods

when more distant contracts were used (Compare Table 2-13). The higher effectiveness of the nearby contract reflects higher parallelism in cash and futures price movement. Since cash and futures prices must converge at contract maturity the nearby contract with at least 10 weeks to maturity leads to better hedging results than the more distant contracts with an outstanding maturity of 3 to 6 or 6 to 9 months. This result of higher hedging effectiveness for nearby contracts is in accordance with empirical results of other investigations for interest rate futures markets (133). EDERINGTON derived opposite results for the GNMA market using data from 1976 to 1977. His results might be the consequence of low trading in the first years of the contract, since our own investigations for 1977 support the result derived above of higher effectiveness for the nearby contract.

6. If we compare the decreasing hedging effectiveness of different futures contracts for T-bonds and GNMAs, we register higher decreasing effectiveness for the GNMA market. Hence the different T-bond contracts move more in line than those of the GNMA market. This fact might also be explained by lower trading activities in the GNMA market (Compare Table 2-13 and 2-14).

Table 2-14 : Open Contracts and Volume of Sales in T-bond and
GNMA Futures Markets

| Date | GNMA | | T-Bond | |
	Volume of [1] Sales	Open [2] Contracts	Volume of [1] Sales	Open [2] Contracts
Mrch 76	7,487	1,610		
June 76	11,935	3,452		
Sept 76	12,568	3,624		
Dec 76	15,030	5,182		
Mrch 77	25,944	8,820		
June 77	29,626	13,219		
Sept 77	11,938	16,211	7,236	1,720
Dec 77	41,787	20,719	7,379	2,864
June 78	75,178	33,503	33,065	8,008
Dec 78	109,602	62,777	98,609	41,246
June 79	111,767	73,339	169,093	61,472
Dec 79	180,349	88,982	260,384	90,676
June 80	248,385	71,853	608,643	111,051
Dec 80	318,735	115,161	1 009,846	243,614
July 81	162,031	133,860	1 094,363	290,930[3]
Dec 81	202,755	77,246	1 377,823	221,680
June 82	156,290	51,891	1 253,026	160,624
Dec 82	134,028	39,958	1 324,723	182,908

1) Number of contracts traded within one month.
2) Number of contracts outstanding at the last day of month.
3) June

Figures are taken from the Statistical Annual of the CBT,
different issues.

5.4. Analysis of Optimal Hedge Ratios

Values for the optimal hedge ratio, derived for the T-bond
market and presented in Table 2-13, are all above one. The
investigation whether these values differ significantly from
one leads to the following results:

The 8% bond hedged with the nearby contract exhibits for the
overall period an optimal hedge ratio of 1.051 a value
significantly greater than one so that to obtain optimal risk
reduction, overhedging would have been the optimal strategy
for the period 1978-1982. For the 8 1/4% bond also
overhedging would have worked out as the best result. Naive
hedging strategy for the 8 1/4% bond would have suggested a
futures position of 1.0245 times the spot position. This
value is derived by adjusting the 1:1 ratio via the
conversion factor, due to the 0 1/4% bond coupon rate and
maturity being different from the fictive bond underlying
futures price quotations (134). The optimal hedge ratio
derived (1.074) is significantly different from 1.0245 (135).

In the two subperiods optimal hedge ratios for all bonds
hedged by the nearby contract are not much different from
values suggested by the naive strategy. The 8% bond figures
(1.023 and 1.075) are not significantly different from one.
Ratios computed for the 8 1/4 and 11 3/4 bond are
significantly above one but not significantly different from
naive 1:1 hedging ratios adjusted by conversion factors.

These adjusted values are 1.025 and 1.024 for the first and second subperiod for the 8 1/4% bond, and 1.349 for the 11 3/4 bond in the second subperiod.

Figures for T-bonds hedged with distant and then following contracts indicate overhedging for the overall and the second subperiod as the optimal strategy whereas a naive ratio is suggested by the figures for the first subperiod.

In addition we observe an increase in the optimal hedge ratio for more distant contracts. This means, that due to a lower correlation between cash and more distant futures contracts and consequently lower hedging effectiveness, the amount of the futures position taken should be increased if more distant contracts are used as hedging instruments.

A final evaluation of the question whether a naive 1:1 hedge ratio or overhedging would have led to better hedging results, turns out to be very difficult to answer on the basis of the above figures. Using the more distant contracts, at least for the overall and second subperiod, overhedging would have been the best strategy. Figures for hedging with the nearby contract suggest overhedging for the overall period. But the results for the two subperiods indicate, that a naive 1:1 strategy cannot be rejected as being the optimal strategy.

We can note that the naive strategy led to extremely good results for the period under investigation, i.e. a hedging effectiveness of 96.8% for the overall period, which might have been slightly improved by overhedging.

Optimal hedge ratios in the GNMA market are - abstracting from two cases (D and DD in 1978 - 6/80) - above one, but in only one case significantly different from one. Hence we can conclude that a naive hedging strategy would have led to optimal results in the period under investigation. These results for the optimal hedge ratios are in accordance with the findings of EDERINGTON and HEGDE (136).

5.5. Evaluation of Results

Before turning to a final discussion of the empirical results, it seems necessary to draw the attention to the procedure in which they were derived. This evaluation seems necessary since the method used might have influenced the findings of this study and hence the conclusions drawn from it.

5.5.1. Critical Analysis of the Applied Procedure

5.5.1.1. Traders' Expectations

This point refers to the adequate incorporation of traders' expectations into the empirical investigation. The situation in which agents have to make decisions is as follows: At time 0 they decide whether and to what extent cash position should be hedged for the following period. Obviously they should know from their own experience or derive from data how cash and futures prices behaved in the past. This knowledge can be based on objective ex-post data.

One hedging strategy would be to apply optimal ex-post hedge ratios as ex-ante measures for the determination of the cash proportion to be hedged (137). A different strategy is the use of expected optimal ratios for the past period corrected to some extent by the forecasting error of the past period. A further method would be one in which agents at time 0 use ex-post data to form in combination with available information on the future, expectations on cash and future price behaviour in the next period (0,1).

Consequently using ex-post data and current available information on factors influencing cash and futures prices in the next period, traders form subjective expectations and determine their ex-ante hedge ratios.

As mentioned above traders expectations are unobservable. Thus we cannot make use of these expectations on price behaviour and derived hedging ratios. We are constrained to an arbitrary assumption on traders' hedging behaviour, such as the naive 1:1 hedging ratio.

In interpreting the results we should bear in mind that traders are assumed to have no information on the past and the future or to hold such information without making use of it. (Abstracting the case where traders believe that the 1:1 ratio is optimal). Hence we investigated routine hedgers, although in reality it seems much more likely that traders in a more or less sophisticated way search for and make use of information to determine the best hedging ratio.

It is against this background that the results of our investigation should be interpreted, i.e. that traders making use of available information and forming individual expectations can always beat the market and can reach hedging results better than those computed in this study. Hence the findings presented can be regarded as a lower boundary of success in risk reduction. Traders forming ex-ante expectations that eventually turn out to be true could have performed better than the routine hedger analysed here.

5.5.1.2. Price Quotations

Another point that needs discussion concerns price quotations on which the empirical investigation is based. We mentioned above (II.4.1.) that bid prices, quoted in statistics and used here, reflect an offer to sell. But it is not guaranteed that a transaction took place at that rate, i.e. that quotations used do adequately reflect market developments.

Futures markets investigated are so active in the last thirty seconds of trading that closing prices should reflect market rates at the end of the day.

Furthermore we have to examine whether cash and futures prices used in this study are quotations on which traders base their decisions and carry out transactions. Cash prices applied were closing bid prices, since other quotations were not available. Consequently, futures quotations employed were closing prices for the same day. This procedure assumes traders to compare cash and futures prices, form their hedging decisions, and establish the relevant positions in the last thirty seconds of futures trading. Whether this assumption is an adequate description of reality must be doubted. Since futures trading starts at 8 am and ends at 2 pm these closing quotations can only be approximate values for prices at which traders take positions. A survey of opening, lowest, highest, and closing futures prices exhibits large price movements in daily trading. Basing the analysis on closing prices (for cash and futures), we might use quotations that are different from those on which traders base their decisions and establish positions. In addition the basis between cash and futures closing prices might be different from the basis that prevailed over the trading day.

Discussing the results, we should bear in mind these eventual shortcomings.
As long as complete daily price series are not available an estimation of the degree of distortion introduced by the use of closing prices turns out to be difficult. To get a rough idea of potential deviations, cash market closing prices were confronted with futures markets opening quotations for the next day (instead of closing prices for the same day).

Results of this evaluation should be interpreted with prudence since futures prices for the following day incorporate all information that emerged between cash market closing and futures trading opening at the next day. Therefore findings derived can be regarded as an extreme distortion exaggerating potential deviations.

Table 2-15: Effects of Hedging on Risk and Return
when Different Price Quotations Were
Used (6/1980-1982)

$\rho_{S,F}$	C	O	
8 % T-bond	0.980	0.949	
$11\frac{3}{4}$ % T-bond	0.991	0.961	
8 % Fedindex	0.930	0.899	
VARIANCE	$Var(R_S)$	$Var(R_{HC})$	$Var(R_{HO})$
8 % T-bond	27.067	1.338	2.824
$11\frac{3}{4}$ % T-bond	21.515	0.385	1.772
8 % Fedindex	25.712	3.493	5.104
RETURN	R_S	R_{HC}	R_{HO}
8 % T-bond	1.032	1.339	1.318
$11\frac{3}{4}$ % T-bond	0.966	1.272	1.251
8 % Fedindex	1.006	1.322	1.300
HE	C	O	
8 % T-bond	0.957	0.900	
$11\frac{3}{4}$ % T-bond	0.985	0.929	
8 % Fedindex	0.848	0.805	

C: Closing futures price of last day of month.
O: Opening futures price of following day.

Results are presented in Table 2-15. Since futures opening prices were not published before 1980 this evaluation is limited to the second subperiod. Findings are not very surprising. Using next morning opening futures prices, led to lower risk reduction for the 8 and 11 3/4% T-bonds and the 8% Fedindex: correlation coefficients between cash and futures prices declined, hedged position variances increased and hedging effectiveness turned out to be smaller. Nevertheless hedging still caused a large reduction in risk, e.g. 90.0% of the 8% T-bonds risk was reduced instead of 95.7%.

The main results of this study were strongly corroberated although prices employed exaggerated potential errors due to the lack of data more accurately reflecting the situation of hedgers.
Hence we can conclude that potential errors caused by price quotations not exactly reflecting prices on which traders act, do not seriously prejudice the results of this investigation.

5.5.2. Summary of Results

In the last section of chapter II we presented results of the empirical investigation of T-bond and GNMA futures markets. We analysed effects of hedging on single assets and portfolios containing a hedged position.

The evidence for the period 1977/78 - 1982 strongly supports the theoretical analysis and the widely held view that hedging reduces risk of single T-bond or GNMA positions and consequently 'protects' traders against interest rate fluctuations. Interest rate futures markets proved to be a highly effective instrument to reduce risk caused by unexpected interest rate changes.

Futures markets efficacy in reducing risk was described using three indicators: correlation coefficients between cash and futures price movements, comparisons of variances of unhedged and hedged positions, and hedging effectiveness. In particular the T-bond market proved to be extremly effective in risk reduction: 95.7% to 98.8% of single bond risk was abolished.

Increasing price variability in the period under investigation, i.e. the 8% bonds variance value grew from 17.506 in the first to 27.067 in the second subperiod, caused larger basis changes but the risk reduction quality of the market did not decrease. A turn around in the interest rate trend, from increasing rates till the end of 1981 to declining rates in 1982, did not affect the risk reduction quality of futures markets.

The GNMA market also proved to be a highly satisfactory instrument of risk reduction. Values of hedging effectiveness are smaller than those for T-bonds. Nevertheless between 80.8 and 90.5% of interest rate risk was abolished.

For both markets futures contracts closest to the end of the hedging period could be verified as better hedging vehicles than following contracts. This result is due to the fact that uncertainty of future interest rate movements and therefore, larger differences in cash and futures price changes, become larger with the period between the end of the hedge and futures contract maturity widening.

These results of hedging effects on asset risk were already derived in the theoretical analysis. The question of the effects of futures trading on hedged position return, and on risk and return of portfolios including a hedged position should be answered by the empirical investigation.
Related to risk of stock and bond portfolios we observed in the period under investigation a definite risk reduction for those portfolios containing a hedged asset. Whereas we could expect a result like this for bondportfolios, given the above findings, the observed significant risk reduction for stock portfolios including a hedged bond position can be regarded as a new result.

With respect to the return we registered an evident increase for hedged positions (either single positions or portfolios containing a hedged position). At first glance this result looks somewhat surprising. If futures markets reduce variability of return we would expect rates of return to be determined by pure interest income. Since in the period under investigation interest rates increased for most of the period, returns were reduced by decreasing cash prices. By trading in futures, hedgers were protected against this price decline and erosion of return. Furthermore we could observe a basis change to the hedgers' advantage. Thus returns of hedged positions not only exceeded spot returns but also exceeded returns due to pure interest income.

Hence we found a clear improvement in a trader's situation in the mean-variance space. In phases of increasing interest rates hedgers could clearly reduce risk and increase return at the same time. Taking positions in the futures markets led to an increase in traders' utility.

It is logical that in such an effective market, returns of hedged position in times of decreasing interest rates were outperformed by earnings from unhedged spot positions. Consequently, an evaluation of traders' utility due to futures trading in relation to sole spot transactions depends on traders attitudes towards risk, i.e. how much return they are willing to sacrifice for risk reduction.

To sum up, interest rate futures market which emerged as a market reaction to growing risk and uncertainty caused by increasing interest rate volatility proved to be a very effective tool for participants in financial markets to cope with the risk of unexpected changes in interest rates.

Footnotes to II.1. (Classical Portfolio Theory)

1) MARKOWITZ, H.M. (1952 and 1959); TOBIN, J. (1958); SHARPE, W.F. (1964 and 1970); LINTNER, J. (1965a and 1965b); MOSSIN, J. (1966).

2) For other approaches dealing with the problem of investment under uncertainty compare: JENSEN, M.C. (1972, pp. 4, 38).

3) See MARKOWITZ, H.M. (1952, pp. 7 f.).

4) For a detailed treatment of decision theory compare e.g. SCHNEEWEISS, H. (1967, pp. 7ff.)

5) KNIGHT, F.H. (1921, P. 20) as quoted in SCHNEEWEISS, H. (1967, p. 12).

6) SHARPE, W.F. (1970, pp. 25 f.).

7) SCHNEEWEISS stated that the categories of risk and uncertainty are two extremes, which can be rarely found in reality. The classical situation of risk is a lottery. The analysis of portfolio theory under the categorie of risk, i.e. the assumption that portfolio selection is based only on stochasticaly moving stock prices, is an approximation of reality justifiable by the fact "dass in fast jeder Ungewissheitssituation, die keine reine Risikosituation ist, doch mehr oder weniger versteckte Risikosituationen enthalten sind" (p. 27). Compare also GEORGESCU-ROEGEN, N. (1958, p. 25).

The preconditions of classical decision theory are not given. A trader in financial markets faces a non-repetitive situation and bases his decision on subjective probabilities. Nevertheless a situation like that can be approximated by probablility theory. A justification for this procedure can be found e.g. in SCHNEEWEISS, H. (1967, pp. 28 f.); WEBER, W.; STREISSLER, E.(1961, pp. 322 f.); MAG, W. (1981, pp. 481 ff.).

Most textbooks and articles on portfolio theory do not mention the fact that an analysis of portfolio theory under the category of risk in probabilistic terms is an approximation.

8) See BOLTEN, S.E. (1970, pp. 423 f.).

9) For the assumptions on which portfolio theory is based compare: FRANCIS, J.C.; ARCHER, S.A. (1979, pp. 5 f., 148); DRUKARCZYK, J. (1980, pp. 294 ff.).

204

10) For a detailed discussion of this point see e.g.
TOBIN, J. (1958, pp. 74 ff.); MARKOWITZ, H.M. (1959.
pp. 286 f.); SCHNEEWEISS, H. (1967, pp. 96 ff. and
120 ff.).

11) See SHARPE, W.F. (1981, pp. 136 ff.).

12) For the theory of expectations and the way expectations
are formed compare the basic contributions of FISHER, I.
(1930); CAGAN, P. (1956); MUTH, J.F. (1961).

13) SHARPE, W.F. (1970. p. 25).

14) A summary of these techniques can be found in FRANCIS,
J.C.; ARCHER, S.A. (1979, pp. 49 ff.).

15) MARKOWITZ H.M. (1952, p.91).

16) SHARPE, W.F. (1970, pp. 21 ff.).

17) BOLTEN, S.E. (1970, p. 425).

18) MARKOWITZ, H.M. (1959, p. 14).

19) See SHARPE, W.F. (1970, p. 35).

20) For this section compare: MARKOWITZ, H.M. (1959, pp.
82 ff.); ELTON, E.J.; GRUBER, M.J. (1981, pp. 43
ff.); FRANCIS, J.C.; ARCHER, S.H. (1979, pp. 43
ff.).

21) MARKOWITZ, H.M. (1952, p. 82).

22) MARKOWITZ, H.M. (1952, p. 82).

23) See point 6 of assumptions underlying portfolio theory.

Footnotes to II.2.   (Application of Portfolio Theory)

24) Compare TAYLOR, F.M.   (1925, pp.   234 f.);   KEYNES, J.M. (1923, p.785 and 1930, p.   129); YAMEY, B.S. (1951, p.   305).

25) See e.g. HIERONYMUS, T.A.   (1977, p.   175).

26) Notice that in contrast to classical portfolio theory formula (II.7) and (II.8) refer to absolute $ returns and not to rates of return.

27) See e.g. TAYLOR, F.M.   (1925, p.   235).

28) See e.g. YAMEY, B.S. (1951, p.   306).

29) For a detailed discussion of the basis and changes in the basis see chapter I.

30) Again this is an anticipation of point II.2.1.3.   But it seems necessary for better understanding of the risk reduction aspect of traditional theory of hedging.

31) Again (II.9) and (II.10) refer to absolute $ returns in contrast to classical portfolio theory.

32) For the mathematical formulations see: FRANCIS, J.C. ARCHER, S.H. (1979, pp.   21 ff.).

33) With E(F) = E(f. - f.), the expected $ return of a futures market position.

34) WORKING, H. (1953a, pp. 325, 326).

35) Compare WORKING, H. (1953a, p.   320).

36) See RUTLEDGE, D.J. (1972, p.   239); EDERINGTON, L.H. (1979, p.   161).

37) TELSER, L.G. (1955/56; pp. 1 ff.); JOHNSON, L.L. (1960, pp.   139 ff.);   STEIN, J.L. (1961, pp.   1012 ff.).

38) JOHNSON, L.L. (1960, p.   141).

39) JOHNSON, L.L. (1960, p.   142).

40) See for example: RUTLEDGE, D.J. (1972, pp.   237 ff.); NEWBERY, D.M.; STIGLITZ, J.E. (1981, pp.   85 ff.); ROLFO, J. (1980, pp. 100 ff.); KAWAI, M. (1981, pp. 1 ff.).

41) Compare II.1.1.

42) An analysis of a short cash market position, for example an investment in assets planned for the next month, is not undertaken here. It would be similar to the following analysis. For such an application see: MANESS, T.S. (1981, pp. 393 ff.) or FRANCKLE, C.T.; SENCHAK, A.J. (1982, pp. 107 ff.).

43) Studies dealing with the problem of determining cash and futures market positions simultaneously: JOHNSON, L.L. (1960, pp. 139 ff.); WARD, R.W.; FLETCHER, L.B. (1971, pp. 71 ff.); ANDERSON, R.W.; DANTHINE, J.-P. (1981, pp. 1182 ff.); ROLFO, J. (1980, pp. 100 ff.).

44) In contrast to portfolio theory return and variance are based on $ returns and not on rates of return.

45) In contrast to equations (II.8) and (II.10) the sign of x_F is positive, reflecting the fact that a number is added. It has still to be determined whether the futures position is a short $(-x_F)$ or long $(+x_F)$ position.

46) Since r is fixed it does not contribute to the risk of spot and hedged positions. σ_F^2 and cov(r,F) are zero.

47) See e.g.: EDERINGTON, L.H. (1979, p. 161); ANDERSON, R.W.; DANTHINE, J.-P. (1981, p. 1183); HILL, J.; SCHNEEWEIS, T. (1981, p. 660).

48) Traders were assumed to be long in cash. Compare third assumption at the beginning of this section.

49) See: STEIN, J.J. (1961, pp. 1012 ff.) and (1964, pp. 762 ff.). For a discussion of Stein see GOSS, B.A. (1972, pp. 61 ff.).

50) STEIN, J.J. (1961, p. 1015). Mathematical formulation in STEIN, J.J. (1964, p. 763).

51) That a higher expected return from unhedged cash positions would increase the ratio of unhedged positions hold can be shown by an upwards shift of point U. See GOSS, B.A. (1972, p. 64).

52) Compare GOSS, B.A.; YAMEY, B.S. (1976, p. 28).

53) JOHNSON, L.L. (1960, pp. 145 ff.). For a discussion of Johnson see GOSS, B.A. (1972, pp. 73 ff.). An application of Johnson's model to production and marketing decisions can be found in WARD, R.W.; FLETCHER, L.B. (1971, pp. 71 ff.).

54) This constraint requires such a size of the futures position x_F that the price risk of holding x_S and x_F from time 0 to 1 is minimized. It is discussed in the following section.

55) The major axis of the ellipse rotates through an angle

$$\frac{1}{2} \text{ arcot } \frac{\sigma_S^2 - \sigma_F^2}{2 \text{ cov}(S,F)}$$

See GOSS, B.A. (1972, P. 78).

56) (II.13) can be written as:

$$x_F = \frac{x_S E(\Delta s) + x_S r + E(H)}{E(\Delta f)}$$

and

$$\frac{\partial x_F}{\partial x_S} = - \frac{E(\Delta s) + r}{E(\Delta f)}$$

57) See JOHNSON, L.L. (1960, pp. 147 f.).

58) In JOHNSON's model the opportunity locus OZ is transferred into an expected return-variance diagram, where it forms a linear line. The trader's optimal E(H) - Var(H) combination is given by the tangential point of one of his indifference curves with this line. If this point is retransferred into figure 2-4 the amounts of x_S and x_F leading to the highest utility for the trader can be determined (1960, pp. 145 ff.).

59) In JOHNSON's analysis x_S is not fixed. The trader expecting a positive (negative) cash price change will increase (decrease) his cash and futures holdings according to the expected cash price movement.

60) Johnson regards $-x_{F1}$ as the trader's normal futures market position since he does not expect any price movement in futures. JOHNSON, L.L. (1960, p. 147).

61) See WARD, R.W.; FLETCHER, L.B. (1971, p. 76).

62) JOHNSON, L.L. (1960, p. 150)

63) Compare for this approach: ROLFO, J. (1980, pp. 102 f.); ANDERSON, R.W.; DANTHINE, J.-P. (1981, pp. 1186 f.). In a later paper ANDERSON/DANTHINE (1983, pp. 249 ff.) extended the two period analysis to a multi-period investigation of hedging that confirmed the relevant results of this approach.

64) In this analysis x $_S$ the spot position was assumed to be given and fixed. For any trader whose cash position is not fixed, e.g. a farmer, an optimal cash position can be derived by maximizing E(U) with respect to x$_S$, for given futures position. See: ANDERSON, R.W.; DANTHINE, J.-P. (1980, pp. 490 f.).

65) For this and the following interpretation see too: KAWAI, M. (1981, pp. 6 ff.); ANDERSON, R.W.; DANTHINE, J.-P. (1981, p. 1187); ROLFO, J. (1980, p. 103).

66) ANDERSON, R.W.; DANTHINE, J.-P. (1983, pp. 255 ff.) proved the validity of the futures position's decomposition also for a multiperiod framework.

67) This risk minimization approach was used by JOHNSON, L.L. (1960, pp. 142 f.) and EDERINGTON, L.H. (1979, pp. 161 f.) to determine the optimal proportion of cash positions to be hedged. The second order condition for a minimum holds:
$$\frac{\partial \text{Var}(H)}{\partial^2 x_F} = 2\sigma_F^2 > 0$$

68) See ANDERSON, R.W.; DANTHINE, J.-P. (1981, p. 1188).

69) See also: ROLFO, J. (1980, p. 103); ANDERSON, R.W.; DANTHINE, J.-P. (1981, PP. 1186 f.).

70) Compare II.2.2.2.2 and Figure 2-5.

71) Described as sitution 4 in II.2.2.2.2.

Footnotes to II.3. (Theoretical Evaluation)

72) The expression single position refers to a single cash
position hedged in futures. This hedged position might
be called a portfolio but in this section the expression
portfolio is used for combinations of several cash
assets among which one cash position might be hedged.

73) For this procedure compare: JOHNSON, L.L. (1960, pp.
142 f.); EDERINGTON, L.H. (1979, pp. 161 ff.).

74) Setting Var(H) in relation to the variance of an
unhedged spot position Var(S), a measure for the risk
reduction effectiveness of futures trading can be
deducted. This measure will be derived in II.4.4.

75) The last line of Figure 2-2 seems to contradict this
statement. E(Δs) and E(Δf) have a positive sign. But
since the expected correlation between cash and futures
prices is -1, a positive cash price change implies a
negative futures price change and vice versa.

76) Compare II.2.2.3.1.

77) Compare II.2.2.3.2.

78) Compare II.2.2.3.2.

79) Compare II.2.2.2.2.

80) This limitation of the theoretical analysis onto the
pure hedge component is necessary, since in the previous
section we could not derive a clear result on the
relation between Var(S) and Var(H) for the overall hedge
component. Hence a comparison of components (b) and (c)
in section 3.2.2., Analysis of Risk, is not possible.

81) Notice that, in contrast to previous sections, the
expected return is no longer calculated as absolute $
return but as rate of return. Up to now x_S was fixed
and standardized at 1 hence absolute $ returns referred
always to an equal invested sum, and comparisons were
possible. In the following analysis returns from
T-bonds must be compared to income from shares, and
correlations between assets with different initial
investments must be taken into consideration. For these
reasons rates of return are used. Like in the previous
analysis we abstract from cost of transactions.

82) Cash and futures prices are kept in line by arbitrage
and spreading. Compare chapter I. 2.3 and 2.4. Hence
this assumption is suitable.

83) Compare II.2.2.3.1

84) Hence we assume that arbitrage and spreading keeps cash and futures prices in line. Compare chapter I.2.3 and 2.4.

85) See: FAMA, E.F.; MILLER, M.H. (1972, p. 281); FAMA, E.F. (1976, p. 60).

86) For the mathematical formulation compare: ELTON, E.J.; GRUBER, M.J. (1981, p. 284).

87) In the next chapter it will be assumed that the portfolio consists out of all assets existing in the market. This portfolio will be called market portfolio.

88) Compare: FAMA, E.F.; MILLER, M.H. (1972, p. 281); FAMA, E.F. (1976, p. 60).

Footnotes to II.4. (Technical Aspects)

89) For a more detailed discussion of this assumption see the following point II.4.3.3.1. Consequences of this procedure on the results of the study are investigated in II.5.5.

90) Later, in September 1978 a second GNMA certificate delivery contract was launched at the CBT which is not investigated here and should not be confused with the first one.

91) See CHICAGO BOARD OF TRADE (ed.) Interest Rate Futures, Statistical Annuals, different years.

92) Compare: FEDERAL RESERVE BANK OF ST. LOUIS, Monetary Trends, 3. March 1983, p. 12.

93) See: FEDERAL RESERVE BANK, Federal Reserve Bulletin, Table 1.54: Mortgage Markets. (before Oct, 1980, Table 1.55), different issues.

94) CHICAGO MERCANTILE EXCHANGE (ed.) (1978, p. 15) (Trading in Tomorrows); LOOSIGIAN, A.M. (1980, p. 422).

95) The T-bond futures contract requires for delivery a cash bond with at least 15 years to delivery or first call date.

96) See also: GARAND, J.J. (1974, p. 284).

97) FEDERAL RESERVE BANK, Federal Reserve Bulletin, Table 1.35: Interest Rates, Money and Capital Markets (before Oct. 1980 Table 1.36).

98) Ibid, Footnote 10.

99) Comparisons of price changes of the 8% bond and the 8% index for 1980/81 showed that on average the amount of price changes did not differ significantly. Nevertheless some months exhibit large differences in price changes, e.g. March 81: bond 1.81 ($) index 0.24, May 81: 3.37 to 1.65, Oct. 1981: 4.12 to 1.02.

100) For the yield curve compare: Treasury Bulletin, June 1983, p. 30; STIGUM, M.L. (1978, pp. 53 ff).

101) Compare: POWERS, M.J.; VOGEL, D.J. (1981, P. 136); STIGUM, M.L.; BRANCH, R.O. (1983, PP. 58 f.).

102) Compare BILDERSEE, J.S. (1975, p. 509); IBBOTSON, R.G.; SINQUEFIELD, R.A. (1976, pp. 14 ff.).

212

103) BILDERSEE, J.S. (1975, p. 509) showed that this assumption might lead to yield differences of maximal 5/100 of 1 percent (a February with a weekend at the 27/28). In most cases, the difference was less than 1/100 of 1 percent.

104) Compare: DARST, D.M. (1981, pp. 307 f.); YEAGER, F.C.; SEITZ, N.E. (1982), p. 74).

105) Compare: SCHWARZ, E.W. (1979, p. 42); FABOZZI, F.J.; ZARB, F.G. (1981, p. 365).

106) Figures refer to T-bonds. See CBT (ed.) (1981, p. 20); CBT, monthly bulletin (Feb. 84, p. 4).

107) MANESS, T.S. (1981, pp. 396 ff.).

108) MCENALLY, R.W.; RICE, M.L. (1979, p. 17).

109) FRANCKLE, C.T. (1980, p. 1274); CICCHETTI, P. e.a. (1981, pp. 384 f.); PARKINSON, P.M. (1981, p. 79); MANESS, T.S. (1981, pp. 396 ff.).

110) EDERINGTON, L.H. (1979, pp. 165 f.); HEGDE, S.P. (1982, pp. 348 ff.).

111) EDERINGTON, L.H. (1979, pp. 165 f.); CICCHETTI, P. e.a. (1981, pp. 384 f.); MANESS, T.S. (1981, p. 400).

112) EDERINGTON, L.H. (1979, pp. 165 f.).

113) HEGDE, S.P. (1982, pp. 348 ff.).

114) PARKINSON, P.M. (1981, p. 83).

115) This measure was first introduced by JOHNSON, L.L. (1960, pp. 142 ff.) for commodity markets.

116) Compare II.2.2.3.1.

117) WHITE, K.J. (1978, pp. 239 f.).

Footnotes to II.5.   (Results of Empirical Investigation)

118) The expression single position refers to single assets
     or portfolios like the Fedindex or Ownindex that are
     either completely hedged or completely unhedged.   In
     section   5.2.   the expression   portfolio refers   to
     combinations of assets among which a single asset but
     never all assets might be hedged.

119) As mentioned in the previous section, hedges including
     a speculative component cannot be investigated since
     traders' ex-ante expectations necessary to determine the
     amount of the overall hedge are not observable.

120) Compare II.3.1.1.

121) The time to maturity factor does not affect this
     statement since the high coupon bonds show the largest
     time to maturity and thus should exhibit the greater
     price volatility.   For the theory of bond pricing
     compare: DARST, D.M. (1931, pp. 307 ff.);   FISCHER,
     D.E.; JORDAN, R.J. (1983, pp. 323 f.).

122) At a first glance one might be indifferent whether a
     percentage return of 0.774% for the first subperiod
     based on cash prices below face value is greater than a
     dollar return of 0.667.   This $ return of 0.667 would
     equal a rate of return of 0.774% if prices were quoted
     at 86.18.   We observe cash prices declining from 97.88
     to 67.25 with an average price of 87.94.   Hence the
     return calculated exceeds pure interest earnings. For
     other periods similar results can be computed.

123) The first subperiod's results for the 10 and 12%
     Fedindex with average returns below pure interest
     earnings seem to contradict this interpretation.   One
     should have in mind that a 10% interest rate was reached
     in the midth of 1979 and the 12% rate at the beginning
     of 1980. Hence these indexes assume a coupon rate too
     high for the underlying first subperiod.

124) Compare I.2.1.2. or the literature on the basis and
     basis changes, e.g. POWERS, M.J.; VOGEL, D.J. (1981,
     pp. 179 ff.).

125) In 49 out of 60 observations the 8% T-bond cash prices
     exceeded futures prices.

126) This observation does not apply to the 77-79 subperiod.
     This is mainly caused by the low return of the hedged
     position in 1977 which is about 0.300% due to a negative
     basis change of -0.367, but anyway above the return of
     0.200% of the spot position.

127) Compare section 3.2. of this chapter.

128) For the construction of the Standard & Poor's Composit Index see section III.3.1.2.

129) Compare section II.5.1.1. and Tables 2-5 and 2-6.

130) Compare: SCHWARZ, E.W. (1979, pp. 42 f.); HEGDE, S.P. (1982, p. 347).

131) EDERINGTON, L.H. (1979, p. 166).

132) HEGDE's results for the GNMA market (hedging effectiveness of 75,4% (Jan to Sept. 1979) and 88,1% (Oct. 1979 to July 1980) cannot be compared to this study, since those figures are based on a two weeks hedge. Nevertheless the figures are in the range of values derived above and support the indication of an improvement of hedging effectiveness in the GNMA market.

133) CICCHETTI, P. e.a. (1981, p. 384); EDERINGTON, L.H. (1979, pp. 165 ff; HEGDE, S.P. (1982, pp. 347 ff.).

134) The ratio of 1.0245 is the average value of conversion factors that declined in the overall period from 1.026 to 1.023, due to decreasing time to maturity of the 8 1/4% bond in the 5 years from 1978 to 1982.

135) The confidence interval at 95% level of significance is 1.0298 - 1.1182; OHR 1.0245.

136) EDERINGTON, L.H. (1979, p. 166). HEGDE investigated hedges of 1 and 2 weeks. HEGDE, S.P. (1982, pp. 350 ff.).

137) For the literature on expectation theory compare footnote 12.

CHAPTER III :   INTEREST RATE FUTURES MARKETS IN THE   CONTEXT
OF THE CAPITAL ASSET PRICING MODEL

1. THEORETICAL BASIS

1.1. The Single-Index Model

The combination of different securities into a portfolio
leads, as discussed in the previous chapter, to a reduction
of risk.   The observation that even a large, well-diversified
portfolio bears   some   remaining   risk,   led   to   the
differentiation of overall security risk into systematic and
unsystematic risk (1).

Unsystematic or diversifiable risk is that part of the risk
attached to an asset which is solely relevant to this special
security (2).   It is caused by security-specific factors,
e.g. management errors, strikes or innovations within the
firm.   Unsystematic risk can be reduced by combining
different assets in a portfolio, therefore it is also called
diversifiable risk.   The larger the number of assets in a
diversified portfolio, the smaller the unsystematic risk of
the portfolio (see Figure 3-1).

Systematic or undiversifiable risk cannot be washed away by
portfolio-building: it is that portion of asset risk that
coincides with general movements in the economic or political

Figure 3-1: Systematic and Unsystematic Risk of a Portfolio

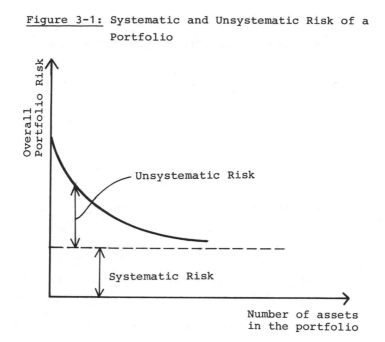

Figure 3-2: Characteristic Line of a Security

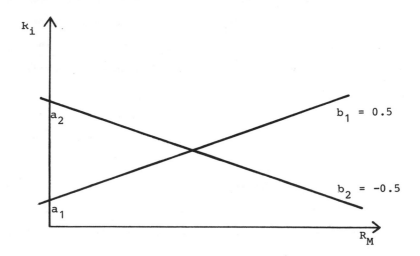

environment, e.g. general strikes, business cycles or tax increase. Systematic risk affects all assets at the same time so that even a large well-diversified portfolio provides no protection against this type of risk. Therefore, systematic risk is also referred to as market-related risk.

Analogous to risk, return can be divided into a systematic market-related and an unsystematic asset-related return. Supposing a linear relationship, the return on any asset i, R_i, can be expressed as follows:

$$(III.1) \quad R_i = b_i R_M + u_i$$

where R_M denotes the market return.

Systematic security return is related to the market return by parameter b_i, the beta-value, which indicates the sensitivity with which the return on asset i is correlated with the market. A b-value of 1.5, for example, states that a market return of 10% would lead to a systematic return of 15% for this assset. Unsystematic return, indicated by u, is independent of the market return and expresses the security-specific return.

The unsystematic return u_i, is usually expressed as

$$u_i = a_i + e_i,$$

where a_i (alpha) refers to the expected value of u_i and e_i to the random element of u_i. The random variable is assumed to have the following properties: an expected value of zero, $E(e_i) = 0$ (for $i = 1,2,...,N$), no correlation with the market return, cov $(R_M, e_i) = 0$, or other stocks, cov $(e_i, e_j) = 0$ for $i \neq j$ (3). Thus equation (III.1) becomes

$$(III.2) \quad R_i = a_i + b_i R_M + e_i$$

This equation, has been introduced by SHARPE in the literature. It is referred to as the single-index or market model (4). SHARPE suggested that returns on various securities were not related among each other but showed a "common relationship with some basic underlying factor" (5). This common factor is usually represented by the return of the stock market, R_M.

The single-index model is not an economic theory explaining assets returns. It just models the empirical observed fact that return on any asset i can be decomposed into a market and a non-market component.

Equation (III.2) of the single-index model can be shown graphically by a regression line, where parameter a indicates the intercept and parameter b the slope (Figure 3-2). This line is the characteristic line of a security. Figure 3-2 exhibits two characteristic lines. The b-value of security 1 is positive, indicating a positive correlation with the market return, while asset 2 shows a negative correlation with the market return, as the b-value of -0.5 specifies

From equation (III.2) systematic and unsystematic asset-related risk, as described in the introduction of this section, can be specified as (6) (7)

$$(III.3) \quad Var(R_i) = Var(a_i + b_i R_M + e_i)$$

$$= b_i^2 \sigma_M^2 + \sigma_{e_i}^2$$

(III.3) describes the risk of an asset as a combination of market-related and non-market risk. The non-market or unsystematic risk is given by the variance of the error term, $\sigma_{e_i}^2$. Systematic risk is directly linked to the market risk, $b_i^2 \sigma_M^2$. Again parameter b indicates the extent with which asset risk follows the market risk.

The risk of a portfolio can be expressed, analogous to single securities, as follows:

$$(III.4) \quad Var(R_p) = b_p^2 \sigma_M^2 + \sigma_{e_p}^2$$

A portfolio's systematic risk, b_p, is equal to the weighted sum of the systematic risk of securities forming the portfolio, $b_p = \sum_{i=1}^{n} x_i b_i$. In the same way, unsystematic portfolio risk is determined by the unsystematic risk of the assets in the portfolio, $\sigma_{e_p}^2 = \sum_{i=1}^{n} x_i^2 e_i^2$ (8).

Figure 3-1 showed unsystematic risk declining as the number of assets in the portfolio increased. If we assume equal amounts invested in each asset, unsystematic risk can be written as

$$\sigma_{e_P}^2 = \sum_{i=1}^{n} \frac{1}{n}^2 \sigma_{e_i}^2 = \frac{1}{n}\left[\sum_{i=1}^{n} \frac{\sigma_{e_i}^2}{n}\right]$$

The term in brackets is the average residual risk of a portfolio. Thus we can write $\sigma_{e_P}^2 = 1/n\, \bar{\sigma}_{e_i}^2$. As n increases, unsystematic portfolio risk declines; with n very large, $\sigma_{e_P}^2$ approaches zero. The sole risk to remain is systematic risk

$$\text{Var}(R_P) = b_P^2 \sigma_M^2 = \left[\sum_{i=1}^{n} x_i^2 b_i^2\right]\sigma_M^2$$

Using ex-post data the parameters a_i and b_i for any asset can be computed by regressing the asset return for a given period of time on the market return:

$$(\text{III.5}) \quad E(R_i) = a_i + b_i R_{M,t} + e_{i,t}$$

The parameters for various stocks were calculated in many studies. The results supported the usefulness of the single-index model in explaining stock returns by a market-related and a security-specific variable (9).

Expected return of assets can be calculated according to

$$E(R_i) = a_i + b_i E(R_M)$$

if the parameters a and b were estimated for past periods and $E(R_M)$ was predetermined for the relevant period.

We have seen that the single-index model distinguishes between systematic or market-related and unsystematic or asset-specific risk and return. Portfolio selection reduces or even abolishes only unsystematic asset risk, σe_i^2, while it leaves systematic risk, $b_i^2 \sigma_M^2$, unaffected. Systematic or market risk σ_M^2 is the same for all securities. Thus the b-value, derived from (III.5) as $b_i = cov(R_i, R_M)/\sigma_M^2$, is the measure of an asset's market related or systematic risk. Beta indicates that portion of risk that a single security contributes to a well-diversified portfolio and cannot be diversified away.

1.2. The Equilibrium of a Single Market Participant with Riskless Lending and Borrowing

In classical portfolio theory investors determined their optimal individual portfolios as a combination of risky assets exclusively according to their individual preferences (10). TOBIN (11) extended this approach by introducing a riskless security with a fixed rate of return. At this rate lending (investment) and borrowing is possible.

1.2.1. Investment Opportunities without Borrowing

Introducing a riskless asset T with a fixed rate of return, r_f, and thus, a variance of zero, enlarges traders' investment opportunities: apart from selecting portfolios containing only risky assets, they can invest their funds into the riskless asset T, shown by point T in Figure 3-3 (12). Investing proportion x into the portfolio of risky assets, P, and (1-x) into the riskless asset T, yields the following expected return and risk for this newly constructed portfolio C:

$$(III.6) \quad E(R_C) = (1-x)r_f + x\,E(R_P)$$

$$(III.7) \quad Var(R_C) = \sigma_C^2 = (1-x)^2\sigma_{r_f}^2 + x^2\sigma_P^2$$
$$+ 2x(1-x)\,cov(r_f, R_P)$$

T is the riskless asset with a fixed return. Therefore $\sigma_{r_f}^2$ and $cov(r_f, R_p)$ are both zero, and we can write

$$(III.7a) \qquad \sigma_C^2 = x^2 \sigma_P^2$$

Additional investment opportunities brought about by the riskless security T can be best demonstrated by Figure 3-3. All efficient portfolios P_n, obtained by combining risky securities, form the efficient frontier (line AB). Linear combinations of the riskless asset T with any portfolio P_n lead to new attainable portfolios, represented by any point on a line from point T to the efficient frontier, e.g. point N on line TP_1.

Figure 3-3 indicates that portfolio N is dominated by other portfolios which exhibit less variance for a given expected return or a higher expected return for a given variance, e.g. portfolio N_1. Any combination of a portfolio P_3 with the riskless asset would be dominated by other combinations of T with portfolios on the efficient frontier located between P_2 and P_3.

An investor acting rationally as assumed in portfolio theory (13), will select only one special portfolio as a combination of risky securities if he invests in risky assets and the riskless asset T. This is portfolio P* determined by the

Figure 3-3: Efficient Frontier with Lending Opporunities
at the Riskless Rate

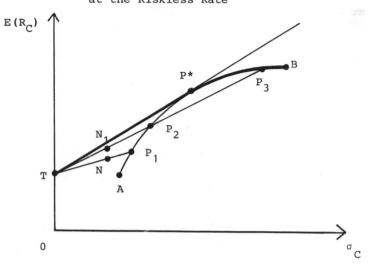

Figure 3-4: Efficient Frontier with Lending and Borrowing
at the Riskless Rate

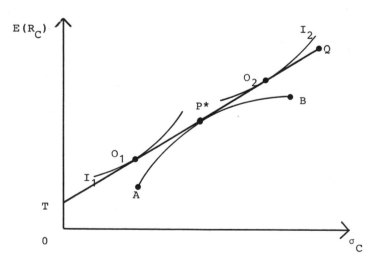

tangent from point T to the efficient frontier. All
combinations of the riskless asset and portfolio P* of risky
securities are represented by line TP*. Section P*B of the
efficient frontier indicates investment opportunities for
traders not investing into T but putting all their funds into
risky assets.

If a riskless investment opportunity is introduced, any
portfolio on the former efficient frontier between A and P*
becomes inefficient: It is dominated by a portfolio on line
TP*. In and beyond point P* all funds would be invested in
risky securities. Line TP*B is the new efficient frontier
(Figure 3-3). Whether an investor chooses point T
(riskless), B (highest possible return) or any other point on
the new efficient frontier depends on his preferences.
Investment in a security without risk can be viewed as
lending (14). Therefore, portfolios represented by line TP*
(point P* being a combination of risky securities is
excluded) are called 'lending portfolios'.

1.2.2. Investment Opportunities with Borrowing

Given the additional possibility of riskless borrowing at a fixed rate, the borrowed amount can be invested in portfolio P* in addition to own funds. Thus x, the proportion of funds invested in the risky portfolio P*, will exceed 1 while (1-x) will become negative, indicating that money is borrowed at the fixed rate. In this way new portfolios of higher expected return - and higher risk - can be achieved (15). The set of attainable portfolios is extended along line TP* to the right. The efficient fronier changes from TP*B to TP*Q (Figure 3-4)

If investors had unlimited borrowing opportunities, the set of new attainable portfolios to the right of line TP* would be infinite. Since borrowers' funding operations are limited by credit lines or collateral requirements, the set of new investment opportunities is also limited e.g. to point Q (16). Portfolios above point P* are called 'borrowing portfolios'.

1.2.3. Conclusions

The introduction of riskless borrowing and lending at a fixed rate into portfolio theory leads to additional investment opportunities and a new efficient frontier TP*Q. The number of investment options is enlarged.

Derivation of an investor's optimal individual portfolio, 0, can be divided into two stages: first he determines the optimal combination of risky securities under the assumption that he invests in risky securities at all. As shown above this selection leads to portfolio P* (17). In contrast to classical portfolio theory, which did not take the riskless asset into consideration, the optimal combination of risky assets P* can be determined without knowledge of the investor's preferences given the above assumption that investors base their decisions only on risk and return as decision variables. This phenomenon of selecting the optimal combination of risky assets irrespective of the investor's risk preferences is called separation theorem (18).

Second the investor, given the optimal combination of risky securities, selects his optimal portfolio along the line TP*Q. Whether he chooses a lending or borrowing portfolio depends on his risk-return preferences. The graphical solution is given by the point where one of his indifference curves touches the efficient frontier. Figure 3-4 shows two indifference curves of more or less risk-averse investors leading to lending (0_1) or borrowing portfolios (0_2).

Having outlined the procedure by which market participants determine their individual optimal portfolios given riskless lending and borrowing opportunities, market equilibrium will be analysed in the following section.

1.3. Market Equilibrium: The Capital Asset Pricing Model

1.3.1. Objectives and Assumptions

The capital asset pricing model (CAPM) is the result of a combination of portfolio theory, analysing the investment behaviour of risk-averse individuals maximizing expected utility, with capital market theory which - as a positive theory - investigates the implications of investors' behaviour on prices and quantities of securities (19). It is derived from analysis of the question of what the implications for capital markets are if all investors behave in the way portfolio theory assumes them to behave (20). Based on special assumptions the CAPM derives a relationship between the expected rate of return and risk of a security or portfolio in equilibrium.

These special assumptions are (21):
1. The assumptions underlying portfolio theory also hold for the CAPM, i.e. risk averse investors want to maximize their expected utility, which is a function of expected return and risk, $E(U) = U(E(R), \sigma^2)$. All investors have a one-period investment horizon (22). Furthermore, the following additional assumptions are made:
2. Unrestricted lending and borrowing is possible at the risk-free interest rate r_f.
3. Homogeneity of investors' expectations, i.e. all

investors have the same estimates of the means, variances
and covariances for all securities.

4. No taxes exist.

5. Perfect capital markets.

   a) No transaction costs

   b) All assets are perfectly divisible

   c) The quantities of all assets are given

   d) Investors are price takers.

6. Capital markets are in equilibrium.

1.3.2. The Capital Market Line

Above we saw that an investor who has - apart from investing
his own funds in risky assets - the opportunity of lending or
borrowing at the riskless rate r_f, determines, irrespective
of his specific preferences, portfolio P^* as the optimal
combination of risky securities. The line from point T
through P* in Figure 3-4 represents all attainable efficient
investment opportunities for an individual investor.

Since all investors agree on future prospects of all
securities in the market (assumption 3 of homogeneous
expectations) they all face the same efficient frontier AB
(23). Consequently, all investors determine portfolio P* as
the optimal combination of risky securities. This portfolio
is called the 'market portfolio' (M) as it is the only
combination of risky securities realized by investors if they

invest in risky assets at all. Figure 3-5 depicts investment
opportunities for all agents. Any combination of the market
portfolio (M) with the riskless asset (T) is indicated by a
point on the line from point T through M. This line, which
represents all efficient investment opportunities in the
market, is the capital market line. Points between T and M
indicate lending portfolios; points above M borrowing
portfolios.

The market portfolio is the only combination of risky
securities investors want to hold. Since capital markets are
in equilibrium (assumption 6), the market portfolio must
contain all risky assets. The proportion of an asset in the

Figure 3-5: The Capital Market Line

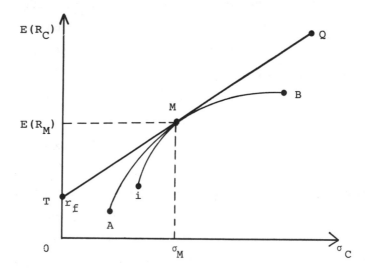

market portfolio is equal to the proportion of its total
value outstanding to the total value of all assets in the
market.
The return of the market portfolio is given by (II.4) as the
weighted average return of all securities in the market,
$E(R_M)$, its risk is $Var(R_M)$.

The equation of the capital market line is derived by
rewriting (III.6) and (III.7a) : expected return and risk of
any efficient portfolio as a combination of the riskless
asset and the market portfolio are

$$(III.8) \quad E(R_C) = (1-x)r_f + xE(R_M)$$

$$(III.9) \quad Var(R_C) = \sigma_C^2 = x^2\sigma_M^2 \quad or \quad \sigma_C = x\sigma_M$$

Substituting for x in (III.8) the expression σ_C/σ_M from
(III.9) and rearranging terms, leads to the equation of the
capital market line:

$$(III.10) \quad E(R_C) = r_f + \frac{\left[E(R_M) - r_f\right]}{\sigma_M}\sigma_C$$

It gives a linear relationship between the expected return

and the risk of any efficient portfolio. The expected return $E(R_C)$ consists of the pure interest rate r_f, which can be regarded as the 'price of time', plus an additional return given by the product of the 'price of risk' $(E(R_M) - r_f)/\sigma_M$ and the risk of the portfolio (24). The 'price of risk' or risk premium which is the slope of the capital market line, indicates the additional return that can be earned for taking on additional risk.

The capital market line gives for all efficient portfolios in equilibrium a linear relationship between expected return and risk. Inefficient portfolios and single assets that bear unsystematic risk cannot be plotted on that line. They lie below the capital market line, e.g. at point i in Figure 3-5 which can be any security.

1.3.3. The Security Market Line

The security market line establishes a relationship between expected return and risk for any security or inefficient portfolio in equilibrium similar to that established by the capital market line for efficient portfolios.

1.3.3.1. Introduction

A security such as asset i in Figure 3-5 is part of the market portfolio since capital markets are in equilibrium. The characteristics of an asset with which an investor is concerned are the contribution of this asset to the risk and expected return of a portfolio (25). Applying (II.5), the risk of the market portfolio is:

$$\text{Var}(R_M) = \sum_{i=1}^{n} x_i^2 \sigma_i^2 + \sum_{i=1}^{n} \sum_{\substack{j=1 \\ i \neq j}}^{n} x_i x_j \text{cov}(R_i, R_j)$$

Asset i contributes to the market portfolio's risk with its own weighted variance, $x_i^2 \sigma_i^2$, plus the (n-1) weighted covariances with all other securities in the portfolio. The market portfolio contains a large number of securities. Therefore, the risk contribution of an asset i is not primarily determined by its own variance but by the (n-1) covariance terms. Instead of $x_i \sum_{j=1}^{n} x_j \text{cov}(R_i, R_j)$ we can simply write $\text{cov}(R_i, R_M)$, as shown in section II.3.2. Thus, the covariance between the return on any security i and the market portfolio is the proper indicator of an asset's risk contribution to a large portfolio like M.

Securities showing low or negative covariances with the return of many other assets in the market portfolio are very suitable for risk-diversification. On the other hand, assets that have high covariances with the return of the market portfolio, i.e. they show high systematic risk, are not useful for risk reduction. Consequently, investors' demand for such assets showing high covariances with the market return will be low. Their prices will also be low and expected rates of return high. Demand and prices for securities that exhibit low or negative covariances with the market will be high and, in consequence, their expected rates of return low. This relationship between assets' expected return and their covariances with the market portfolio can be described by

$$(III.11) \qquad E(R_i) = r_f + \frac{\left[E(R_M) - r_f\right]}{\sigma_M^2} \, cov(R_i, R_M)$$

Figure 3-6 shows this relationship between expected return and the risk contribution of an asset to the market portfolio. The line indicating higher rates of return for increasing risk contributions is the security market line. It is also called the CAPM.

235

Figure 3-6: The Security Market Line

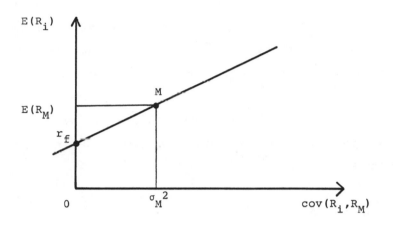

Figure 3-7: The Security Market Line with Two Different
Measures for a Security's Systematic Risk

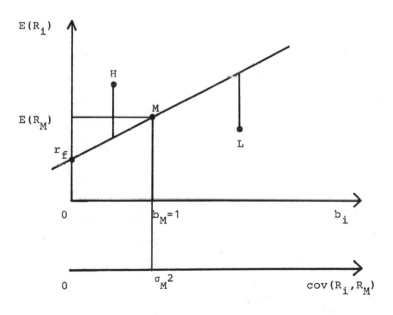

1.3.3.2. Formal Derivation

Figure 3-5 presented the capital market line and the risky
security i. A portfolio Z consisting of the risky security i
and the market portfolio can be represented, according to the
proportions invested in each asset, by a point on line iM
(26). The slope of iM at any point is determined by the
correlation between the two securities returns (ρi,M).
At point M the slope of iM, is (27)

$$\left. \frac{\partial E(R_Z)}{\partial \sigma_Z} \right|_{\substack{a=0 \\ \sigma_Z = \sigma_M}} = \frac{\left[E(R_i) - E(R_M) \right] \sigma_M}{\text{cov}(R_i, R_M) - \sigma_M^2}$$

Line iM is tangent to the capital market line at point M
since this line represents all efficient portfolios in
equilibrium. If line iM intersected the capital market line
at M because it is steeper or flatter than the capital market
line there would be some portfolios above the capital market
line. That would imply that these portfolios dominated some
portfolios on the capital market line. Since the capital
market line represents - by construction - all efficient
combinations this situation cannot occur. Therefore, at M
the slope of line iM and the capital market line are equal.

$$\left. \frac{\partial E(R_Z)}{\partial \sigma_Z} \right|_{\substack{a=0 \\ \sigma_Z = \sigma_M}} = \frac{\partial E(R_C)}{\partial \sigma_C}$$

$$\frac{\left[E(R_i) - E(R_M)\right] \sigma_M}{\text{cov}(R_i, R_M) - \sigma_M^2} = \frac{E(R_M) - r_f}{\sigma_M}$$

Simplifying and rearranging leads to the formula of the security market line

$$(\text{III}.11) \quad E(R_i) = r_f + \frac{\left[E(R_M) - r_f\right]}{\sigma_M^2} \cdot \text{cov}(R_i, R_M)$$

1.3.3.3. Interpretation

Thus, the security market line states that in equilibrium the expected return on any asset i, $E(R_i)$, is equal to the risk-free rate of return, r_f, plus an amount given by the product of the market's risk premium, $E(R_M) - r_f / \sigma_M^2$, and the risk of asset i, $\text{cov}(R_i, R_M)$. An asset's return is a linearly increasing function of its risk.

The adequate measure for the risk of a security is not its variance but the covariance of its return with the market, $\text{cov}(R_i, R_M)$, also called systematic risk. Since unsystematic security risk can be washed away by diversification, the market does not pay a price for it. Systematic risk, expressed by the covariance of a security with all assets in the market portfolio, cannot be diversified away by portfolio building (28). For this non-diversifiable risk of an asset the market pays a risk premium. Hence, the more systematic risk a security bears the higher is its expected return. A security with no correlation with the market portfolio, $\text{cov}(R_i, R_M) = 0$, that is, a security without systematic risk, yields the pure interest rate.

In equilibrium all securities lie on the security market line (29). Let us take for example an asset that is placed at point H in Figure 3-7. In relation to its risk it pays an unusually high return. Consequently, investors will bid up its price till the return is in an adequate relation to the risk the asset bears, i.e. till H lies on the security market line. On the other hand an asset L with a return too low for its sytematic risk will be sold till it can be plotted on the security market line.

As shown above, section II.3.3., the covariance of an asset with the market portfolio is proportional to the marginal contribution of an asset i to the risk of the market portfolio, $\partial \sigma_M / \partial x_i = \text{cov}(R_i, R_M) \sigma_M$. Therefore, the security market line can also be written as

$$(III.12) \qquad E(R_i) = r_f + \frac{E(R_M) - r_f}{\sigma_M} \cdot \frac{\text{cov}(R_i, R_M)}{\sigma_M}$$

where $E(R_M) - r_f / \sigma_M$ is the market price of risk and the covariance term standardized by the standard deviation of the market portfolio is the measure of an asset's risk (30).

At the beginning of this chapter we considered the beta-value as the measure of systematic asset risk. Here we used the covariance term of an asset with the market return as the indicator of an asset's risk for which the market pays a risk premium. Both measures can be used to define the security market line (31). Applying $b_i = \text{cov}(R_i, R_M)/\sigma_M^2$ as the factor indicating an asset's systematic or market risk, the security market line is

$$(III.13) \qquad E(R_i) = r_f + (E(R_M) - r_f) \, b_i$$

The security market line is most often expressed in this way. Equation (III.13) is the version in which the CAPM is tested. The two version of the security market line, (III.11) and (III.13), are graphed in Figure 3-7, showing different notations for the horizontal axis. $\text{cov}(R_i, R_M)$ and b_i. The covariance of the market portfolio with itself is $\text{cov}(R_M, R_M) = \sigma_M^2$. Thus, it is intuitive that the market portfolio has a b-value of one, $b = \text{cov}(R_M, R_M)/\sigma_M^2 = 1$.

The CAPM leads to the result that investors want to hold only one portfolio of risky securities, the market portfolio. Combinations of this market portfolio with the riskless asset create all efficient portfolios in the market, represented by the capital market line.

The CAPM determines an asset's return in equilibrium as a positive linear relationship with its systematic risk, measured as the risk contribution of an asset to the market portfolio. All assets and portfolios can be described by the security market line (32).

1.3.4. Extensions and Tests

The CAPM in its original version has been criticized for its unrealistic assumptions. As a consequence of this criticism the model has been modified by relaxing one or the other assumptions: introduction of taxes and transaction cost, different borrowing and lending rates, constraints on the amount borrowed, substitution of the riskless asset by a minimum variance, zero-beta portfolio, disallowance of short sales, inclusion of non-marketable assets, introduction of heterogeneous expectations, and multiperiod analysis (33). Although the analysis led in some cases to somewhat obscure results most of the extensions proved the robustness of the model. The basic suggestions of the original version remained valid with altered assumptions (34) (35).

Another reply to criticism of the CAPM is that the value of a model does not depend only on the reasonabless of its assumptions since reality is so complex that abstractions are necessary. If a model contributes to a better understanding of how the markets work and if the implications of the model can be verified by tests, then the oversimplified assumptions do not lessen its value (36).

Many tests of the CAPM were carried out (37). The model given by (III.13) $E(R_i) = r_f + (E(R_M) - r_f) b_i$ is formulated in terms of expectations. Since expectations are not measurable tests can only be carried out using observable ex-post data. Further, the lack of a reliable proxy for the market portfolio makes the analysis more doubtful. Normally the Standard and Poor's Index of 500 common stocks or the equally weighted index of the New York Stock Exchange are used as a proxy (38).

Most tests follow a two-step cross-sectional procedure (39). In a first-pass regression the market model of (III.5) is applied to estimate the beta-values of single assets from regressing a time series of security returns for some period on the return of the market index.

$$(\text{III.5}) \quad R_{i,t} = a_i + b_i R_{M,t} + e_{i,t}$$

Then, in a second-pass cross-sectional regression, the average returns of different assets, $\overline{R}_i$, are regressed on their beta-values determined in the first-pass regression:

$$(\text{III.14}) \quad \overline{R}_i = \lambda_o + \lambda_1 \hat{b}_1 + \varepsilon_1$$

Comparing the parameters derived from (III.14) with the equation of the security market line (III.13) expressed in realized average return form,

$$(III.15) \quad \bar{R}_i = \bar{r}_f + (\bar{R}_M - \bar{r}_f) \, b_i + \eta_i$$

we would expect λ_0 equal to $\bar{r}_f$, λ_1 equal to $(\bar{R}_M - \bar{r}_f)$ and $\eta_i = \varepsilon_i = 0$ or small if the CAPM holds true (40). The average rate of a riskless asset, $\bar{r}_f$, is normally approximated by the return of a 90 day T-bill.

There is sufficient evidence from testing that beta is a useful measure of asset risk (41) and that the positive linear relationship between return and risk is an adequate description of reality (42). Security market lines derived from empirical investigations were flatter than theoretical lines, i.e. estimated λ_0 exceeded observed values for the riskless rate of return, $\bar{r}_f$, while λ_1-values were less than observed risk premiums, $(\bar{R}_M - \bar{r}_f)$ (43) (44). Therefore, we can conclude that the tests gave neither a full confirmation nor a complete discrediting of the CAPM.

1.3.5. Critical Evaluation of the CAPM

1.3.5.1. Assumptions

Among the assumptions on which the CAPM is based, that of
homogeneous expectations will be taken into closer
consideration. This assumption implies that all investors
share an identical view of the future prospect of all
securities, i.e. all investors agree on expected rates of
return, variances and correlations between security returns.
This assumption is necessary because otherwise no meaningful
analysis of "expected return and risk from the viewpoint of
the market" would be possible (45).
Homogeneous expectations can only emerge in the market in a
systematic way if every individual investor has the same
information on all factors that are of relevance in deriving
an investment decision (46). In addition it is necessary to
assume that every single investor draws the same conclusions
from this public set of information, i.e. all investors will
process the information in the same way, or to use modern
terminology, they show rational expectations.

Modifications of the homogeneous-expectations-assumption
followed two lines:
a) Some studies relaxed this assumption by allowing for
heterogeneous expectations. In this way it was possible to
derive an equilibrium pricing equation similar to the CAPM.
But the expressions for expected returns, variances and

covariances turned out to be very complex weighted averages of individual investors' expectations (47). Via this complex weighted averages, individual risk-return preferences enter the equation. Therefore a theory like this is not testable (48).

To derive a general equilibrium solution with heterogeneous expectations it is necessary to introduce by assumption a special type of utility function or to limit the degree of heterogeneity allowed for (49).

b) The strong assumption of homogeneous expectations or complete consensus has sometimes been relaxed to a "considerable consensus" that is necessary for the model to be workable (50) but which is too vague for formal derivation (51). The considerable consensus is based on a group of traders and money managers who have sufficient market weight to determine prices (52). These traders are assumed to be well-informed from a similar set of information and to use similar analytical tools to process the information. The ill-informed or incompetent have no influence on prices since their over-optimistic or over-pessimistic evaluations cancel each other out. Even if they bring the price to a value that is regarded as "wrong" by the well-informed, this latter group will bring the price immediately back to the value they deem "adequate".

Against this view has to be contrasted the way in which in futures markets information emerges and is being used to form expectations on which trading decisions are based.

In classical theory, futures trading was based on the assumption that risk-averse traders (hedgers) shift the risk of price changes to speculators who receive a premium for taking over the risk. This description of futures trading, as a mechanism of risk-shifting among traders with different attitudes towards risk, became known as KEYNES' theory of normal backwardation (53). HOFFMAN and WORKING opposed that view by stating that hedging is done to take advantage of favourable price changes, i.e. profit is the aim of hedging (54).

If profit is the motive for futures trading, then a trader - either hedger or speculator - will only establish a position if he believes that the actual price at which he purchases or sells a position is a wrong forecast of the futures price to prevail till maturity of the contract and that he will be able to close out his position at a later date with a profit (55). The other party to the contract also regards the price as wrong since otherwise he would not trade. This means that both contractors establish positions at a price which they subjectively consider as "false" (56). It follows from this that divergent beliefs are essential for futures trading, or, as HIRSHLEIFER puts it, "only those individuals deviating from representative beliefs in the market will hedge or speculate" (57).

Divergent beliefs cannot be based on a public set of information accessible to every investor and processed in the same way. Either traders base their decisions on different information or they draw different conclusions from the same set of information.

The above analysis leads to the conclusion that the assumption of a considerable consensus, and all the more of homogeneous expectations on which the CAPM rests, is not an adequate description of the way information arises and is processed by individual traders, nor of how trading takes place in futures. Hence this assumtion is an over-simplification, which throws doubts on whether the CAPM is an adequate theory to analyse interest futures. Furthermore it may be wondered whether the CAPM can be tested via markets that do not fit the assumptions on which the model is based. Before giving a definite answer to these questions, we shall shed more light on methods by which the CAPM is tested. In the literature the CAPM is defended against criticism by the argument that naturally oversimplified assumptions do not lessen the model's value if its implications can be verified by tests (58).

1.3.5.2. Testing

Any empirical investigation of the CAPM faces the following difficulties:
1. The CAPM describes the expected return of an asset or portfolio as being determined by its expected risk. Testing

this theory is confronted by the difficulty that investors' expectations are unobservable. Therefore any empirical verification is limited to ex-post data. A procedure like this would be adequate if the ex-post distributions of security returns were those on which traders base their decisions, i.e. return distributions remained stationary over a period of time. If return distributions change, this procedure does not lead to adequate tests of the model.

This test is defended by two arguments:

a) that expectations are on average and on the whole correct. Consequently, realised returns are good proxies for expectations over long periods (59).

b) BLACK, JENSEN, SCHOLES demonstrated a method by which it is possible to test the ex-ante model using realized returns (60). They assume that realized returns are described by the single-index model as

$$(III.16) \quad R_{i,t} = E(R_i) + b_i \ (R_{M,t} - E(R_M) + e_{i,t}$$

The CAPM is given by (III.13): $E(R_i) = r_f + b_i(E(R_M) - r_f)$. Substituting from this equation the expression of $E(R_i)$ into (III.16) yields

$$(III.17) \quad R_{i,t} = r_f + b_i \ (R_{M,t} - r_f) + e_{i,t}$$

$$= (1 - b_i)r_f + b_i R_{M,t} + e_{i,t}$$

Running a regression of the form $R_{i,t} = a_i + b_i R_{M,t} + e_{i,t}$ on the basis of observed data would support the CAPM if the calculated parameter $\hat{a}_i$ would equal $(1-b_i)r_f$.

A test following this procedure is not only a test of the CAPM but also of the single-index model: the test is based on the assumptions that the single-index model and the CAPM hold true in all periods. Furthermore b is assumed to be stable. If one of these assumptions is violated the test is useless.

2. Cross-sectional tests of the form (III.14) $\overline{R}_i = \lambda_o + \lambda_1 b_i + \varepsilon_i$ require true values for the explanatory variable b. In practice true values for the measure of systematic risk are unobservable. Therefore betas are derived from the first-pass time series regression. As a consequence, estimated b-values, $\hat{b}_i$, may contain measurement errors. Hence the use of estimated b-values might cause severe difficulties with cross-sectional tests and lead to biased estimates of λ_o and λ_1; as long as $\hat{b}_i$ contains measurement errors λ_o will be upward biased whereas λ_1 will be biased downwards (61).

Therefore interpretation of the estimators λ_o and λ_1, as well as comparisons of these estimators with the riskless rate of return and with the risk premium lead to results that should be interpreted with caution.

This difficulty of measurement error can be solved by a grouping of data procedure (62). BLACK, JENSEN, SCHOLES for example formed ten portfolios each containing 58 to 109 assets selected according to their b-values of the previous period. Then the risk measures $\hat{b}$ were calculated for these portfolios using the first-pass regression. In this way inconsistencies in the estimators of the second-pass regression due to measurement errors in estimated b-values could be reduced substantially (63).

Hence we can conclude that reliable tests of the CAPM can only be carried out using a large number of assets. The CAPM which claims to describe the relationship between asset or portfolio return and their risk in equilibrium turns out to be testable only for large portfolios, but not for single assets.

3. Furthermore the b-value is only then a useful measure of asset risk if this value is stable over a period of time. Empirical tests of the CAPM are based on this assumption as discussed above. Studies investigating the stability of betas for one-year and seven-year periods came to the conclusion that betas for portfolios containing about 50 securities are very stable whereas betas for single assets fluctuated significantly (64). These investigations measured the stability of beta by correlating betas for different periods. Since calculated b-values contain measurement

errors, the result of low beta stability for single assets
might partly be due to this mesasurement errors.

Consequently these findings lead to doubts whether the
distributions of $R_{M,t}$ and $R_{i,t}$ are stationary through a
period of time thus giving the stable b-values which are
required for testing the CAPM (65). This insufficiency can
once again be resolved by forming portfolios of many assets.

To sum up, this critical evaluation of the CAPM backed up
already existing scepticism concerning the oversimplifying
assumptions of the model. Homogeneous expectations cannot
explain the informational situation in futures markets nor
the way trading takes place.

A frequently used argument against this criticism was that
the implications of a model - verified by tests - determine a
model's value, and not the adequateness of naturally
oversimplified assumptions.

But these tests intended to verify the CAPM can be criticised
as well: Besides ROLL's general statement that the theory is
not testable at all because of the impossibility of observing
the true value-weighted market portfolio, further doubts on
the adequateness and reliability of the testing procedure
were outlined above.

Hence tests giving support to the CAPM, but also
investigations that led to contradictory results (66) have to
be considered with the necessary care.

From this it seems to follow that the CAPM is not an adequate theory for analysing interest rate futures markets nor does it seem appropriate to test the model via futures trading. Besides general doubts as to the testability of this model (67), a test of the CAPM via interest rate futures markets is also excluded for technical reasons, i.e. as stated above a test based on single assets is inappropriate and leads to biased results. Since futures trading in interest-rate bearing securities started only 7 years ago neither a sufficient number of assets nor a sufficiently large observation period is given.

Hence we do not intend to test the CAPM in this study. However the question which remains to be discussed is whether we can gain some insight into the effects of interest rate futures markets by applying the beta-value, which emerged from the above analysis as the measure of systematic risk, to fixed-income securities.

2. ANALYSIS OF INTEREST RATE FUTURES MARKETS IN THE
   FRAMEWORK OF THE CAPITAL ASSET PRICING MODEL

The point to be investigated in this section is whether
fixed-income securities like government debt or GNMAs bear
risk; if so, what kind of risk; and to what extent it is
possible to apply the framework analyzed above to these
securities. Furthermore we have to discuss whether the
concept of systematic and unsystematic risk can also be
applied to futures and hedged positions.

2.1. Risk of Interest-Bearing Securities

2.1.1. Spot Positions

The risk of fixed-income securities such as T-bills, T-bonds,
corporate bonds, GNMAs or certificates of deposit (CDs) can
be divided into business or default risk and market risk
(68).

Default risk of these securities is similar to unsystematic
risk of stocks. This risk is related to the standing of the
issuer of the debt instrument, e.g. a bank, corporation or
the state, which guarantees the periodical interest payment
and repayment of principal at maturity. Analogous to stocks
this default or unsystematic risk of fixed-income securities
can be reduced by forming portfolios. Combining bonds that

bear the possibility of default but from totally unrelated reasons into a portfolio, reduces most of the unsystematic risk of single bonds (69).

The default risk of single T-bill or T-bond positions is regarded as non-existent since these assets are backed by the US government, which is regarded .as being able to serve all debt payments through taxation (70). Therefore government debt is free of unsystematic risk. The same refers to GNMA positions since these assets are guaranteed by government authorities.

Market risk is the risk associated with liquidating a position before its maturity. Changes in interest rates influence the value of fixed-income securities. If rates go up, prices will decline and owners of interest-bearing securities will suffer a loss from liquidating their positions in the cash market. Consequently market risk which is relevant for all types of fixed-income securities, including government debt, can also be referred to as interest rate or systematic risk (71).

Within the CAPM the T-bill rate is usually referred to as a measure of the riskless rate of return. (72). The T-bill is assumed as default risk free. But the T-bill is only free of interest rate risk if the date of maturity and the investment horizon of the investor are identical. If the end of these two periods differs, a T-bill is affected by interest rate changes in the same way as every other fixed-income security.

The sensitivity of interest-bearing securities to changes in interest rates increases with increasing periods to maturity (73).

Bearing this in mind it is obvious that a default free T-bond or GNMA position with 15 or more years to maturity is affected by interest rate changes. Therefore these positions can be considered as risky assets like stocks. T-bonds or GNMAs bear risk caused by interest rate fluctuations, i.e. they have systematic risk (74).

If this holds true, the single-index model should not only be applicable to stocks but also to fixed-income securities. Applying the model, we expect to derive significant and positive b-values for T-bond or GNMA positions held in the cash market. Findings of empirical investigations analyzing government or corporate bond portfolios support this view (75).

2.1.2. Futures Positions

As discussed in the first chapter, a position in the futures market is a contract to buy or sell a standardized quantity of fixed-income securities to be delivered at a specified date in the future. Daily trading takes place at an exchange where the price is found by open outcry. A clearing house guarantees the fulfilment of each contract. Consequently default or unsystematic risk of futures positions is negligible.

Futures prices are linked to cash prices by arbitrage transactions (section I.2.3.). In this way variations in cash market rates or changing expectations concerning future cash rates are transmitted to futures markets (and vice versa). Factors affecting cash rates also have an impact on futures rates. Therefore futures prices will follow cash prices.

It follows from this that futures positions should bear interest rate or systematic risk provided that the relevant spot asset on which the futures contract is based is a risky asset. Once again the single-index model should be applicable to determine the systematic risk of positions established in interest rate futures markets. If arbitrage between cash and futures markets works perfectly, cash and futures positions should even show the same amount of systematic risk, i.e. their beta-values should be equal. Beta-values for futures positions quite different from spot-betas would indicate low parallelism between cash and futures price movements, i.e. the arbitrage mechanism would be disturbed.

The author is not aware of any study investigating the systematic risk of interest rate futures contracts within the framework of the single-index model. Most studies of

commodity futures except one reached the conclusion that
nearly all contracts investigated showed no systematic risk;
most beta-values derived did not differ significantly from
zero (76).

2.1.3. Hedged Positions

One of the most important functions of interest rate futures
markets is that they provide the opportunity to reduce or
abolish the risk associated with interest rate changes.
Theoretically, hedging should lessen or even abolish the
systematic risk of cash positions:
Analyzing the measures of systematic risk for a spot and a
hedged position, we have to compare

$$bs = \frac{cov(R_S, R_M)}{\sigma_M^2} = \frac{\sigma_S \rho_{S,M}}{\sigma_M}$$

$$bh = \frac{cov(R_H, R_M)}{\sigma_M^2} = \frac{\sigma_H \rho_{H,M}}{\sigma_M}$$

The empirical investigation (II.5) proved that $\sigma_S > \sigma_H$ and
$\rho_{S,M} > \rho_{H,M}$. Thus, theoretically bh is smaller than bs, i.e.
hedging reduces systematic risk.

Applying the single-index model to hedged positions we expect
b-values significantly smaller than beta-values for spot
positions. Furthermore, with cash and futures prices moving

in close harmony, implying bs = bf, hedged positions would not bear interest rate or systematic risk, i.e. the b-values of hedged positions would be zero or at least not significantly different from zero. Therefore bh is not only a measure for the systematic risk of hedged positions but can also be interpreted as an indicator for the hedging effectiveness of interest rate futures markets.

We conclude this section with the result that the concept of systematic and unsystematic risk is not only applicable to stocks but also to interest-bearing securities. Government debt is considered as default-risk free, therefore it should not show unsystematic risk. But since these assets are affected by interest rate changes they should bear systematic risk. This conclusion refers to spot and futures positions. Hedged positions on the other hand should bear low or no systematic risk if hedging does really reduce interest rate risk. These statements will be evaluated in the following section by calculating beta-values for spot, futures and hedged positions.

3. EMPIRICAL INVESTIGATION

3.1. Technical Aspects

3.1.1. Estimation Procedure

Beta-values for single fixed-income securities and for indices representing the government bond market were calculated applying the classical single-index model regression

$$(III.5) \quad R_{i,t} = a_i + b_i R_{M,t} + e_{i,t}$$

where

$R_{i,t}$ refers to the monthly rate of return of the assets under investigation either as spot, futures, or hedged positions. Rates of return were calculated as outlined in section II.4.3.

$R_{M,t}$ is the monthly rate of return of a market index, which will be described on the following pages.

Once again the investigation period covers the years 1978-1982 for the government bond market and 1977-1982 for GNMAs.

The equation was estimated using the ordinary least squares (OLS) technique (77). Occasionally the Cochrane-Orcutt procedure was applied to correct for autoregressive tendencies (78).

3.1.2. Index Representing "The Market"

According to general practice (79) and despite ROLL's critique the market is approximated to by the Standard and Poor's (S&P) Composite Index (80). Since the composition of the index representing the market might influence the results of the study, we allowed at a later stage for fixed-income securities within the stock index. These results are compared to beta-values resting on a pure stock index in section III.3.3.

The S&P Composite Index is a value-weighted index including stocks of 500 different companies: 400 industrials, 40 utilities, 20 transportation companies and 40 financial institutions (81). Market-value-weighted means that the weight of each stock in the index equals the number of stocks outstanding multiplied by their prices. Hence any price change of a stock will influence the index in proportion to the relative index value of this stock. The 500 stocks included in the S&P Composite Index represent about 80 percent of the value of all stocks listed at the New York Stock Exchange. Therefore the S&P Composite Index is generally accepted as a good proxy for the US stock markets.

The data were taken from the Financial Times for the last day of the month. Monthly rates of the market return (R_M) are calculated according to the formula

$$R_{M,t} = \frac{I_t - I_{t-1}}{I_{t-1}}$$

where I_t is the value of the index at the end of month t.

Calculating monthly rates of return for the stock index we abstract from dividend payments because we are not actually interested in the return an investor earns for holding a proportion of the market index. Above all we are concerned with the beta-coefficients. And beta-values are not influenced whether the T-bond returns are regressed on the market index inclusive or exclusive of dividends. Inclusion or exclusion of dividends affects the estimation of the intercept term of the regression, but has only a marginal influence on the beta-value. This claim, first suggested by SHARPE, W.F. and COOPER, G.M. (82) for stocks, has been confirmed for fixed-income securities by running regressions on a market index with and without dividends (See Table 3-1) (83).

Table 3-1 : Comparison of Regression Results   for   Different
             Calculations of the Market Return

Market Return	a	b	R^2	F	DW
T-bond Futures Contract					
RM	-0.726 (-1.337)	0.364 (3.111)	0.143	9.681	1.668
RMDIV	-0.886 (-1.601)	0.367 (3.134)	0.145	9.820	1.672
8% T-bond Spot					
RM	0.326 (0.567)	0.383 (3.095)	0.142	9.580	1.617[1]
RMDIV	0.158 (0.270)	0.387 (3.117)	0.144	9.714	1.619[1]
8% T-bond Hedged					
RM	1.032 (8.393)	0.032 (1.208)	0.025	1.460	1.687
RMDIV	1.018 (8.124)	0.032 (1.213)	0.025	1.471	1.687
8% GNMA Spot					
RM	0.407 (0.835)	0.327 (3.011)	0.115	9.069	1.906
RMDIV	0.267 (0.553)	0.330 (3.034)	0.116	9.208	1.908

RM   : Return of market portfolio
RMDIV : Return of market portfolio with dividends included.

T-statistics in paranthesis, 60 observations

1) Values within the inconclusive region (1.55 - 1.62). Analysis
   for autoregressive processes did not lead to significant
   results.

3.2. Empirical Results

Above we derived theoretically that T-bond or GNMA cash and futures positions should bear systematic risk, i.e. beta-values are proposed to be positive and significantly different from zero.

Ho: bs > 0

Ho: bf > 0

Furthermore we expected the two beta-values to be more or less equal, since arbitrage transactions should keep cash and futures prices in line.

Ho: bs = bf

If hedging reduces systematic (interest rate) risk the beta-values of hedged positions should be significantly smaller than the beta-values for the related spot and futures positions

Ho: bh < bs

Ho: bh < bf

and close to, or even equal to, zero.

Ho: bh = 0

3.2.1. Systematic Risk of Spot Positions

Regressing monthly rates of return of different cash positions on the market return led to positive beta-values significantly different from zero. (Compare Table 3-2).

Values computed for the T-bond market in the overall period 1978 to 1982 are in the range between 0.383 and 0.335. Single bonds exhibit the highest betas (0.383 and 0.379), indices representing portfolios of bonds the smaller ones. For the Fedindex systematic risk factors decrease as coupon rates increase (8%: 0.358, 10%: 0.344, 12%: 0.335) This observation is in accordance with bond pricing theory, stating that due to yield changes, other things being equal, return variability decreases as coupon rates increase (84). The newly constructed Own Bondindex exhibits with a b-value of 0.342 systematic risk in the range between the 10% and 12% Fedindex.

For the GNMA market a significant beta-value of 0.337 was computed. This indicates that the GNMA market bore less systematic risk in the period under investigation than the T-bond market. Calculations of beta-values for the six year period (1977 to 1982) including the 'relatively stable' year 1977 led to a smaller beta-value of 0.327.

Alpha-values for all assets investigated are not significantly different from zero, supporting the hypothesis that fixed-income securities backed by the US government do not bear unsystematic risk (85).

Table 3-2: Regression Results for Spot Positions
1978 - 1982

Asset	a	b	R^2	F	DW
8% T-bond	0.326 (0.567)*	0.383 (3.095)	0.142	9.580	1.617[1]
$8\frac{1}{4}$% T-bond	0.301 (0.535)*	0.379 (3.124)	0.144	9.760	1.598[1]
8% Fedindex	0.320 (0.548)*	0.358 (2.844)	0.122	8.089	1.509[2]
10% Fedindex	0.367 (0.653)*	0.344 (2.840)	0.122	8.067	1.509[2]
12% Fedindex	0.400 (0.732)*	0.335 (2.840)	0.122	8.065	1.511[2]
Own Bondindex	0.291 (0.568)*	0.342 (3.100)	0.142	9.611	1.589[1]
GNMA	0.375 (0.652)*	0.337 (2.716)	0.113	7.378	1.897
1977-1982	0.407 (0.853)*	0.327 (3.011)	0.115	9.069	1.906

60 Observations, T-ratios in parenthesis,
* Values not significant on the 95% level.

1) Values within the inconclusive region (1.55 - 1.62).
   Analysis for autoregressive processes did not lead to
   significant results.
2) Values indicate autoregression for the disturbance term.
   It was not possible to trace significant autoregressive
   processes.

265

Subperiods: The analysis of variance-values for spot
positions indicated an increase in return variability from
the first to the second subperiod (Compare II.5.1.1.2.).
Therefore we expect a similar development of b-values as
indicators of systematic or interest rate risk.
Table 3-3 lists b-values for the two periods 1978- 6/80 and
7/80-1982. In accordance with the overall period single
bonds exhibit higher betas than indices. And, as expected,
beta-values for the first subperiod are smaller than betas
for the overall period, whereas the second subperiod shows
the highest b-values, e.g. for the 8% bond the following
b-values were computed: 0.290 and 0.457 for the subperiods,
0.383 for the overall period. The equivalent values for the
10% Fedindex are: 0.261, 0.418 and 0.344. But all these
values that would support the hypothesis of different levels
of systematic risk for the T-bond and GNMA market in the two
periods, are not significantly different (for all assets and
all three periods), as F-tests on the 95% level of
significance showed (86). Hence the hypothesis of a risk
increase in the market could not be verified by the
application of the single-index model to fixed-income
positions.

These indications for an increasing beta with increasing
interest rate volatility may explain why beta-values derived
in this study are higher than values of other investigations
analysing previous years.
For the period 1953 to 1972 YAWITZ, MARSHALL derived for a

Table 3-3:   Regression Results for Spot Positions   (Subperiods)

Asset 1978-6/80	a b	R^2	F	DW
8% T-bond	-0.006 0.290 (-0.009)* (1.755)*	0.099	3.079	1.359[1]
$8\frac{1}{4}$% T-bond	-0.038 0.286 (-0.050)* (1.731)*	0.097	2.995	1.355[1]
8% Fedindex	-0.017 0.272 (-0.021)* (1.546)*	0.079	2.391	1.380[1]
10% Fedindex	0.040 0.261 (0.053)* (1.545)*	0.079	2.385	1.379[1]
12% Fedindex	0.081 0.254 (0.109)* (1.543)*	0.078	2.381	1.381[1]
Own Bondindex	-0.010 0.290 (-0.014)* (1.930)*	0.117	3.723	1.339[2]
GNMA	0.158 0.293 (0.244)* (2.048)	0.130	4.196	1.419[1]

continued on the following page

Table 3-3: Regression Results for Spot Positions (Subperiods)
(continued)

Asset 7/80-1982	a	b	R^2	F	DW
8 % T-bond	0.666 (0.746)*	0.457 (2.436)	0.175	5.933	1.742
8¼% T-bond	0.640 (0.749)*	0.462 (2.569)	0.191	6.600	1.695
8% Fedindex	0.657 (0.753)*	0.435 (2.371)	0.167	5.621	1.599
10% Fedindex	0.694 (0.826)*	0.418 (2.367)	0.167	5.601	1.599
12% Fedindex	0.720 (0.880)*	0.407 (2.367)	0.167	5.604	1.602
Own Bondindex	0.592 (0.757)*	0.388 (2.358)	0.166	5.558	1.622
CNMA	0.592 (0.604)*	0.375 (1.835)*	0.107	3.367	2.036
11¾% bond	0.649 (0.812)*	0.395 (2.350)	0.165	5.521	1.684

30 Observations

1) Values within the inconclusive region (1.35 - 1.49).
   Analysis for autoregressive processes did not lead to
   significant results.

2) Value indicates autoregression. It was not possible to
   trace a significant autoregressive process.

portfolio containing T-bonds with 20 years to maturity a bs of 0.059. MODIGLIANI, POGUE found for a portfolio of government and high grade bonds a bs of 0.07 for the period 1960 to 1971. SHARPE computed for the same portfolio for the period 1966 to 1975 a bs of 0.170.

WEINSTEIN, who analyzed the corporate bond market for the years 1966 to 1972 estimated beta-values in the range between 0.126 and 0.205 (87).

These figures indicate that the values derived above for government bonds and GNMAs seem plausible for a period of extremely volatile interest rates.

R-square values of Table 3-2 and 3-3, explaining the extent by which a change in the return of the spot position is explained by a movement in the market return, seem quite low. This result is in accordance with many other studies of the single-index model. WEINSTEIN, for example, derived for the riskier corporate bond market R-square values between 0.095 and 0.191. For grain and wheat futures contracts for the period 1952 to 1967 DUSAK's regressions showed R-squares around zero (0.003 to 0.013) (88).

Empirical investigations of the single-index model for the stock market exhibit R-square values between 0.250 and 0.490 (89) and SHARPE wrote that "a typical value of R-square of a single stock is about 0.30" (90).

Since the above analysis regresses returns of relatively

riskless T-bonds or GNMAs on a share market index, R-square values in the range between 0.122 and 0.144 seem acceptable.

Hence the beta-values derived above support the hypothesis that T-bonds - either single issues or portfolios - and GNMAs bear positive systematic risk at a significant level. The beta-values were higher than the results of studies for the same assets in years with lower interest rate variability. In comparison to typical stock betas (e.g. air transport 1.80, motor vehicles 1.27, banks 0.81 , energy utilities 0.60 (91)) these values are low, reflecting the much lower risk of T-bonds and GNMAs compared to stocks.

3.2.2. Systematic Risk of Futures Positions

Computations for T-bond and GNMA futures positions led to significant beta-values of 0.364 for the T-bond futures contract and of 0.296 for the GNMA contract (1978 - 1982, see Table 3-4). The GNMA-beta for the six year period is slightly smaller (0.284) than the beta-value of the five year interval. This result is similar to the GNMA cash market. Furthermore the finding that GNMA cash positions bear less systematic risk than T-bond positions is also confirmed for the futures market.
Alphas derived are not significantly different from zero, indicating that futures positions show no unsystematic risk.

Table 3-4:   Regression Results for Futures Positions

Asset 1978-1982	a b	R^2 F DW
T-bond	-0.726 0.364 (-1.337)* (3.114)	0.143 9.681 1.668
GNMA (1978-82)	-0.663 0.296 (-1.446)* (2.996)	0.134 8.974 1.582[1]
GNMA (1977-82)	-0.515 0.284 (-1.346)* (3.258)	0.312 10.615 1.570[1]
1978-6/80		
T-bond	-0.805 0.292 (-1.118)* (1.833)	0.107 3.361 1.448[1]
GNMA	-0.765 0.259 (-1.294)* (1.990)	0.124 3.960 1.408[1]
7/80-1982		
T-bond	-0.648 0.429 (-0.777)* (2.448)	0.176 5.991 1.680
GNMA	-0.562 0.329 (-0.780)* (2.167)	0.144 4.696 1.628
Use of different futures contracts (1977-1982)		
GNMA N	-0.515 0.284 (-1.35)* (3.258)	0.132 10.615 1.570[1]
GNMA D	-0.551 0.290 (-1.41)* (3.260)	0.132 10.630 1.606[1]
GNMA DD	-0.573 0.282 (-1.51)* (3.263)	0.132 10.644 1.621[1]

1) Values within the inconclusive region.
   Analysis for autoregressive processes did not lead
   to significant results.

For the GNMA market the regressions were reestimated for the next following contracts. Beta-values of 0.290 and 0.282 are very close to the beta of the nearby contract (0.284). The equivalent variance values for the futures position returns were 11.872, 12.329 and 11.681. This gives indication that the analysis of futures markets via the single-index model leads to results similar to the investigation within the portfolio theory framework.

As for the spot market, we observe beta-values smaller for the first subperiod and greater for the second subperiod than beta-values for the overall period. As in the spot market the F-test does not prove a significant difference of these values.

Estimates of beta-values for GNMA and T-bond futures positions led to betas significantly different from zero. Therefore we can conclude that futures positions exhibit systematic or interest rate risk.

3.2.3. Comparison of Systematic Risk of Spot and Futures Positions

Beta-values for spot and futures positions show only slight differences (See Table 3-2 and 3-4). The hypothesis that bs equals bf could not be rejected for all assets under investigation on the 95% level of significance (92). The results of regression analysis do not contradict the hypothesis that T-bond and GNMA cash and futures positions bear systematic risk of the same level.

The beta-value for the 8% cash bond was 0.383 whereas the futures contract shows a beta of 0.364. For the 8 1/4% bond we observe a bs of 0.379 slightly closer to the bf. The 8% Fedindex with maturity and coupon rate similar to the fictive bond on which futures price quotations are based, is with a bs of 0.358 closest to the b-value of the futures contract (0.364). The remaining difference might reflect either computation insufficiencies (e.g. weekly average prices, rounding errors) or imperfect arbitrage between cash and futures. The bs-values for the other indices (0.344, 0.342, 0.335) are below the beta of the futures market in the same range as the bs for the single issues are above that value. Since beta-values computed for cash and futures positions show no large differences, we expect the beta-values for hedged T-bond positions to be very close to zero.

Betas for GNMA cash and futures markets show the largest absolute difference: 0.337 to 0.299 and 0.327 to 0.284 for the six year period (Nevertheless those values are not significantly different). On the basis of these findings we expect GNMA beta-values to be greater than T-bond betas for the following analysis of systematic risk of hedged positions. Furthermore, bh for the six year period should be greater than the beta-value for the five year period.

3.2.4. Systematic Risk of Hedged Position

Regressing the returns of hedged positions on the market return led to bh-values in the range of 0.032 to -0.024 for the T-bond positions and to a bh of 0.043 for the GNMA position for the period 1978 to 1982 (See Table 3-5). The first hypothesis to test was whether bh is significantly different and smaller than either bs or bf, Ho: bh < bs, bh < bf.

This hypothesis could not be rejected on the 95% level of significance (93). Furthermore statistical evidence supports the hypothesis of a non significant beta-value for hedged positions. Hence the hypothesis Ho: bh = 0 can not be rejected at the 95% level of significance for all assets.

The results of the above analysis within the framework of portfolio theory, stating that T-bond and GNMA futures markets are very effective in reducing risk, is also confirmed by the application of the single-index model, i.e. betas derived not only support the hypothesis that hedged positions clearly bear less systematic risk than spot positions but also indicate a level of risk close to and not significantly different from zero.

Comparing bh-values for single positions we see that the Own Bondindex and the 8% Fedindex bear the lowest systematic risk (in absolute terms) with a bh of -0.0059 and -0.0091. The single bonds bh-values of 0.032 and 0.031 indicate very good hedging results.

The GNMA market also shows sufficient systematic risk
reduction capacity. For the five year period the bh is
0.043, slightly higher - as we expected - than in the T-bond
market. Also as expected, the six year period shows the
highest bh with 0.052.

The a-values of hedged positions are positive and
significantly different from zero. Hence hedged positions
which are free of systematic risk, exhibit unsystematic risk.
This result reflects the fact that hedged positions earn a
monthly interest income. Calculating the regression line for
hedged positions, but abstracting from the monthly interest
income, led to a-values not significantly different from zero
(94).

Hence the results support the view that the T-bond and GNMA
futures markets are very efficient markets for reducing the
systematic (interest rate) risk existing in these markets.

Table 3-5: Regression Results for Hedged Positions
1978 - 1982

Asset	a	b	R^2	F	DW	ς_1
8% T-bond	1.032 (8.393)	0.032 (1.208)*	0.025	1.460	1.687	
$8\frac{1}{4}$% T-bond	1.037 (9.637)	0.031 (1.328)*	0.030	1.764	1.785	
8% Fedindex	1.069 (8.966)	-0.0091 (-0.270)*	0.073	2.001[2]		-0.500[1] (-4.469)
10% Fedindex	1.112 (10.233)	-0.0176 (-0.566)*	0.320	2.057[2]		-0.527[1] (-4.801)
12% Fedindex	1.143 (11.057)	-0.024 (-0.792)*	0.627	2.092[2]		-0.548[1] (-5.071)
Own Bondindex	1.002 (12.210)	-0.0059 (-0.335)*	0.002	0.112	1.775	
GNMA	1.034 (5.691)	0.043 (0.896)*	0.802	2.051[2]		-0.341[1] (-2.810)
(1977-82)	0.905 (5.833)	0.052 (1.183)*		1.399	2.019[2]	-0.314[1] (-2.802)

1) Significant autoregressive process of first order.

2) Investigation for second order autoregressive processes did not lead
   to significant results.

3.3. Evaluation of Results

ROLL pointed out that the selection of the index representing the market might influence the regression results (95). Since we are investigating the systematic risk of fixed-income securities such as government bonds or GNMAs, an index reflecting solely the stock market might be inadequate for this analysis. Therefore we reestimated beta-values for the 8% T-bond, the 8% Fedindex, the Own Bondindex and the GNMA position, using as proxy for the market an index that also included fixed-income securities.

According to the Flow of Fund Analysis of the Federal Research Board (96), the combined index includes 14.3% government bonds. As indicator for the government bond market we used the Fedindex, assuming a coupon rate of 10% (97). The stock market was represented by the S&P index.

Running the regressions on a market index inclusive of fixed-income securities we expect beta-values greater than those derived from regressions on a pure stock index, since this combined index should better explain the return variability of fixed-income securities. Furthermore the values of the test statistics are expected to increase.

Results of the regressions based on the combined index are presented in Tables 3-6 to 3-8.
As expected, we observe for spot, futures, and hedged

Table 3-6 : Regression Results for Spot Positions Based on a
Combined Index

1978–82	a	T(a)	b	T(b)	R^2	F	DW
8 % T-bond	0.206	(0.383)*	0.555	(4.388)	0.249	19.256	1.648
8 % Fedindex	0.194	(0.354)*	0.538	(4.180)	0.232	17.470	1.542 [2]
Own Bondindex	0.192	(0.399)*	0.492	(4.345)	0.246	18.879	1.605 [1]
GNMA	0.249	(0.461)*	0.516	(4.067)	0.222	16.538	1.887
1978–6/80							
8 % T-bond	-0.091	(-0.129)*	0.453	(2.623)	0.197	6.881	1.326 [2]
8 % Fedindex	-0.108	(-0.144)*	0.444	(2.403)	0.171	5.774	1.353 [1]
Own Bondindex	-0.077	(-0.119)*	0.429	(2.726)	0.210	7.429	1.315 [2]
GNMA	0.088	(0.143)*	0.421	(2.816)	0.221	7.930	1.375 [1]
7/80–1982							
8 % T-bond	0.499	(0.603)*	0.639	(3.420)	0.295	11.694	1.769
8 % Fedindex	0.492	(0.607)*	0.616	(3.361)	0.288	11.298	1.665
Own Bondindex	0.458	(0.627)*	0.545	(3.279)	0.277	10.750	1.654
GNMA	0.407	(0.449)*	0.597	(2.905)	0.232	8.438	2.038
$11\frac{3}{4}$% T-bond	0.508	(0.679)*	0.549	(3.242)	0.273	10.512	1.737

60 Observations (1978–1982), 30 Observations for subperiods.
* Values not significant on the 95% level.

1) Values within the inconclusive region. Analysis for
   autoregressive processes did not lead to significant results.
2) Values indicate autoregression for the disturbance term. It was
   not possible to trace significant autoregressive processes.

Table 3-7 :   Regression Results for Futures Positions Based on a Combined Index

1978-1982	a	T(a)	b	T(b)	R^2	F	DW
T-bond	-0.838	(-1.646)*	0.525	(4.390)	0.249	19.275	1.722
GNMA	-0.756	(-1.751)*	0.429	(4.229)	0.236	17.881	1.576 [1]
1978-6/80							
T-bond	-0.886	(-1.304)*	0.449	(2.696)	0.206	7.269	1.428 [1]
GNMA	-0.827	(-1.469)*	0.371	(2.712)	0.208	7.355	1.373 [1]
7/80-1982							
T-bond	-0.796	(-1.022)*	0.591	(3.353)	0.287	11.242	1.760
GNMA	-0.688	(-1.024)*	0.478	(3.133)	0.260	9.815	1.643

1) Values within the inconclusive region. Analysis for autoregressive processes
   did not lead to significant result.

Table 3-8 :   Regression Results for Hedged Positions Based on a Combined Index

1978-82	a	T(a)	b	T(b)	R^2	F	DW
8 % T-bond	1.021	(8.382)	0.049	(1.694)*	0.047	2.871	1.668
8 % Fedindex	1.054	(8.927)	0.010	(0.272)*			2.011 [1]
Own Bondindex	1.006	(12.223)	-0.007	(-0.385)*	0.003	0.149	1.768
GNMA	0.992	(5.579)	0.086	(1.660)*			2.055 [2]

1) Significant autoregressive process of first order, d : -0.493 (-4.388).
   No significant autoregressive process of second order.

2) Significant autoregressive process of first order, d : -0.340 (-2.799).
   No significant autoregressive process of second order.

positions for all periods and all assets under investigation, beta-values greater than those derived from regressions on a pure stock index: betas for spot positions changed from 0.383 to 0.555 (8% T-bond) or from 0.337 to 0.516 (GNMA). In the same range beta-values for futures positions increased. A T-test could not prove a significant difference for betas based on the pure stock or the combined index (95% level of significance).

For hedged positions betas increased from 0.032 to 0.049 (8% T-bond) or from 0.043 to 0.086 (GNMA). These values are not significantly different from zero. Hence this result supports the risk reduction effectiveness of interest rate futures markets, and shows that the important findings of the underlying study do not depend on the composition of the market index.

As related to the question of unsystematic risk (a-value) the results did not change when the regressions were reestimated on the combined index.

T-ratios for betas as well as R-square and F values are all greater when the combined index was used, expressing the higher explanatory power of this index. These observations are in accordance with WEINSTEIN's findings who also observed increasing values when he allowed for an index including fixed-income securities (98).

Application of a combined index including fixed-income securities instead of a pure stock market index led to increased beta-values. But these values are in complete accordance with the hypothesis derived above (99). Thus we can conclude that the choice of the index representing the market affects the beta-values derived, but is not crucial for the results of the study, which are:

- Spot positions of fixed-income securities such as government debt or GNMAs bear interest rate or systematic risk at a significant level, i.e. these assets are risky assets within the concept of the CAPM. They are free of unsystematic or default risk since they are issued or backed by the US government.

- T-bond or GNMA futures positions are risky too. The level of systematic risk is similar to the relevant spot positions. This observation indicates that arbitrage between cash and futures markets works quite well on average. No unsystematic risk of futures positions could be traced.

- Hedged positions turned out to be free of systematic risk, i.e. hedging abolishes the risk of T-bond or GNMA spot positions due to interest rate changes.

The application of the single-index model to interest rate futures markets, i.e. calculations of beta-values for spot, futures and hedged positions, led to another proof of the risk reduction effectiveness of futures markets. This effect has already been demonstrated in the previous chapter via the indicators: correlation coefficient, variance and hedging effectiveness.

Footnotes to III.1. (Theoretical Basis)

1) These expressions were introduced by SHARPE, W.F. (1964, pp. 436 and 439).

2) Compare for this section: MODIGLIANI, F; POGUE, G.A. (1974a, pp. 76 ff.); FRANCIS, J.C.; ARCHER, S.H. (1979, pp. 155 ff.); MULLINS, D.W. (1982, pp. 107 f.).

3) SHARPE, W. F. (1963, pp. 281 ff.).

4) SHARPE, W.F. (1963, pp. 281 ff.). He called the model, the diagonal model. It was introduced as a solution to the problem of generating the statistical input for portfolio analysis, which requires a lot of calculations. A portfolio of n assets wants $1/2$ (n^2 - n) covariance terms to be calculated.

5) SHARPE, W.F. (1963, p. 281).

6) For the formal derivation of (III.3) and the equations for $E(R_i)$ and $cov(R_i, R_j)$ compare: SHARPE,W.F. (1963, p. 282); ELTON, E.J.; GRUBER, M.J. (1981, pp. 110 ff.).

7) Remember that $cov(R_M, e_i) = 0$.

8) Remember that $cov(e_i, e_j) = 0$.

9) A survey of studies estimating b-values can be found e.g. in: ELTON, E.J.; GRUBER, M.J. (1981, pp. 116 ff.).

10) See point II.1.4.

11) Tobin regarded cash as the riskless asset with an expected return of zero. No borrowing was possible in his model. Inflation was excluded. TOBIN, J. (1958, pp. 65 ff.).

12) For the following section compare: TOBIN, J. (1958, pp. 71 ff.); HALEY, C.W.; SCHALL, L.D. (1973, pp. 119 ff.), DRUKARCZYK, J. (1980, pp. 303 ff.).

13) See II.1.1. assumption 6.

14) SHARPE, W.F. (1981, p. 131); HALEY, C.W.; SCHALL, L.D. (1973, p. 119).

15) Expected return and risk can be computed according equations (III-6) and (III-7).

16) Compare FRANCIS, J.C.; ARCHER, S.H. (1979, p. 165).

17) It is assumed that the riskless rate is equal for borrowing and lending. Otherwise there would be more than one optimal combination of risky securities. This case is analysed e.g. in ELTON, E.J.; GRUBER, M.J. (1981, pp. 66 f.).

18) SHARPE, W.F. (1970, p. 70); FRANCIS, J.C.; ARCHER, S.H. (1979, p. 152).

19) MODIGLIANI, F; POGUE, G.A. (1974a, p. 68); ROSENBERG, B. (1981, p. 6).

20) To mention only a few names that contributed to the development of the CAPM: SHARPE, W.F. (1964); TREYNOR, J.L. (1965); LINTNER, J. (1965a); MOSSIN, J. (1966); FAMA, E.F. (1968).
The CAPM as presented here is the so-called SHARPE-LINTNER version.

21) See SHARPE, W.F. (1964, PP. 428 and 433 ff.); JENSEN, M.C. (1972, p. 5); FULLER, R.J. (1981, p. 20).

22) For an explicit discussion of assumptions on which portfolio theory is based see point 1.1 of chapter 2.

23) For the following section compare: SHARPE, W.F. (1970, pp. 83 ff.); FULLER, R.J., pp. 23 ff.; DRUKARCZYK, J. (1980, pp. 320 ff.).

24) SHARPE, W.F. (1970, p. 84).

25) For the following analysis compare HALEY, C.W.; SCHALL, L.D. (1973, pp. 144 ff.); FRANCIS, J.C.; ARCHER, S.H. (1979, pp. 158 ff.); DRUKARCZYK, J. (1980, pp. 324 ff.).

26) In this way the security market line was originally derived by SHARPE, W.F. (1964, pp. 437 ff.). Compare also SHARPE, W.F. (1970, pp. 86 ff.). Different ways to derive the security market line were used by LINTNER, J. (1965b, pp. 597 ff.) and FAMA, E.F. (1968, pp. 29 ff.).

27) With proportion (a) invested in security i and (1-a) in the market portfolio, expected return and risk of portfolio Z are:

$$E(R_Z) = aE(R_i) + (1-a)\ E(R_M)$$

$$\sigma_Z = \left[a^2 \sigma_i^{\,2} + (1-a)^2 \sigma_M^{\,2} + 2a(1-a)cov(R_i,R_M) \right]^{1/2}$$

Differentiating with respect to a ,

$$\frac{\partial E(R_Z)}{\partial a} = E(R_i) - E(R_M)$$

$$\frac{\partial_Z}{\partial a} = \frac{a\left[\sigma_i^{\,2} + \sigma_M^{\,2} - 2\ cov(R_i,R_M) \right] - \sigma_M^{\,2} + cov(R_i,R_M)}{\sigma_Z}$$

The slope of iM is $\dfrac{\partial E(R_Z)}{\partial \sigma_Z} = \dfrac{\partial E(R_Z)/\partial_a}{\partial \sigma_Z / \partial \sigma_a}$. At point M

a=O and $\sigma_Z = \sigma_M$. Thus

$$\frac{\partial E(R_Z)}{\partial_Z} = \frac{\left[E(R_i) - E(R_M) \right]\sigma_M}{cov(R_i,R_M) - \sigma_M^{\,2}}$$

28) Compare section 1.1. of this chapter.

29) SHARPE, W.F. (1964, p. 442).

30) This formulation of the security market line is used e.g. by JENSEN, M.C. (1972, p. 6) and ELTON, E.J.; GRUBER, M.J. (1981, pp. 283 ff.).

31) FRANCIS, J.C.; ARCHER, S.H. (1979, p. 160)

32) The proof that efficient portfolios plot on the capital market and security market line can be found, e.g., in FULLER, R.J. (1981, p. 25).

33) For a description of these extensions see e.g.: JENSEN, M.C. (1972, pp. 14 ff.); FAMA, E.F. (1976, pp. 277 ff.); ROSS, S.A. (1978, pp. 894 ff.); SHARPE, W.F. (1981, pp. 172 ff.).

34) FRANCIS, J.C.; ARCHER, S.H. (1979, p. 316); ELTON, E.J.; GRUBER, M.J. (1981, p. 316).

35) Among other asset pricing models the arbitrage pricing model (APM) which is more general than the CAPM should be mentioned, ROSS, S.A. (1976, pp. 341 ff.). This model

explains expected returns on risky assets as a linear
function of a number of unspecific factors. If the
market return were the only factor explaining asset
return, the APM would be identical to the CAPM.

36) Compare e.g. FAMA, E.F. (1976, p. 277); SHARPE, W.F.
(1981, p. 143).

37) See e.g.: MILLER, M.H.; SCHOLES, M. (1972); BLACK,
F.; JENSEN, M.C.; SCHOLES, M. (1972); FAMA, E.F..
MacBETH, J.D. (1973).
ELTON, E.J.; GRUBER, M.J. (1981, pp. 337 ff.), provide
a summary of these tests.

38) The use of a proxy for the market portfolio was
criticised by ROLL stating that "no correct and
unambiguous test of the theory has appeared in the
literature", ROLL, R. (1977, p. 129). He argued that
it is impossible to measure the return of the true market
portfolio. Consequently, the theory is not testable
unless the "exact composition of the true market
portfolio" is determined (130).

39) See e.g. BLACK, F.; JENSEN, M.C.; SCHOLES, M. (1972,
pp. 91 ff.).

40) If the CAPM is tested in the risk premium version,
(III.15) would be $(\bar{R}_i - \bar{r}_f) = (\bar{R}_M - \bar{r}_f) b_i + \eta_i$
Then λ_0 should be zero, whereas the interpretation of λ_1
remains unchanged if the CAPM is tested in the risk
premium formulation.

41) DOUGLAS, G. (1968) traced a significant positive
relationship between assets returns and their variances
of return. MILLER, M.H.; SCHOLES, M. (1972) showed
that these findings were due to measurement errors in
beta and correlation between beta and residual risk (p.
60 ff.).

42) There has been a discussion in the literature whether
the linear form of the CAPM is the most adequate.
Functional forms were proposed. Empirical investigations
could not reject the linear risk-return relationship
(LEE, C.F., 1976) respectively supported the application
of the linear CAPM in estimating systematic risk
(McDONALD, B., 1983).

43) BLACK, F.; JENSEN, M.C.; SCHOLES, M. (1972); BLUME,
M.E.; FRIEND, I. (1973); FAMA, E.F; MacBETH, J.D.
(1973).

44) These results seem to conform better with BLACK's (1972)
zero-beta version of the CAPM. On the other hand ROLL,
R. (1977, p.131) shows that the results are in

accordance with the Sharpe-Linter version of the CAPM due to a misspecification of the market index used for testing. See also FAMA, E.F. (1976, p. 370).

45) FAMA, E.F. (1976, p. 272).

46) See e.g. SHARPE, W.F. (1981, pp. 144).

47) LINTNER, J. (1969, p. 358 ff.); FAMA, E.F. (1976, pp. 314 ff.).

48) FAMA, E.F. (1976, p. 319).

49) See e.g. LINTNER, J. (1969, p. 352 ff.; GONEDES, N.J. (1976, pp. 2 ff.); RABINOVITCH, R.; OWEN, J. (1978, pp. 581 ff.).

50) FULLER, R.J. (1981, p. 21).

51) FAMA, E.F. (1976, 272).

52) See HIRSHLEIFER, J. (1977, p. 979); SHARPE, W.F. (1981, p. 143). HIRSHLEIFER uses the term "concordant beliefs".

53) KEYNES, J.M. (1930, pp. 128 f.); see also HICKS, J.R. (1946, pp. 137 f.).

54) HOFFMAN, G.W. (1932, pp. 409, 418); WORKING, H. 1953, pp. 325 f.).

55) Compare for this: STREIT, M.E. (1983a, pp. 70 f.).

56) STREIT, M.E. (1983b, pp. 7 f.).

57) HIRSHLEIFER, J. (1975, p. 539).

58) FAMA, E.F. (1967, p. 277); SHARPE, W.F. (1981, p.143); ELTON, E.J.; JOHN, M.J. (1981, p. 275 and 294).

59) ELTON, E.J.; GRUBER, M.J. (1981, p. 332).

60) BLACK, F.; JENSEN, M.C.; SCHOLES, M. (1972, pp. 83 ff.).

61) BLACK, F.; JENSEN, M.C.; SCHOLES, M. (1972, pp. 91 ff. and 118); LEVY, H. (1982, p. 56).

62) BLACK, F.; JENSEN, M.C.; SCHOLES, M. (1972); FAMA, E.F.; MacBETH, J. (1973).

63) FAMA, E.F. (1976, p. 347).

64) BLUME, M.E. (1971, p. 7); LEVY, R.A. (1971, p. 57).

65) FABOZZI, F.J.; FRANCIS, J.C. conducted a study leading to the result that many stock's betas move randomly (1978, p. 101). ALEXANDER, G.J.; BESON, P.G. (1982, pp. 33 ff.) contradict their findings.

66) See e.g. FRIEND, I.; WESTERFIELD, R. (1981); LEVY, H. (1983).

67) ROSS, S.A. (1978, pp. 898); FAMA, E.F. (1976, 370).

Footnotes to III.2 (Analysis of IRFM in the CAPM Framework)

68) Compare LORD, T.J. (1980, pp. 24 ff.); SHARPE, W.F. (1981, pp. 308 ff.); WEINSTEIN, M. (1981, pp. 257 ff.).

69) SHARPE, W.F. (1981, p. 313).

70) Compare e.g. YEAGER, F.; SEITZ, N. (1982, p. 83); FISCHER, D.E.; JORDAN, R.J. (1983, p. 340).

71) WEINSTEIN, M. (1981, p. 258) showed that the default risk of corporate bonds contains also a systematic risk component. Since default probability of corporations increases in the downswings of the business cycle there is a link between default risk of low grade bonds and general economic movements. Government debt is free of default risk. Therefore this point is not of relevance for the underlying study.

72) See e.g. MULLINS, D.W. (1982, p. 106); FAMA, E.F.; MILLER, M.H. (1972, p. 228).

73) For an explicit discussion of the reactions of bond prices to yield changes see e.g. DARST, D.M. (1981, pp. 307 ff.).

74) See e.g. GOULDEY, B.K.; GRAY, G.J. (1981, p. 161).

75) MODIGLIANI, F; POGUE, G.A. (1974b, p. 72); SHARPE, W.F. (1981, p. 314); WEINSTEIN, M. (1981, p. 272).

76) BODIE, Z.; ROSANSKY, V.I. (1980); DUSAK, K. (1973); GRAUER, F.L. (1977) as quoted in BREEDEN. BREEDEN, D.T. (1980) came to the same results applying the standard single-index model. He also calculated consumption beta-values. These betas were significantly different from zero, indicating that commodity contracts bear systematic risk according the consumption beta. CARTER, C.A.; RAUSSER, G.C.; SCHMITZ, A. (1983) derived significant positive beta-values using the standard single-index model.

Footnotes to III.3 (Empirical Investigation)

77) We assumed that the classical conditions for the application of the OLS estimation were given:

$E(e_t)$ $= 0$ for $t=1,2,\ldots,T$
$E(e_t)$ $= \sigma_t^2$ for $t=1,2,\ldots,T$
$E(e_t,e_j)$ $\overset{+}{=} 0$ for all $t \neq j$
$E(e_t,R_{M,t})= 0$ for $t=1,2,\ldots,T$

Compare: SCHNEEWEISS, H. (1978, pp. 36 ff.); KMENTA, J. (1971, pp. 201 ff.).

78) COCHRANE, D.; ORCUTT, G.H. (1949, pp. 32 ff.).

79) See for example: IBBOTSON, R.G.; SINQUEFIELD, R.A. (1976); BLACK, F.; JENSEN, M.C.; SCHOLES, M. (1972); YAWITZ, J.B.; MARSHALL, W.J. (1980).

80) Roll's critique points to the fact that by the use of any stock market index, always a proxy for the market is used, but never the true market portfolio which consists out of all assets. ROLL, R. (1977, pp. 129 ff.).

81) For a description of the S&P index see: INDEX AND OPTION MARKET (ed.), (1982, pp. 5 f.); REILLY, F.K. (1981, pp. 300 ff.).

82) SHARPE, W.F.; COOPER, G.M. (1972, pp. 49 ff.).

83) BLACK, F.; JENSEN, M.C.; SCHOLES, M. (1972, p. 118) came to the same result when evaluating a similar question. They found that betas are not affected if monthly returns are regressed on a market index defined in risk-premium respectively in absolute return form.

84) Compare e.g. FISCHER, D.E.; JORDAN, R.J. (1983, pp. 323 f.).

85) This observation does not depend on the procedure by which the market return is calculated (Compare Table 3-1).

86) Tests carried out on $(bs_{II} - bs_I)/\sigma(bs_{II})$, assuming bs_I to be the true value. KMENTA, J. (1971, p. 236).

87) YAWITZ, J.B.; MARSHALL, W.J. (1980, p. 20); MODIGLIANI, F.; POGUE, G.A. (1974b, p. 72); SHARPE, W.F. (1981, p. 314); WEINSTEIN, M. (1981, p. 272).

88) DUSAK, K. (1973, p. 1402).

89) See: FRANCIS, J.C.; ARCHER, S.A. (1979, p. 60).

289

90) SHARPE, W.F. (1981, p. 158).

91) FRANCIS, J.C.; ARCHER, S.H. (1979, p. 64).

92) Test carried out according (bf - bs)/σ(bf), assuming bs to be the true value.

93) The test for significant difference of bh from bs (bf) was conducted according (bs - bh)/σbs assuming bh to be the true value.

94) 8 % T-bond :   a: 0.175, T(a): 1.490
    8 % T-bond :   a: 0.774, T(a): 1.712

95) ROLL, R. (1977, p. 130).

96) Figures were taken from FRIEND, I., WESTERFIELD, R. (1981, p. 293). They report the following proportions of different assets in the US capital markets: government bonds 10%, corporate bonds 30%, stocks 60%.

97) For practical purposes the government bond market was approximated by the Own Index when beta-values for this index were computed and by the GNMA market, when these betas were estimated.

98) WEINSTEIN, M. (1981, pp. 272 f.).

99) For completeness of the study, the regressions were also estimated with bond proportions of 20, 30 and 40%. With the bond proportion increasing, beta-values became larger. Once again these values support the findings of the study. One special case needs further explanation: for a bond proportion of 30 and 40% we could trace systematic risk for hedged positions at a significant level. The beta-values were 0.069 (2.296) and 0.083 (2.697). Although these figures indicate that systematic risk is not completely abolished via hedging, they strongly support the risk reduction effectiveness of interest rate futures markets, since the equivalent betas for spot positions were 0.770 and 0.842.

CHAPTER IV :   SUMMARY AND CONCLUSIONS

The main intention of the underlying research was to contribute to a better understanding of the functioning of interest rate futures markets and to evaluate the effects on single economic agents, capital markets and the economy. To achieve this aim we pursued the question whether classical capital market theory such as portfolio theory and the capital asset pricing model can be applied to interest rate futures markets.

1. EFFECTS OF INTEREST RATE FUTURES MARKETS ON SINGLE ECONOMIC AGENTS

The application of portfolio theory to interest rate futures led to the following results:

- interest rate futures markets can be analysed within this concept,
- portfolio theory does not lead to a completely new theory of hedging but incorporates elements of two quite different elder hedging theories,
- decision criteria of portfolio theory are useful instruments for agents in futures markets to determine their optimal transactions and thus contribute to a better understanding of agents' behaviour in these markets,

- agents can realize a clear reduction of risk if they
  establish positions according to the decision criteria
  of portfolio theory. This reduction of risk can occur
  in combination with either a reduction or an increase in
  return,
- portfolio theory provides useful measures of hedging
  effectiveness and optimal hedge ratios which can be
  estimated empirically.

The empirical investigation of interest rate futures markets
by applying these measures traced a tremendous risk reduction
effectiveness irrespective of the direction of interest rate
movements and the degree of interest rate volatility. This
important result could be confirmed when we made use of a
further indicator derived from the CAPM.

Thus interest rate futures markets proved to be a very useful
and effective instrument for participants in financial
markets to reduce their exposure to risk stemming from
unexpected interest rate changes. Reduction of interest rate
risk is a very important benefit interest rate futures
markets bring about for single economic agents.

Participants engaging in futures trading to reduce their
exposure to interest rate risk can be divided into three main
groups:

o Holders of cash positions

Short hedges provide protection of cash holdings against
unexpected increases in interest rates which cause prices of
interest-bearing securities to decline and thus losses for
owners of cash positions (1). Consequently, short hedges
facilitate carrying of inventories at lower cost (2). This
type of short hedge may be advantageous for private
investors, financial institutions, insurance companies as
well as corporate treasurers holding securities in their
portfolios. Security dealers and financial institutions
carrying an inventory of securities to meet demand of their
clients can benefit from short hedging in the same way as
financial institutions that hold temporarily as underwriter
or issuer a position of securities to be sold in the capital
market.

o Investors who want to lock in a special lending rate

Lenders who plan an investment in securities but cannot
dispose of the funds at the moment can be protected against a
decline in interest rates and, consequently, lower earnings,
by establishing a long hedge (3). Locking in a current high
interest rate, may be attractive for private investors,
corporate treasurers, bank and other fund managers for new
engagements or rolling-over of outstanding investments.

o Borrowers who want to lock in a special borrowing rate

Financial institutions, private borrowers or corporate treasurers who plan to raise funds in the future but expect interest rates and thus costs of borrowing to increase in the interim, can lock in the actual rate by establishing a short hedge (4). Outstanding engagements can be rolled-over at the current favourable rate. Banks may use this type of short hedge to create medium-term fixed-rate loans without running the risk of a classical squeeze. Furthermore banks or mortgage institutions may provide loans to be paid out in some months hence without bearing an interest rate risk.

Besides risk reduction interest rate futures markets provide the following benefits for single economic agents:

Improvement of planning and decision situation: The economical and political environment within which economic agents have to come to investment decisions is characterized by sudden and unpredictable changes. Hence every decision on plans and activities is a decision under uncertainty. Given the opportunity to fix at least one decision variable - the actual interest rate for a transaction to take place in the future - planning and decision making is improved.

Profit opportunities: Interest rate futures provide the opportunity for speculative trading at very low cost and thus the opportunity for large profits (5).

Procurement of Capital: Cash positions can be used as
collaterals. But if the cash position is exposed to price
risk banks are reluctant to grant loans. Given the
opportunity to hedge the collaterals and thus to reduce price
risk, banks may be more ready to grant loans on such an
inventory (6).

2. EFFECTS OF INTEREST RATE FUTURES MARKETS ON CAPITAL MARKETS AND THE ECONOMY

The analysis of interest rate futures markets in the context
of portfolio theory led to important insights into the
effects of futures trading on individual economic agents.
Another point of importance was the question of the effects
of futures trading on capital markets. Therefore we
investigated whether interst rate futures markets can be
analysed in the context of the CAPM. Since this model is an
extension of portfolio theory to the meso level, an
application of the CAPM might have led to a better
understanding of the impacts of interest futures on capital
markets.

From an a priori point of view the CAPM proved not to be
applicable to interest rate futures markets since the
assumption of homogeneous expectations on which the model is
necessarily based to aggregate different expectations of many
individuals, does not describe adequately the informational

situation of participants in these markets. Homogeneous expectations cannot reflect the way information arises and is processed by individual traders, nor of how trading takes place in speculative markets such as futures markets.

In addition, tests of the CAPM via futures markets turned out to be impossible: firstly, doubts on the adequateness and reliability of the testing procedure emerged and, secondly, the period of futures trading in interest-bearing securities was too short and the number of assets traded too small to carry out unbiased tests of the CAPM.

However, the analysis of the CAPM led to another useful measure of the risk reduction effectiveness of interest rate futures markets: the beta value as an indicator for the systematic or interest rate risk of an asset. We could demonstrate that hedging abolishes the systematic risk of interest-bearing securities and thus confirm previous results.

Since it was not possible to prove theoretically or empirically the impacts of interest rate futures markets on capital markets we shall discuss this question on the following final pages. Given the advantages brought about by futures trading for single agents, we shall speculate on the question of the effects of futures trading in interest-bearing securities on capital markets.

2.1. Informational Situation

Futures trading takes place at a central market place. Information which is dispersed all over the country is revealed at that place and incorporated into prices (7). Transaction costs in futures markets are quite low and thus attract large participation: Borrowers and investors in financial markets transmit their personal knowledge, expectations, capital demand and supply to the market via hedging transactions. Speculators trade in futures in expectation of profits. They will gain if they predict price movements correctly. Therefore speculators are specialized in collecting and processing price-relevant information, an activity for which they spend quite a lot of resources. Trading in futures, they disseminate their knowledge and individual expectations to the market.

New information coming up will be incorporated into prices immediately. Participants not in agreement with futures prices quoted can trade at once and thus express their divergent views. Price distortions will be corrected immediately. Access to futures markets is not limited. Prices are established in an open bargain.

Cash markets reflect above all opinions of optimistic market participants since there is no difficulty for traders expecting prices to increase, to establish a long position. Traders expecting prices to decline have more difficulties to express their pessimistic views in cash markets, since only those who are long in cash are able to sell a position. Costs of forward transactions are quite high. In futures also pessimistic traders can easily express their opinion by going short (8). Costs of transaction are very low. Consequently prices quoted in futures do also reflect pessimistic views.

Hence the informational situation in capital markets is improved through futures trading since futures prices are established in open competition at a central market place with open access to which different groups of traders from all over the country contribute with their best knowledge.

Futures prices are public prices available at zero cost even to those not active in these markets and quickly spread over the country. Thus lasting information monopolies cannot emerge. This tends to reduce market power in information of large entities able to spend more resources in the collection and processing of information than small entities. As a consequence, barriers to entry are reduced and competition in the market is improved (9).

Reflecting the best knowledge in the market, futures prices are a useful basis for planning and the best indicator of the market's expectation on the futures course of interest rates.

2.2. Volatility of Interest Rates

Whether futures trading leads to more or less price stability is one of the most frequently and most controversially discussed effects of futures markets.

General reasoning suggests several a priori reasons for stabilizing price effects of interest rate futures (10):

- We have shown above that futures trading improves the informational situation of capital markets. Market participants wide-spread all over the country contribute with their best knowledge to the price formation process at one central market place. Prices not reflecting fundamental market factors cannot emerge or will be corrected immediately. Large price swings due to mispricing, imperfect informtion or imperfect processing of information are improbable to emerge.

  In addition, futures prices established at a central market place and communicated all over the country serve as reference prices. Capital market participants may reflect upon their plans in the light of prices quoted for future delivery dates and may adopt their lending and borrowing plans thus contributing to more price stability.

- Without the existance of futures markets holders of cash positions have to sell their assets if they expect interest rates to increase, to get protection against losses due to declining prices. Such and similar transactions affect cash markets and create price movements. Given interest rate futures markets that provide hedging oppotunities, traders do not have to use cash markets for liquidating or establishing a position as protection against unfavourable interest rate movements. Instead they trade in futures thus shifting demand and supply from cash to futures markets. Cash prices are not affected.

- Hedgers' and speculators' transactions in futures produce price movements which cause reactions by scalpers, a special type of speculative market participant. They just trade on small price ticks brought about by normal orders (11). Their activities add liquidity to the market and dampen price swings originated by hedgers and speculators thus contributing to less heavy price fluctuations. This type of speculative transaction dampening price swings cannot be carried out as conveniently in cash markets due to cost of transactions and the difficulty of taking short positions.

- Given the opportunity to lock in lending or borrowing rates for investment or funding operations to take place at future dates, hedgers affect futures prices and rates today. If those transactions lead to basis values that exceed cost of carry and transactions, arbitrage operations will be carried out, causing an adjustment of current cash prices to expected futures prices. E.g. if market participants regard current interest rates as high and expect rates to decline they will lock in that actual rate by establishing a long hedge. Those transactions will raise futures prices. (Preasure on futures rates may be strengthened by speculators sharing the view of an increase in prices). Futures prices will be above cash prices. If the contango exceeds cost of carry and cost of transactions arbitrage operations will take place. Traders selling futures contracts and simultaneously buying back the relevant cash positions to be delivered against the futures commitment will lower the futures price and increase current cash prices.

The same mechanism will work if traders regard current rates as low and expect them to increase.

Thus transactions in futures markets to lock in a special rate in combination with arbitrage adjust current rates to expected future rates and prevent too large price swings. An intertemporal allocation of resources takes place, adjusting current rates to the direction of the expected level of future rates and vice versa. Consequently, interest rate movements are dampened by futures markets.

- Speculators' activities tend to stabilize prices. Already classical economic writers argued that speculators will buy if they regard prices as low, store the commodity and will sell if they regard prices as unusually high (12). "The tendency of their operations is to equalize price, or at least to moderate its inequalities" (13).

The following arguments are put forward supporting
destabilizing effects of futures trading on prices, given the
assumption of perfectly competitive markets (14):

- Contrary to the view presented above, speculation is
  regarded as the main source of price distortions.
  Speculators, encouraged by very low cost of trading, are
  assumed to exaggerate price swings causing price levels in
  futures not justified by market fundamentals. These
  excessive futures price movements are transmitted to the
  cash market via arbitrage. Thus cash prices and interest
  rates are distorted due to speculative trading activities
  in futures markets.

  FRIEDMAN argued that destabilizing speculation on average
  would cause losses to speculators (15). A situation like
  this cannot last for long since speculators will be ruined
  except for a situation in which a group of sophisticated
  traders profits at the expense of a second continually
  changing group of speculators which realizes losses (16).

- Participants unable to offset their futures possitions
  because the daily price limit had already been reached,
  will switch to the spot market and distort spot prices.
  However, market observations showed that the daily limit
  was reached only for few times and spillovers to the cash
  market could not be registered (17).

- Futures trading is assumed to draw funds away from spot markets ("diverted funds hypothesis"). Spot markets will become quite thin and wider price variations will be the result. However, since futures markets reduce the risk of holding cash inventories and facilitate arbitrage transactions we would expect an increase in cash market liquidity.

The discussion of the impacts of futures trading on cash price stability has shown that most arguments for destabilizing effects could be questioned whereas there are strong a priori reasons for stabilizing effects.

A definite answer to this point may be brought about by empirical investigations. Studies on classical futures markets support the view that futures trading tends to stabilize cash prices (18). Only few studies investigated interest rate futures markets and the effects on cash prices. FIGLEWSKI arrived at the conclusion that GNMA futures contribute among other factors to price volatility in cash markets (19). SIMPSON/IRELAND and FROEWISS came to opposite results for the same market (20). They conclude their studies with the observation that interest rate futures had at least not contributed to more price instability. FROEWISS ovserved less price volatility but could not prove that this improvement was due to futures trading. GARDNER reached similar results for the T-bill market (21).

Therefore we can conclude that empirical evidence does not support the view of destabilizing effects of futures trading. On the other hand, theoretical arguments and to some extent also empirical studies support the view that interest rate futures markets tend to stabilize underlying cash prices.

Much more concern on destabilizing effects of futures trading emerges if the assumption of perfect competition is relaxed (22). If deliverable supply of securities is small in relation to outstanding futures contracts or if a trader controls the major part of deliverable assets, price distortions cannot be excluded. This aspect is of great concern for monetary authorities. A shortage in supply could force the Treasury to issue more debt than planned in order to prevent price distortions. Such actions may run counter to the aims of monetary policy. If manipulation in the market for governmant debt did really cause price distortions investors will shun the market. Consequently, cost of borrowing for the Treasury will increase.
Empirical studies did not register price distortions due to manipulative trading. In few cases T-bills appeared to have traded at a premium, but it is not clear whether this premium had been caused by activities in futures markets (23).

Hence fears that manipulation causes price distortions cannot be completely dismissed, but an event like this seems highly improbable due to the large amount of outstanding assets and the active role of the CFTC.

2.3. Capital Market Efficiency

Futures markets provide the opportunity to carry out transactions more efficiently (24). Since trading takes place at a central market place search cost and cost for collecting information are reduced significantly. Default risk is shifted to the clearing house.

Futures trading improves the liquidity of cash markets. The opportunity of hedging enhances traders' willingness to hold securities since the price risk is reduced. More and better information on market conditions should also contribute to additional trading and investment activities. Arbitrage transactions increase liquidity and transmit futures prices to the cash market. Thus the informational value of cash prices is improved and the possibility that prices are out of line with market fundamentals is reduced. More liquidity, an increase of information and less risk in a market should cause lower cost of trading. In a competitive market lower cost of trading should lead to a reduction of costs for issuers and dealers of securities and, consequently, lower interest rates for borrowers.

Additional pressure on interest rates should stem from the fact that interest rate risk is reduced. Security dealers and banks carrying inventories of assets to meet clients demand can diminish their exposure to unfavourable price changes and thus risk premiums charged to clients. As a consequence, bid-ask spreads are likely to tighten. BURNS observed a development like this in the GNMA market after the introduction of futures trading (25). Underwriters of security issues who temporarily hold these assets prior to resale also have the opportunity, of hedging their price risk. Therefore they should quote lower prices to issuers. Finally, banks as creditors can create medium term fixed-rate loans, or loans to be paid in the future with less risk and thus at conditions more favourable to their clients.

As a consequence of less risk and increased liquidity futures trading should improve the operational efficiency of capital markets and should lead to lower levels of interest rates.

Futures trading tends to improve the supply of long-term capital in the economy. Due to interest rate changes long-term assets exhibit large price swings. Therefore cash markets show a rapid decline in liquidity with increasing maturity of securities. Since hedging provides the opportunity to reduce the price risk caused by interest rate changes investors' propensity to provide long-term capital increases.

Futures trading contributes to a better integration of capital markets (26). Regional markets with price differences due to lack of information cannot continue to exist with a central futures market providing information on market conditions all over the country.

In the final passage we investigated the effects of interest
futures on capital markets. Based on the main results of the
empirical analysis, the tremendous risk reduction
effectiveness, this speculative discussion of the effects of
futures trading on capital markets and thus on the whole
economy led to the conclusion that interest rate futures
markets

- improve the informational situation in the economy,
- prevent lasting information monopolies,
- reduce cost of trading,
- increase competition via a reduction of barriers to
  entry,
- improve liquidity in cash markets,
- tend to reduce the amplitude of price swings and to
  stabilize interest rates,
- tend to reduce the level of interest rates,
- bring prices of different places in line and contribute
  to a better integration of capital markets,
- reduce uncertainty and improve the basis for planning,
- enhance the supply of long-term capital.

Footnotes to IV (Summary and Conclusions)

1) Compare example of short hedge in chapter I.

2) LOOSIGIAN, A.M. (1980, pp. 375 ff.); BURNS, J.M. (1983, pp. 64 f.).

3) Compare example of a long hedge in chapter I.

4) Compare e.g. KOBOLD, K. (1985, p. 68).

5) See chapter I.2.2.

6) Compare e.g.: HARDING, J. (1979, p. 37); FITZGERALD, D.M. (1983, p. 119).

7) Compare for the following arguments: HARDING, J. (1979, pp. 37 ff.); STREIT, M.E. (1980c, pp. 515 ff.); CFTC (1981, part III, p. 13 ff.).

8) FITZGERALD, D.M. (1983, p. 181).

9) Compare: POWERS, M.J.; VOGEL, D.J. (1981, pp. 5 f.); BURNS, M.J. (1983, p. 69).

10) See e.g.: FROEWISS, K.C. (1978, pp. 23 f.); MILLER, R. (1979, pp. 6 ff.); STREIT, M.E. (1980b, pp. 496 ff.).

11) Compare chapter I.2.2.

12) MILL, J.S. (1848, p. 715); MARSHALL, A. (1932, p. 262).

13) MILL, J.S. (1848, p. 715).

14) Compare TREASURY/FEDERAL RESERVE STUDY (1979, pp. 6 ff.); CFTC (1981, part III, pp. 61 ff.).

15) FRIEDMAN, M. (1953, p. 175).

16) See also KALDOR, N. (1939, pp. 2 f.).

17) TREASURY/FEDERAL RESERVE STUDY (1979, p. 6).

18) Those studies are enumerated in: GOSS, B.A.; YAMEY, B.S. (1976, pp. 29 ff.) or CFTC (1981, part III, pp. 64 ff.).

19) FIGLEWSKI, S. (1981).

20) FROEWISS, K.C. (1978); SIMPSON, W.G.; IRELAND, T.C. (1982).

21) GARDNER, R.M. (1979).

22) TREASURY/FEDERAL RESERVE STUDY (1979, pp.   7 f.);
    CFTC (1981, part III, pp. 50 ff.).

23) TREASURY/FEDERAL RESERVE STUDY (1979, p.   7);   CFTC
    (1981, part III, p. 61)

24) For the following arguments compare e.g.:   HARDING,
    J. (1979, pp. 37 ff.); LOOSIGIAN, A.M. (1980, pp.
    375 f.); BURNS, J.M. (1983, pp. 63 ff.).

25) BURNS, J.M. (1979, p. 77).

26) BURNS, J.M. (1983, p. 69).

BIBLIOGRAPHY

ALEXANDER, G.J.; BENSON, P.G. (1982), More on Beta as a Random Coefficient, in: Journal of Financial and Quantitative Analysis, vol. 17, pp. 27-36.

ANDERSON, R.W.; DANTHINE, J.-P. (1980), Hedging and Joint Production: Theory and Illustrations, in: Journal of Finance, vol. 35, pp. 487-501.

ANDERSON, R.W.; DANTHINE, J.-P. (1981), Cross Hedging, in: Journal of Political Economy, vol. 89, pp. 1182-1196.

ANDERSON, R.W.; DANTHINE, J.-P. (1983), The Time Pattern of Hedging and the Volatility of Futures Prices, in: Review of Economic Studies, vol. 50, pp. 249-266.

ARAK, M.; McCURDY, C.J. (1979/80), Interest Rate Futures, in: Federal Reserve Bank of New York Quarterly Review, pp. 33-46.

ARDITTI, F.D. (1978), Interest Rate Futures: An Intermediate Stage Toward Efficient Risk Reallocation, in: Journal of Bank Research, vol. 9, pp. 146-150.

ARNIM, R. von (1982), Das Warenterminrecht in den USA, in: Recht der Internationalen Wirtschaft, vol. 82, pp. 313-325.

BERNHOLZ, P. (1979), Grundlagen der Politischen Oekonomie, Band 3, Tuebingen.

BILDERSEE, J. (1975), Some New Bond Indexes, in: Journal of Business, vol. 50, pp. 506-525.

BLACK, F. (1972), Capital Market Equilibrium with Restricted Borrowing, in: Journal of Business, vol. 45, pp. 444-455.

BLACK, F.; JENSEN, M.C.; SCHOLES, M. (1972), The Capital Asset Pricing Model: Some Empirical Tests, in: Jensen, M.C. (ed.), Studies in the Theory of Capital Markets, New York, pp. 79-121.

BLUME, M.E. (1971), On the Assessment of Risk, in: Journal of Finance, vol. 26, pp. 1-10.

BLUME, M.E.; FRIEND, I. (1973), A New Look at the Capital Asset Pricing Model, in: Journal of Finance, vol. 28, pp. 19-33.

BODIE, Z.; ROSANSKY, V.I. (1980), Risk and Return in Commodity Futures, in: Financial Analysts Journal, vol. 36, pp. 27-39.

BOLTEN, S.E. (1970), Security Analysis and Portfolio Management, New York.

BRANSON, W.H. (1972), Macroeconomic Theory and Policy, New York.

BREEDEN, D.T. (1980), Consumption Risk in Futures Markets, in: Journal of Finance, vol. 35, pp. 503-520.

BURNS, J.M. (1979), A Treatise on Markets: Spot, Futures, and Options, Washington.

BURNS, J.M. (1983), Futures Markets and Market Efficiency, in: Streit, M.E. (ed.), Futures Markets: Modelling, Managing and Monitoring Futures Trading, Oxford, pp. 46-74.

CAGAN, P. (1956), The Monetary Dynamics of Hyperinflation, in: Friedman, M. (ed.), Studies in the Quantity Theory of Money, Chicago, pp. 25-117.

CAGAN, P. (1981), Financial Futures Markets -- Is More Regulation Needed? Paper presented at Conference on Regulation and Futures Markets, Graduate School of Business, Center for Study of Futures Markets, January 29-30, 1981.

CARTER, C.A.; RAUSSER, G.C.; SCHMITZ, A. (1983), Efficient Asset Portfolios and the Theory of Normal Backwardation, in: Journal of Political Economy, vol. 91, pp. 319-331.

CHICAGO BOARD OF TRADE (ed.) (different years), Interest Rate Futures, Statistical Annuals, Chicago.

CHICAGO BOARD OF TRADE (ed.) (1981), An Introduction to Financial Futures, Chicago.

CHICAGO BOARD OF TRADE (ed.) (1982a), A Guide to Financial Futures at the Chicago Board of Trade, Chicago.

CHICAGO BOARD OF TRADE (ed.) (1982b), Financial Futures: The Delivery Process in Brief, Chicago.

CHICAGO BOARD OF TRADE (ed.) (1982c), GNMA CDR Futures, Chicago.

CHICAGO BOARD OF TRADE (ed.) (different issues), The Financial Futures Professional, A monthly marketing bulletin, Chicago.

311

CHICAGO MERCANTILE EXCHANGE (ed.) (1978), Facts About
    Futures Trading: Trading in Tomorrows, Chicago.

CICCHETTI, P.; DALE, C.; VIGNOLA, A. J. (1981),
    Usefulness of Treasury Bill Futures as Hedging
    Instruments, in: Journal of Futures Markets, vol. 1,
    pp. 379-388.

CLAASSEN E.-M. (1980), Grundlagen der makrooekonomischen
    Theorie, Muenchen.

COCHRANE, D.; ORCUTT, G.H. (1949), Application of Least
    Squares Regression to Relationships Containing
    Autocorrelated Error Terms, in: Journal of the
    American Statistical Association, vol. 44, pp. 32-61.

COMMODITY FUTURES TRADING COMMISSION (1981), Report to the
    Congress, Washington.

COMPTROLLER OF THE CURRENCY (ed.) (1983), Banking Circular
    BC 79 (3rd Rev.), Washington.

COOTNER, P. H. (1968), Speculation, Hedging, and
    Arbitrage, in: International Encyclopedia of the
    Social Science, vol. 15, New York, pp. 117-121.

DARST, D.M. (1981), The Handbook of the Bond and Money
    Markets, New York.

DAVIA, T.R.; HARDING, C.J. (1979), Understanding the
    T-bond & Commcercial Paper Futures Markets, in:
    Commodity Yearbook 1978, New York, pp. 45-53.

DEW, J.K.; MARTELL, T.F. (1981), Treasury Bill Futures,
    Commercial Lending, and the Synthetic Fixed-Rate Loan,
    in: Journal of Commercial Bank Lending, vol. 63, pp.
    27-38.

DRABENSTOTT, M.; McDONLEY, A. (1982), The Impact of
    Financial Futures on Agricultural Banks, in: Economic
    Review, Federal Reserve Bank of Kansas City, vol. 67,
    pp. 19-30.

DRUKARCZYK, J. (1980), Finanzierungstheorie, Muenchen.

DUSAK, K. (1973), Futures Trading and Investor Returns: An
    Investigation of Commodity Market Risk Premiums, in:
    Journal of Political Economy, vol. 81, pp. 1387-1406.

DUSHEK, C.J.; HARDING, C.J. (1979), Trading the Foreign
    Currency Futures Markets, in: Commodity Yearbook 1978,
    New York, pp. 20-33.

EDERINGTON, L.H. (1979), The Hedging Performance of the New Futures Markets, in: Journal of Finance, vol. 34, pp. 157-170.

EDWARDS, F.R. (1983), The Clearing Association in Futures Markets: Guarantor and Regulator, in: Journal of Futures Markets, vol. 3, pp. 369-392.

ELTON, E.J.; GRUBER, M.J. (1981), Modern Portfolio Theory and Investment Analysis, New York.

FABOZZI, F.J.; FRANCIS, J.C. (1978), Beta as a Random Coefficient, in: Journal of Financial and Quantitative Analysis, vol. 13, pp. 101-116.

FABOZZI, F.J.; KIPNIS, G. (1984), Stock Index Futures, Homewood.

FABOZZI, F.J.; ZARB, F.G. (ed.) (1981), Handbook of Financial Markets: Securities, Options, Futures, Homewood.

FAMA, E.F. (1968), Risk, Return and Equilibrium: Some Clarifying Comments, in: Journal of Finance, vol. 23, pp. 29-40.

FAMA, E.F. (1976), Foundations of Finance, New York.

FAMA, E.F.; MacBETH, J.D. (1973), Risk, Return and Equilibrium: Empirical Tests, in: Journal of Political Economy, vol. 71, pp. 607-636.

FAMA, E.F.; MILLER, M.H. (1972), The Theory of Finance, Hinsdale.

FEDERAL RESERVE BANK (ed.) (different years), Federal Reserve Bulletin, Washington.

FEDERAL RESERVE BANK OF ST. LOUIS (ed.) (different issues), Monetary Trends.

FIGLEWSKI, S. (1981), Futures Trading and Volatility in the GNMA Market, in: Journal of Finance, vol. 26, pp. 445-456.

FISCHER, D.E.; JORDAN, R.J. (1983), Security Analysis and Portfolio Management, Englewood Cliffs, (3rd. ed.).

FISHER, I. (1930), The Theory of Interest, New York.

FITZGERALD, D.M. (1983), Financial Futures, London.

313

FRANCIS, J.C.; ARCHER, S.H. (1979), Portfolio Analysis, Englewood Cliffs, (2nd. edition).

FRANCKLE, C.T. (1980), The Hedging Performance of the New Futures Markets: Comment, in: Journal of Finance, vol. 35, pp. 1273-1279.

FRANCKLE, C.T.; SENCHACK, A.J. (1982), Economic Considerations in the Use of Interest Rate Futures, in: Journal of Futures Markets, vol. 2, pp. 107-116.

FRIEDMAN, M. (1953), Essays in Positive Economics, The Case for Flexible Exchange Rates, Chicago.

FRIEND, I.; WESTERFIELD, R. (1981), Risk and Capital Asset Prices, in: Journal of Banking and Finance, vol. 5, pp. 291-315.

FROEWISS, K. C. (1978), GNMA Futures: Stabilizing or Destabilizing?, in: Federal Reserve Bank of San Francisco - Economic Review, pp. 20-29.

FULLER, R.J. (1981), Capital Asset Pricing Theories - Evolution and New Frontiers, Charlottesville.

GARAND, J.J. (1974), Fixed Income Portfolio Performance: A Discussion of the Issues, in: Journal of Bank Research, pp. 280-297.

GARDNER, R. M. (1979), The Effects of the T-bill Futures Market on the Cash T-bill Market, Chicago.

GEORGESCU-ROEGEN, N. (1958), The Nature of Expectation and Uncertainty, in: Bowman, M.J., Expectations, Uncertainty, and Business Behaviour, New York, pp. 11-29.

GEMMILL, G.T. (1981), Financial Futures in London: Rational Market or New Casino? in: National Westminster Bank, Quarterly Review, pp. 2-13.

GEMMILL, G.T. (1983), Regulating Futures Markets: A Review in the Context of British and American Practice, in: Streit, M.E. (ed.): Futures Markets: Modelling, Managing and Monitoring Futures Trading, Oxford, pp. 295-318.

GONEDES, N.J. (1976), Capital Market Equilibrium for a Class of Heterogenous Expectations in a Two-Parameter World, in: Journal of Finance, vol. 31, pp. 1-15.

GOSS, B.A. (1972), The Theory of Futures Trading, London, Boston.

GOSS, B.A.; YAMEY, B.S. (1976), The Economics of Futures Trading, London.

GOULDEY, B.K. and GRAY, G.J. (1981), Implementing Mean-Variance Theory in the Selection of US Government Bond Portfolios, in: Journal of Bank Research, vol. 12, pp. 161-173.

GRAY, R.W. (1960), The Characteristic Bias in Some Thin Futures Markets, in: Food Research Institute Studies, vol. 1, pp. 296-312.

HALEY, C.W.; SCHALL, L.D. (1973), The Theory of Financial Decisions, New York.

HALL, W. (1979), The Struggle for Control of the US Futures Market, in: The Banker, pp. 35-39.

HALL, W. (1981), Enthusiasm runs high in Chicago, in: US Futures Markets, Financial Times Survey, p. VIII.

HARDING, J. (1979), Financial Interest Futures in the United Kingdom, in: International Commodities Clearing House (ed.): Financial Futures in London? London, pp. 1-41.

HEGDE, S.P. (1982), The Impact of Interest Rate Level and Volatility on the Performance of Interest Rate Hedges, in: Journal of Futures Markets, vol. 2, pp. 341-356.

HESTER, D.D. (1981), Innovations and Monetary Control, in: Brooking Papers on Economic Activity, vol. 1, pp. 141-189.

HICKS, J.R. (1946), Value und Capital, Oxford, (2nd. edition).

HIERONYMUS, T.A. (1977), Economics of Futures Trading for Commercial and Personal Profit, New York.

HILL, J.; SCHNEEWEIS, T. (1981), A Note on 'the Hedging Effectiveness of Foreign Currency Futures, in: Journal of Futures Markets, vol. 1, pp. 659-664.

HIRSHLEIFER, J. (1975), Speculation and Equilibrium: Information, Risk and Markets, in: Quarterly Journal of Economics, vol. 89, pp. 519-542.

HIRSHLEIFER, J. (1977), The Theory of Speculation under Alternative Regimes of Markets, in: Journal of Finance, vol. 32, pp. 975-999.

HOBSON, R.B. (1978), Futures Trading in Financial Instruments, Washington.

315

HOFFMAN, G. W. (1932), Future Trading upon Organised Commodity Markets in the United States, Philadelphia.

HOPKINSON, M. (1981), The Financial Futures Market - A Guide for Corporate Treasures, in: Multinational Business, No. 4, pp. 1-15.

IBBOTSON, R.G.; SINQUEFIELD, R.A. (1976), Stocks, Bonds, Bills, and Inflation: Year-by-Year Historial Returns (1926-1974), in: Journal of Business, vol. 49, pp. 11-43.

INDEX AND OPTION MARKET (ed.) (1982), Inside S&P 500 Stock Index Futures, Chicago.

INTERNATIONAL MONETARY MARKET (ed.) (1982), Currency Futures: Trading for Financial Institutions, Chicago.

JAFFE, N.L.; HOBSON, R.B. (1979), Survey of Interest-Rate Futures Markets, Washington.

JENSEN, M.C. (1972), The Foundations and Current State of Capital Market Theory, in: Jensen, M.C. (ed.), Studies in the Theory of Capital Markets, New York. pp. 3-43.

JOHNSON, L.L. (1960), The Theory of Hedging and Speculation in Commodity Futures, in: Review of Economic Studies, vol. 27, pp. 139-151.

KALDOR, N. (1939), Speculation and Economic Stability, in: Review of Economic Studies, vol. 7 pp. 1-27.

KAUFMANN, P.J. (1984), Handbook of Futures Markets: Commodity, Financial, Stock Index and Options, New York.

KAWAI, M. (1981), Price Volatility of Storable Commodities Under Rational Expectations in Spot and Futures Markets. The John Hopkins University, Department of Political Economy, Working Papers in Economics 83.

KEYNES, J.M. (1923), Some Aspects of Commodity Markets, in: Manchester Guardian a Commercial European Reconstruction Series, Section 13, March 29, pp. 784-786.

KEYNES, J.M. (1930), A Treatise on Money, vol. 2, The Applied Theory of Money, London (edition used: 8th, 1971).

KMENTA, J. (1971), Elements of Econometrics, New York.

KNIGHT, F.H. (1921), Risk, Uncertainty and Profit, Boston.

KOBOLD, K. (1985), Terminkontraktmaerkte fuer verzinsliche Wertpapiere, in: Sparkasse, vol. 10, pp. 64-69.

KOCH, D.L.; STEINHAUSER, D.W.; WHIGHAM, P. (1982), Financial Futures as a Risk Management Tool for Banks and S&Ls, in: Economic Review, Federal Reserve Bank of Atlanta, pp. 4-14.

KOLB, R.W.; CHIANG, R. (1981), Improving Hedging Performance Using Interest Rate Futures, in: Financial Management, pp. 72-79.

LEE, C.F. (1976), Investment Horizon and the Functional Form of the Capital Asset Pricing Model, in: Review of Economics and Statistics, vol. 58, pp. 356-363.

LEVY, H. (1982), A Test of CAPM via a Confidence Level Approach, in: Journal of Portfolio Management, vol. 9, pp. 56-61.

LEVY, H. (1983), The Capital Asset Pricing Model: Theory and Empiricism, in: Economic Journal, vol. 93, pp. 145-165.

LEVY, R.A. (1971), On the Short-Term Stationarity of Beta Coefficients, in: Financial Analysts Journal, vol. 27, pp. 55-62.

LINTNER, J. (1965a), The Valuation of Risk Assets and the Selection of Risky Investments in Stock Portfolios and Capital Budgets, in: Review of Economics and Statistics, vol. 47, pp. 13-37.

LINTNER, J. (1965b), Security Prices, Risk and Maximal Gains from Diversification, in: Journal of Finance, vol. 20, pp. 587-615.

LINTNER, J. (1969), The Aggregation of Investors' Diverse Judgment and Preferences in Purely Competitive Security Markets, in: Journal of Financial and Quantitative Analysis, vol. 4, pp. 347-400.

LOOSIGIAN, A.M. (1980), Interest Rate Futures, Hoomewood.

LORD, T.J. (1980), The Structure of Prices Between the Futures and Cash Markets for 90-day Treasury Bills, Iowa.

LOWER, R.C. (1982), Futures Trading for Financial Intstruments - The Regulatory Environment, Chicago.

MAG, W. (1981), Risiko und Ungewissheit, in: Handwoerterbuch der Wirtschaftswissenschaftler, Bd. 6, pp. 478-495.

MANESS, T.S. (1981), Optimal versus Naive Buy-Hedging with T-Bill Futures, in: Journal of Futures Markets, vol. 1, pp. 393-403.

MARKOWITZ, H.M. (1952), Portfolio Selection, in: Journal of Finance, vol. 7, pp. 77-91.

MARKOWITZ, H.M. (1959), Portfolio Selection: Efficient Diversification of Investment, New York.

MARSHALL, A. (1932), Industry and Trade, London (3rd edition 1920, reprinted 1932).

McDONALD, B. (1983), Functional Forms and the Capital Asset Pricing Model, in: Journal of Financial and Quantitative Analysis, vol. 18, pp. 319-329.

McENALLY, R.W.; RICE, M.L. (1979), Hedging Possibilities in the Flotation of Debt Securities, in: Financial Management, vol. 10, pp. 12-18.

MILL, J.S. (1848), Principles of Political Economy, London.

MILLER, M.H.; SCHOLES, M. (1972), Rates of Return in Relation to Risk: A Re-examination of Some Recent Findings, in: Jensen, M.C. (ed.), Studies in the Theory of Capital Markets, New York, pp. 47-78.

MILLER, R. (1979), Interest Rate Futures in Britain?, in: International Commodities Clearing House (ed.): Financial Futures in London, London, pp. 1-31.

MODIGLIANI, F.; POGUE, G.A. (1974), An Introduction to Risk and Return, in: Financial Analysts Journal, vol. 30, 1974a March/April, pp. 68-80, 1974b May/June, pp. 69-86.

MOSSIN, J. (1966), Equilibrium in a Capital Asset Market, in: Econometrica, vol. 34, pp. 768-783.

MULLINS, D.W. (1982), Does the Capital Asset Pricing Model work? in: Harvard Business Review, vol. 60, pp. 105-114.

MUTH, J.F. (1961), Rational Expectations and the Theory of Price Movements, in: Econometrica, vol. 29, pp. 315-335.

NEWBERY, D.M.; STIGLITZ, J.E. (1981), The Theory of Commodity Price Stabilization, Oxford.

OECD, (ed.) (1979) The Market for International Floating Rate Notes, in: Financial Market Trends, no. 11, pp. 99-113.

318

PARKINSON, P.M. (1981), The Usefulness of Treasury Bill Futures for Forecasting and Hedging, University of Wisconsin - Madison 1981.

POWERS, M.J.; VOGEL, D.J. (1981), Inside the Financial Futures Markets, New York.

RABINOVITCH, R.; OWEN, J. (1978), Nonhomogeneous Expectations and Information in the Capital Asset Market, in: Journal of Finance, vol. 33, pp. 575-587.

REILLY, F.K. (1981), Corporate Stocks, in: Fabozzi, F.J.; Zarb, F.G. (eds.), Handbook of Financial Markets, Homewood, pp. 269-311.

ROLFO, J. (1980), Optimal Hedging under Price and Quanity Uncertainty: The Case of a Cocoa Producer, in: Journal of Political Economy, vol. 88, pp. 100-116.

ROLL, R. (1977), A Critique of the Asset Pricing Theory's Tests, Part I: On Past and Potential Testability of the Theory, in: Journal of Financial Economics, vol. 4, pp. 129-176.

ROSENBERG, B. (1981), The Capital Asset Pricing Model and the Market Model, in: Journal of Portfolio Management, vol. 7, pp. 5-16.

ROSS, S.A. (1978), The Current Status of the Capital Asset Pricing Model (CAPM), in: Journal of Finance, vol. 33, pp. 885-901.

RUTLEDGE, D.J. (1972), Hedgers' Demand for Futures Contracts: A Theoretical Framework with Applications to the US Soybean Complex, in: Food Research Institute Studies, vol. 11, pp. 237-256.

RUTLEDGE, D.J. (1977/78), Estimation of Hedging and Speculative Positions in Futures Markets: An Alternative Approach, in: Food Research Institute Studies, vol. 16, pp. 205-211.

SANDER, G. (1981), Financial Futures dinamici: Contratti a termine su interessi - ora anche in Europa, in: Il mese, vol. 8, pp. 12-15.

SANDOR, R.L.; SOSIN H.B. (1983), Inventive Activity in Futures Markets: A Case Study of the Development of the First Interest Rate Futures Market, in: Streit, M.E. (ed.), Futures Markets: Modelling, Managing and Monitoring Futures Trading, Oxford, pp. 255-272.

SCHNEEWEISS, H. (1967), Entscheidungskriterien bei Risiko, Berlin.

SCHNEEWEISS, H. (1978), Oekonometrie, Wuerzburg, (3rd. edition).

SCHOLES, M.S. (1981), The Economics of Hedging and Spreading in Futures Markets, in: Journal of Futures Markets, vol. 1 pp. 265-286.

SCHWARZ, E.W. (1979), How to Use Interest Rate Futures Contracts, Homewood.

SHARPE, W.F. (1963), A Simplified Model for Portfolio Analysis, in: Management Science, vol. 9, pp. 277-293.

SHARPE, W.F. (1964), Capital Asset Prices: A Theory of Market Equilibrium under Conditions of Risk, in: Journal of Finance, vol. 19, pp. 425-442.

SHARPE, W.F. (1970), Portfolio Theory and Capital Markets, New York.

SHARPE, W.F. (1981), Investments, Englewood Cliffs, (2nd. edition).

SHARPE, W.F.; COOPER, G.M. (1972), Risk-Return Classes of New York Stock Exchange Common Stocks, 1931-1967, in: Financial Analysts Journal, vol. 28, pp. 46-54.

SIMPSON, W.G.; IRELAND, T.C. (1982), The Effects of Futures Trading on the Price Volatility of GNMA Securities, in: Journal of Futures Markets, vol. 2, pp. 357-366.

STEIN, J.L. (1961), The Simultaneous Determination of Spot and Futures Prices, in: American Economic Review, vol. 51, pp. 1012-1025.

STEIN, J.L. (1964), The Opportunity Locus in a Hedging Decision: A Correction, in: American Economic Review, vol. 54, pp. 762-763.

STIGUM, M.L. (1978), The Money Market: Myth, Reality and Practice, Homewood.

STIGUM, M.L.; BRANCH, R.O. (1983), Managing Bank Assets and Liabilities, Homewood.

STREIT, M.E. (1980a), Zur Funktionsweise von Termin-kontraktmaerkten (An Analysis of the Functioning of Futures Markets), in: Jahrbuch fuer Nationaloekonomie und Statistik, vol. 195, pp. 533-549.

STREIT, M.E. (1980b), On the Use of Futures Markets for Stabilization Purposes, in: Weltwirtschaftliches Archiv, vol. 116, pp. 493-513.

STREIT, M.E. (1980c), Moeglichkeiten der Funktionsverbesserung von Rohstoffmaerkten durch Terminkontrakthandel, in: Zeitschrift fuer Wirtschafts- und Sozialwissenschaften, vol. 100, pp. 507-530.

STREIT, M.E. (1981), Terminkontrakthandel mit Waehrungen, (Futures Trading in Currencies), in: G. Bombach et al (eds.): Zur Theorie und Politik internationaler Wirtschaftsbeziehungen, Tuebingen, pp. 183-210.

STREIT, M.E. (1983a), Heterogene Erwartungen, Preisbildung und Informationseffizienz auf spekulativen Maerkten, in: Zeitschrift fuer die gesamte Staatswissenschaft, vol. 139, pp. 67-79.

STREIT, M.E. (1983b), Modelling, Managing and Monitoring Futures Trading: Frontiers of Analytical Inquiry, in: Streit, M.E. (ed.), Futures Markets: Modelling, Managing and Monitoring Futures Trading, Oxford, pp. 1-26.

TAYLOR, F.M. (1925), Principles of Economics, New York, (9th. edition).

TELSER, L.G. (1955/56), Safety First and Hedging, in: Review of Economic Studies, vol. 23, pp. 1-16.

TEWELES, R.J.; HARLOW, C.V.; STONE, H.L. (1977), The Commodity Futures Game, New York.

TOBIN, J. (1958), Liquidity Preference as Behaviour Towards Risk, in: Review of Economic Studies, vol. 25, pp. 65-86.

TREASURY/FEDERAL RESERVE STUDY OF TREASURY FUTURES MARKETS (1979), Summary and Recommendations, Washington.

TREYNOR, J.L. (1965), How to Rate Management of Investment Funds, in: Harvard Business Review, vol. 43, pp. 63-75.

VEIT, E.T.; REIFF, W.W. (1983), Commercial Banks and Interest Rate Futures: A Hedging Survey, in: Journal of Futures Markets, vol. 3, pp. 283-293.

WALT, H.R. (1981), Financial Futures: A Primer, in: Federal Home Loan Bank Board Journal, vol. 14, pp. 4-11.

321

WARD, R.W.; FLETCHER, L.B. (1971), From Hedging to Pure Speculation: A Micro Model of Optimal Futures and Cash Market Positions, in: American Journal of Agricultural Economics, vol. 53, pp. 71-78.

WARDREP, B.N.; BUCK, J.F. (1982), The Efficacy of Hedging with Financial Futures: A Historical Perspective, in: Journal of Futures Markets, vol. 2, pp. 243-254.

WATLING, T.F.; MORLEY, J. (1978), Successful Commodity Futures Trading, London (2nd. edition).

WEBER, W.; STREISSLER, E. (1961), Erwartungen, Unsicherheit und Risiko, in: Handwoerterbuch der Sozialwissenschaften, Bd. 3, pp. 330-339.

WEINSTEIN, M. (1981), The Systematic Risk of Corporate Bonds, in: Journal of Financial and Quantitative Analysis, vol. 16, pp. 257-278.

WHITE, K.J. (1978), A General Computer Program for Econometric Methods - SHAZAM, in: Econometrica, vol. 46, pp. 239-240.

WORKING, H. (1953a), Futures Trading and Hedging, in: American Economic Review, vol. 43, pp. 314-343.

WORKING, H. (1953b), Hedging Reconsidered, in: Journal of Farm Economics, vol. 35, pp. 544-561.

WORKING, H. (1962), New Concepts Concerning Futures Markets and Prices, in: American Economic Review, vol. 52, pp. 431-459.

YAMEY, B.S. (1951), An Investigation of Hedging on an Organized Produce Exchange, in: The Manchester School of Economics and Social Studies, vol. 19, pp. 305-319.

YAMEY, B.S. (1971), Short Hedging and Long Hedging in Futures Markets: Symmetry and Asymmetry, in: Journal of Law and Economics, vol. 14, pp. 413-434.

YAMEY, B.S. (1983), The Economics of Futures Trading: Some Notes and Queries, in: Streit, M.E. (ed.), Futures Markets: Modelling, Managing and Monitoring Futures Trading, Oxford, pp. 22-45.

YAWITZ, J.B.; MARSHALL, W.J. (1980), Risk and Return in the Government Bond Market, in: Bernstein, P. (ed.), The Theory and Practice of Bond Portfolio Management, vol. 2, New York, pp. 14-26.

YEAGER, F.C.; SEITZ, N.E. (1982), Financial Institution Management, Reston.